qb

WITHDRAWN

FRANCIS PARKMAN, HISTORIAN AS HERO

American Studies Series
William H. Goetzmann, Editor

Francis Parkman, ca. 1855, the hero-historian in his prime,
about the time of the publication of the *Conspiracy of Pontiac*.
(From a daguerreotype; courtesy Daniel Sargent
and Mrs. John Forbes Perkins.)

FRANCIS PARKMAN, HISTORIAN AS HERO

THE FORMATIVE YEARS

by Wilbur R. Jacobs

University of Texas Press, Austin

First Edition, 1991

Requests for permission to reproduce material from this work should be sent to
Permissions, University of Texas Press, Box 7819, Austin, Texas 78713-7819.

∞   The paper used in this publication meets the minimum requirements of American
National Standard for Information Sciences—Permanence of Paper for Printed Library
Materials, ANSI Z39.48-1984.

LIBRARY OF CONGRESS CATALOGING-IN-PUBLICATION DATA

Jacobs, Wilbur R.
   Francis Parkman, historian as hero : the formative years / by
Wilbur R. Jacobs. — 1st ed.
      p.   cm. — (American studies series)
   Includes bibliographical references and index.
   ISBN 0-292-72467-5 (cloth)
   1. Parkman, Francis, 1823–1893. 2. Historians—United States—
Biography.   I. Title.   II. Series.
E175.5.P28J3   1991
970'.007202—dc20
   [B]   91-10285
                                                                  CIP

FOR PRISCILLA, WILLIAM AND EMILY, NONA,
WALTER, AND SHIRLEY, AND BETSY AND CATHY

Parkman was certainly one of the most heroic figures in the history of American letters.

—CONCLUDING SENTENCE IN
CHARLES H. FARNHAM'S BIOGRAPHY,
A LIFE OF FRANCIS PARKMAN, 1899

Frank Parkman, Harvard College Student.
(From a daguerreotype and a print;
W. R. Jacobs Photography Collection.)

CONTENTS

Nature affords for our contemplation subjects from the minutest to the most grand . . . the farther we investigate her secrets the wider appears the range she opens to us. The nearer view we take of her, the more captivating does she appear.

—"STUDIES IN NATURE," 1839

America was . . . the Domain of Nature.

—"ROMANCE IN AMERICA," 1844

Against absolute authority there was a counter influence, rudely and wildly antagonistic. Canada was at the very portal of the great interior wilderness. The St. Lawrence and the Lakes were the highway to that domain of savage freedom.

—THE OLD RÉGIME, 1874

The eighteen-year-old explorer tells of his exploits:
"Dear Father,
I write, as in duty bound, to relieve your spirit of the overwhelming load of anxiety which doubtless oppresses you, seeing that your son is a wanderer in a strange land—a land of precipices and lakes, bears, wolves, and wildcats." (Parkman to his father, July 22, 1841, from Conway, New Hampshire; courtesy Daniel Sargent and Massachusetts Historical Society.)

PREFACE

MY INTEREST IN FRANCIS PARKMAN goes back to college days at the University of California, Los Angeles, when I studied under Louis Knott Koontz, a specialist in colonial American history. He often spoke of Parkman as a great historian who wrote the kind of early American frontier history that influenced generations of readers. Grant that I was infected by Koontz's enthusiasm, I came to have reservations about Parkman's work. As a younger professor I came upon Parkman's Oregon Trail letters in an old secretary, still intact, in his original, unused study at 50 Chestnut Street, Boston, then owned by an elderly relative. My admiration for Parkman was rekindled by this discovery and the editing of his correspondence, but as I later considered his full influence in early American history, I began writing critical essays, some of these given as papers before groups scattered throughout the United States. I took three of my published articles and bound them as a makeshift book for students at the University of California, Santa Barbara. My "book," entitled "Highlights of Parkman's Formative Period," had so much appeal in the college library that I had to replace the copy several times.

With the hope that other readers might find the subject of Parkman's youthful, heroic years of interest, I have drawn upon pieces I have published in the *Pacific Historical Review*, *New England Quarterly*, and *American Quarterly* and have composed eight additional essays. Unless otherwise indicated, all citations to Parkman's works are to his last versions of his *History* (*France and England in North America*) in the Frontenac edition, sixteen volumes, published in 1899 in Boston by Little, Brown & Co.

I have concentrated on Parkman's emergence as a writer. As a young poet and fiction writer before taking up history, Parkman saw history as a form of literature. If we think of literature as the evocation of human experience that tells us about the quality of human life, or how people felt about their lives, we can better understand Parkman.

My central theme is that Parkman considered himself a hero figure and transposed this novelistic image onto historical figures he studied. His *History* had lifelike vigor and an enduring quality because he lived the kind of history he wrote, as a bold explorer on the Oregon Trail and afterwards as a writer battling to overcome a debilitating illness. This theme resonates through my research on Parkman involving documentary analysis of primary sources in Indian and colonial frontier history, as well as extended probings into historiography and literary, medical, ethno-, and environmental history.

In the end I found much controversy among modern critics and admirers. Few are neutral about Parkman, as I try to point out in my bibliographical note. My feeling is that he will outlive those who seek his decanonization because he was a brilliant writer who brought historical narrative to the near point of novelistic perfection.

Without doubt, able scholars have an honest difference of opinion about Parkman. Mine is based upon some three decades of study into a wide variety of sources. Like some of Parkman's other critics, I have had the advantage of specializing in the kinds of historical materials Parkman studied, mainly early American and Canadian sources of Indian-white frontier history. My views on Parkman's "heroic" career and novelistic histories are set forth in ensuing chapters. I am convinced that his *History*, despite its novelistic style, has a place in the canons of colonial American history because of Parkman's literary skills, his remarkable penetration of the sources, and his original interpretation of the data. The younger Parkman had a spiritual intensity about his work in ferreting out any kind of material that enhanced his literary designs. He was particular, for example, in testing the veracity of controversial accounts where he sometimes found plagiarism, as in the case of Father Hennepin's journals.

Parkman knew more about woodland and plains Indians than any other historian of his generation, and, although he admired their lifestyles, he considered them all savages, denizens of the wilderness. He had his biases about Indians, but he nevertheless was a recognizable pioneer in comparable ethnology and in what we now call ethnohistory. Additionally he was an accomplished naturalist-horticulturalist, who had a fundamental knowledge about the interdependence of plant and animal life and the relationship of Indian culture to the surrounding wilderness. As an eyewitness he observed and described in his writings environmental panoramas that will never be seen again. Besides all this, his investigations into climatic and geographical history gave vital power to his wilderness scenes. In the interdisciplinary arena of ethno-environmental history Parkman set a standard that can inspire scholars of our own time.

Modern readers, however, find it difficult to overlook the prejudices that crept into Parkman's pages. Although he did not see himself as bigoted, he believed in the inferiority of women, lower classes of white Americans, and people of color. In writing about the Catholic Church, he found it almost impossible to conceal his hostility.

Throughout his life, during spates of crisis, rest, recuperation, and writing, Parkman battled his "enemy," a formidable combination of mental and physical complaints, including semiblindness, insomnia, extremely painful headaches, and palpitations of the heart. This struggle with his "enemy" provided an opportunity for him to fashion a heroic image of himself. There is no question that sick or well, Parkman thought of himself as an honest, dedicated historian who had the literary skills to give his readers a reconstruction of past events. Parkman, in my mind, evidenced courage and strength of character in his attempt to leave a legacy that would endure beyond his death. His papers disclose that he thought of himself as an ardent patriot who yearned to make a contribution to his country's historical literature.

Even though his heroic image was self-fashioned, it was not essentially an untrue projection of himself. It is temptingly facile to try to make a seamless whole of Parkman's work, his life, and his legacy, but Parkman was a trailblazing historian whose story is complex, as chapters in this book demonstrate.

The process of decoding Parkman's life and work is fraught with challenges. Comparable to the savage Indian image in his books, Parkman is a rebuffing figure, sometimes deceptive and even obstructionist. His autobiographical accounts, for example, are misleading, although he appears not to have wanted to deceive. I had the feeling that Parkman would have disliked what I wrote about him and that he would be hostile to me, an academic with the wrong credentials, a graduate of a state university with a German-Irish-Jewish heritage and a grandmother who was a shanty Irish, Roman Catholic, vegetarian-pacifist. Parkman never would have given my grandmother the right to vote.

If the reader grows weary from descriptions of Parkman's illness, bear with me. There is an element of humor here. Like the Sleeper in one of Woody Allen's movies, Parkman got well by gobbling up all the wrong things as prescribed by his doctor: cream, butter, fat, and arsenic. He built up his cholesterol and ate poison, but he overcame his "enemy," his illness, and went on to complete his lifetime work. In more ways than one, Parkman is unique. Like the novelist Willa Cather, who admired him and borrowed from his writings, Parkman evades identification. There was nobody like him.

FOR COURTESY AND HELP extended to me some years ago when I began editing Parkman's letters in preparation for writing this book, I am grateful to Parkman's family. The late Elizabeth Cordner, Parkman's niece, permitted me to examine his account books, Oregon Trail letters, and other manuscripts then preserved in his study at 50 Chestnut Street. Mr. and Mrs. Daniel Sargent, Mr. and Mrs. John Forbes Perkins, Mr. and Mrs. John Templeman Coolidge of Milton, Mrs. John Templeman Coolidge of Boston, and Mary B. Coffin extended every courtesy to me. Mary Coffin's excellent genealogy of the Parkman family was particularly useful to me in studying the Parkman family correspondence. I am grateful to these Parkman descendants for permission to publish his letters and photographs and for leads in research.

I am especially indebted to members of the Massachusetts Historical Society staff and to the Society for permission to publish Parkman materials. For patient assistance I owe a great deal to Stephen T. Riley, former director, and to Winifred Collins, former manuscripts curator, who assisted me in searching the rich documentary collections of the Society. The late Walter Muir Whitehill, who supervised the reconstruction of Parkman's study at the Colonial Society of Massachusetts, made the resources of the Society and the Boston Athenaeum available to me.

For many courtesies extended to me, I am deeply grateful to the Harvard College Library, the Harvard Archives, the Huntington Library, and the Library of the University of California, Santa Barbara. I have had financial support from the UCSB Committee on Research and the Huntington Library. The physicians and psychoanalysts of the Santa Barbara Mental Hygiene Clinic gave me professional advice in analyzing Parkman's illness.

At the Huntington Library I owe thanks to Robert Skotheim, President, to Martin Ridge, Director of Research, to William A. Moffett, Librarian, to Robert Schlosser, Head of the Photography Department, to Alan Jutzi, Curator of Rare Books, to Virginia Renner, Head of Reader Services, and to Linda Williams, Acquisitions Librarian, and Carol B. Pearson, index specialist. I am particularly under obligation to Martin Ridge, who tamed the Huntington coyotes so they would not threaten

PREFACE

noontime walks and talks about Parkman amid the wild areas of the Library's botanical gardens.

I express my thanks to the *New York Times Book Review* for publishing an inquiry that led to the discovery of many Parkman letters. Christine Gilbert of the University of Texas Press has given me valuable assistance. I am thankful to my wife, and to my two small children, William and Emily, who patiently allowed me to work long hours when I could have been with them. Six friends have given me special assistance: Alexander DeConde, Henry F. Dobyns, Leland Carlson, Peter Loewenberg, Andrew Rolle, and David Levin. For friendly counsel and exchange of views over the years, I express my gratitude to a number of scholars, some of them no longer here to see the publication of this volume. They include Francis Jennings, Nancy and Sean O'Neill, Yasu Kawashima, Karen Langlois, Samuel E. Morison, Allan Nevins, Bernard DeVoto, William D. Altus, Otis Pease, William Taylor, Mason Wade, Howard Doughty, Lewis O. Saum, Patricia Cline Cohen, Roderick Nash, Merle Curti, Henry R. Murray, Michael Mullin, Alfred Hurtado, Calvin Martin, Gregory Schaaf, Christopher Miller, Duane Mosser, Jean Bonheim, Chad Wozniak, Mabel and Ray Billington, Paul M. Zall, Kent Clark, Michael McConnell, Peter Neushul, and Gregory E. Dowd.

The Parkman family mansion at 5 Bowdoin Square, Boston, the historian's home from 1838 until he married. Built in 1788 by his paternal grandfather, Samuel Parkman, the house had beveled wood to imitate stone blocks. (From Charles H. Farnham, *A Life of Francis Parkman*.)

*If the people will learn that no expansion of territory, no
accumulation of wealth, no growth of population, can compensate for
the decline of individual greatness; if they can learn to recognize the
reality of superior minds, and to feel that they have need of them; to
feel too, that in rejecting and ignoring them they prepare the sure but
gradual ruin of popular government,—that beneficent lesson would
be cheaply bought by years of calamity and war.*

—"WHERE ARE OUR LEADERS?" PARKMAN TO THE
BOSTON DAILY ADVERTISER, 8 JANUARY 1862

The Reverend Dr. Francis Parkman, the historian's father, known as the son of a rich merchant and father of a famous historian. (Courtesy Massachusetts Historical Society.)

Caroline Hall Parkman, the historian's mother. She was a person, Parkman wrote, "of rare
affection, disinterestedness, and self-devotion." (From a miniature; courtesy Massachusetts
Historical Society.)

PROLOGUE

A VISITOR OF BEACON HILL in 1851 might have encountered a hand-some young man in his late twenties walking with a cane because of a disabled knee and wearing tinted spectacles to shield his hypersensitive eyes from the sun. Despite these signs of physical handicaps, he was ob-viously a person of bearing and composure. Behind the glasses, his glance was open and direct. His brown hair, parted on the side and combed over a high forehead, was combined with sideburns that reached down to his white collar. His features, open and pleasant to look at, were marked by a generous mouth and slightly protruding lower lip and chin. He weighed nearly 170 pounds and stood five feet eleven. His shoulders were muscular, his hands broad and strong. Meticulously dressed, with a folded white handkerchief in his coat pocket and buttoned spats covering his ankles and part of his shoes, he would seem like a man practiced in giving orders. The observant person would have also detected an air of alertness, even a ner-vousness of manner. This was Francis Parkman in 1851, at age twenty-eight, when his publishers were sending out the first copies of his new book, *The Conspiracy of Pontiac*, known as *Pontiac* to generations of readers.

He was to become one of the most significant historians in the United States, and in the early 1850s he was at a crossroads in his career. He had, in a sense, been marking time in writing fiction and travel accounts, but now he had broken away to strike out in a new direction, to begin a career as a serious writer of history. Successful Bostonian historians George Bancroft and William H. Prescott had already demonstrated that there was prestige and honor in writing history. But Parkman was untried and unknown as a historian. In his apprenticeship, he was determined to show that he would not live in the shade of Bancroft and Prescott; he would have his own place.

FRANCIS PARKMAN

THIS BOOK ON THE EMERGING Francis Parkman has four divisions. Part One concentrates on his apprenticeship years, the onslaught of his illness, and the lifelong struggle he had in coping with his maladies. A central theme is that Parkman's illness, and the contrived hero-image that he cultivated, were reflected in images and episodes of the storylike narratives he wrote. In *The Oregon Trail*, Parkman's early efforts at painting a self-portrait are revealed in his account of hunting buffalo and in his adventurous contacts with frontiersmen. This autobiographical story, rich in the bravery, audacity, and courage of the author, is revealed, on close examination and in comparison with journal accounts, to be especially designed for reader interest. The narration had to conform to storylike literary techniques. The book, when compared to Parkman's journals, is, in some cases, an altered version of what happened, a volume designed to appeal to a wide audience. If the book succeeded, it would embellish the reputation of the author as an intrepid explorer-traveler.

This analysis of Parkman's first book-length narrative offers clear insights on his literary methods in structuring chapters around colorful individuals and elements of suspense. We have an indication of what he will do when he turns to giving his readers a history of the role of Chief Pontiac in "the old French War."

Part Two is entirely devoted to escalating problems the young author had in bringing a formidable historical narrative to a stage of completion. In the sources, Pontiac turned out to be a very shadowy figure, but Parkman did not shrink from the task of molding the character of a treacherous conspirator. He addressed himself to the seemingly impossible task of recreating a vision of the past that covered much of the whole history of the English and French in North America as a background setting for Pontiac's War of 1763.

The enormous effort required that he amass basic sources of information and then arrange them in a topical and chronological sequence, especially subordinated to a suspenseful conspiracy plot. There was an additional complication: the event sequence depended upon the identification and construction of portraits of whole tribes or Indians and a detailed characterization of Pontiac himself. Noble and ignoble savages emerge from Parkman's pen. A myriad of details, in a twisted conspiratorial series of motivated incidents, had to be arranged and rearranged. They had to be buttressed with documentary proof of treachery upon treachery, step by step. In middle life Parkman had to revise his narrative to provide details on the giving of infectious smallpox blankets to Indians at Fort Pitt. This grisly episode, based on circumstantial evidence Parkman discovered in Colonel Henry Bouquet's papers, could not be ignored.

PROLOGUE

Part Three concerns Parkman's art of storytelling. How did he do it, and specifically how did he incorporate himself into his pages? For an answer to this question a chapter backtracks to one of Parkman's first efforts at fiction, demonstrating how he freely borrowed from his journals to inject a believable element of realistic danger and suspense. Another chapter in Part Three analyzes some of Parkman's novelistic literary devices that made him a master of historical storytelling. He became an expert in building subclimaxes and final grand climaxes, as in the fatal confrontation between Generals Montcalm and Wolfe on the Plains of Abraham.

Part Four describes and analyzes the origins and persistence of elitist social perspectives that permeate all of Parkman's writings. His social views, militantly spread through pamphlets and newspaper articles in middle life, are in a subdued fashion, softly trumpeted in his *History*. Nowhere does one find more blatant expression of his ideas than in his anticlericalism and in his hostility to the women's movement of the nineteenth century. Both of these find ready expression in his historical narratives, giving his entire *History* a particular bent of interpretation. What is more, Parkman defiantly refused to accept revisionist social ideas promulgated by intellectuals of his own class.

The epilogue focuses on what became the legend of the hero-historian following the publication of *The Oregon Trail* and *Pontiac* and the onset of illness that made him a virtual invalid. The argument is made that Parkman, more well than sick, made the most of his illness by using it to fashion a tragic image of himself through skillfully contrived autobiographical letters. Largely through the impact of these remarkable letters, the tragic hero and the author of heroic narratives are blended as one in the memory of America as part of our literary heritage. Within the prism of bias and hero worship, Parkman fashioned a multivolumed novelistic history that has a sustained popularity with generations of readers.

Parkman's wife and daughters. On the left is Katharine, who married John Templeman Coolidge, artist and trustee-director of Boston museums and owner of the Portsmouth mansion in New Hampshire where Parkman wrote his final pages of *A Half-Century of Conflict*. On the right is his wife, Catherine Bigelow Parkman (died 1858), and daughter Grace. She married Charles P. Coffin, Boston attorney, who shared Parkman's love of Sir Walter Scott's novels. (Courtesy Massachusetts Historical Society.)

Ida Agassiz, daughter of Louis Agassiz, Harvard scientist, the woman Parkman had planned to marry after his wife's death. (From a photograph in the Parkman Papers; courtesy Massachusetts Historical Society.)

PART ONE

THE HERO-HISTORIAN CONQUERS ADVERSITY

The hero on horseback, hunting buffalo,
an illustration by Frederic Remington
for *The Oregon Trail*, 1892 edition.
Parkman supplied the artist with photographs of himself
and descriptions of clothing he wore on the plains.

In achievement *I expect to fail, but I shall never
recoil from endeavor . . .*

—LETTER TO MARY DWIGHT PARKMAN, 1852

Parkman at Fort Laramie with Henry Chatillon, his guide, on the right. An illustration by
Frederic Remington, who had a photograph of Chatillon sent by Parkman. Parkman advised
Remington to examine Karl Bodmer's Indians for authentic details. On Chatillon, Remington replied, he "looks like a Boston fisherman and not like a wild horseman of the American
desert." (From *The Oregon Trail*, 1892 edition.)

CHAPTER ONE

THE HERO-HISTORIAN AND HIS ILLNESS

FRANCIS PARKMAN'S LIFE contained all the elements of a romantic legend because he purposely cultivated a heroic image of himself for future biographers.[1] During his lifetime he made a conscious effort to mold this kind of self-portrait by composing herolike autobiographical descriptions of himself and by writing a popular account of his experiences on the Oregon Trail, which emphasized his brave exploits. This same image is also found in his correspondence with relatives, friends, fellow-writers, and historians, as well as in the interviews he held with journalists. Although contrived, Parkman's portrayal of himself was so convincing that it was wholeheartedly accepted by people around him and by his biographers.

History, written with the imagery of the "Parkmanesque" style, is possible when the author has lived through, at least vicariously, the kinds of events and activities he depicts. The youthful Parkman possessed the necessary imaginative powers to an extraordinary degree. By examining his life and some of the psychological aspects of his mysterious illness, we can understand more easily how he was able to put himself into the situations of his characters. The major figures in his writing were frequently men of the type that Parkman hoped to be.[2] The result of this close relationship between Parkman, the author, and his writings is that his personal history throws light upon the development of his career as a historian.

Parkman was born in Boston on 16 September 1823, into a family important in the commercial and religious life of New England.[3] His father, the Reverend Dr. Francis Parkman, a prominent Unitarian minister, was, in later years, known as both the son of a prominent merchant and the father of a famous historian. Caroline Hall Parkman, his mother, had distinguished Puritan ancestors, including John Cotton and Cotton Mather.

Frank, as Francis was called, had a younger brother, John Eliot, and three sisters. They grew up on Boston's Bowdoin Square in an elegant and spacious mansion, built in 1788 and originally owned by paternal grandfather Samuel Parkman.

The home life of the Parkmans was in keeping with their means and their standing in the community. Their frequent parties and dinners were attended by many of the business and intellectual leaders of Boston. A summer house at Philip's Beach provided a refuge from the city's stifling summer heat. The family was an active, closely knit group. On Thanksgiving and other holidays the family mansion on Bowdoin Square was the scene of intense activity. The children occupied themselves with continual games, playacting, and sketching, in which Frank was the leader. He was exposed to important formative influences at home, especially in the circle of Dr. Parkman's friends, and soon came to appreciate the wealth of knowledge to be found in his father's library, which contained books on history, literature, and theology. Despite his complaints of illness, he grew quickly to nearly six feet—handsome, strong, athletic, and precocious.

He entered Harvard in 1840, a well-prepared student, having already completed basic work in mathematics and literature. His precollege studies included Milton, Byron, and Shakespeare, and practice in translating selections from Homer and Virgil. Unexpectedly, his college record proved to be mediocre. He later recalled that he was bored with recitation and drill and, as a result, was absent from classes. Where was he? In the college library he hungrily read books on ethnology and early frontier history.[4]

In language classes, he studied enough to acquire a working knowledge of French and Italian. As a young adult he learned to read Spanish and German. His ability to translate seventeenth- and eighteenth-century documents written in these languages demonstrated that Parkman was skilled in paleography, which deepened his approaches to research.[5]

His enthusiasm for history was soon observed by Jared Sparks, his teacher and one of America's first historians to use archival resources, who provided encouragement by suggesting reference works in English and in French. Sparks, during ensuing years, smoothed the way for his protégé to search out foreign libraries and archives. Theirs was a lifelong friendship, and in later years Parkman stood by his old teacher when he was publicly humiliated for defacing original George Washington letters.

Parkman's later study of law at Harvard, which he considered intellectual drudgery, did not persuade him to become a lawyer, but it would exercise an important influence upon his writings. He seems never to have forgotten the lessons learned in pouring over texts such as Simon Greenleaf's book on *Evidence*. Despite his concentration on sources that tended to support his storylike narratives, he nevertheless exhibited a lawyer's persistence in sifting facts and making a critical appraisal of evidence. There can be little doubt that his legal training shaped his approach to writing history, especially in the matter of making judgments and giving attention to specific kinds of evidence that might be used to support his argument. This can be detected, for instance, in his attempts to document a Pontiac conspiracy as a model for historical explanation.[6]

While books and teachers helped to form Parkman's views, he worked out his own methods of collecting information. His correspondence and journals disclose that he developed the technique of gathering data by what he termed "observation."[7] Many of his "observations" were jotted down in travel journals. At the time when he was still an undergraduate, he explored New England and parts of eastern Canada by train, horse, and canoe as well as on foot—often exhausting the patience and stamina of his companions. And in Europe on a grand tour, he visited Italy, France, England, and Germany and had a first-hand experience studying the inner life of the Catholic Church by taking part in a Passionist retreat in Rome.[8]

Upon his return to the United States, Parkman completed requirements for a B.A. degree, part of which was the composition of a graduation oration, "Romance in America."[9] This single piece, still extant among his papers, reveals his captivation with James Fenimore Cooper and Sir Walter Scott. Cooper's *Leatherstocking Tales*, especially *The Last of the Mohicans*, gave Parkman a literary model for writing Indian history. Scott's chivalric borderland novels proved to have a particular value for Parkman, as well as other writers who focused on Indian history. It can be argued that Scott inspired American interest in aboriginal life, tribal customs, and Indian eloquence in speech. Scott's manner of reconstructing forgotten events with colorful descriptions of flora and fauna were not lost on the youthful Parkman. Scott may well have been an inspiration for Parkman's preoccupation with romantic opposites, such as dying and emerging settlements in New France and along the early American frontier. As Parkman wrote in his college oration: "The charm of the Cheviot Hills . . . will never be ours, though our forests have seen struggles more savage and bloody . . . no nation could afford truer elements of romance."[10]

Despite his concentration on the romantic aspects of his theme, Parkman did manage to finish his study of law. At the same time, working at a frenzied pace, he made extensive preparations for a book on "the Old French War." To obtain special background material, he inspected historic sites in the Old Northwest and then made provisions for an extensive journey to the far western frontier. In an earlier visit to Onondaga, the ancient Six Nations' stronghold, he saw Iroquois men dressed in overalls quietly smoking cigars. What a disappointment! It was imperative that he seek out the untainted "Mohawk warrior" of the plains, who could be found in the person of the Sioux fighting man and hunter of the 1840s, living out an age-old lifestyle only partly changed by contacts with whites.

In March 1846, Parkman began his journey to the western prairies. Although he learned to speak only a few words of Oglallah, the Lakota language, for basic communication, he nevertheless was able to record in his notebooks particulars of Sioux lifestyles. These gave him insight into the powerful aboriginal societies of America's colonial period. He was then better able to evaluate accounts of Indian medicine men and their rituals, as witnessed by seventeenth-century Jesuit missionaries.

In a letter to his father, written 14 September 1846, from Westport, Missouri, Parkman told about the part of his tour that took him from the Medicine Bow range of the Rockies southward to Bent's Fort and the Upper Arkansas River.[11] He recounted contacts with Pawnee and Arapaho Indians and with American soldiers on the march to California. His health complaints at the end of his journey were mentioned, although they were concealed from his parents in earlier letters. His illness, which he described as "temporary," had left him vulnerable in Indian villages, where his weakness had been perceived. Yet it was all worth the effort. As he told his parents: "One season on the prairies will teach a man more than a half a dozen in the settlements. There is no place on earth where he is thrown more completely on his own resources."[12]

Although Parkman maintained that he was "completely well" in his letter, he did confess that his eyes still bothered him and that he had been so sick in an Indian encampment that he could not saddle his own horse and was practically an "invalid."[13] Thus, we are alerted to the complex and sometimes mysterious shadow of infirmity that lurked around every corner of his life. We must backtrack to trace its origins before making judgments on the significance of his maladies.

BACKGROUND OF PARKMAN'S ILLNESS

Parkman's relationship with his parents and siblings offers an insight into the early periods of his illness. In terms proposed by Erik Erikson, Parkman enjoyed a boyhood of deepest trust. He identified with his father, Dr. Francis Parkman, a formidable role model. There can be little question that the father's periodic complaints of depression were an omnipresent factor in the adolescence and youth of Frank, who developed strikingly similar moods of dejection. There was a visible identification between father and son. As a small boy, he had been considered frail by his parents and was sent to live with his grandparents on a farm in nearby Medford. He returned in better health after three years to rejoin his family in a new and spacious home, the Parkman mansion on Boston's Bowdoin Square.

A key figure in handling accounts and managing servants in the Parkman household was Frank's mother, Caroline Hall Parkman, who appears in the Parkman papers as the healthiest member of his family. She surfaces as a loving, strong person, managing stressful family affairs with intelligence and affection and due regard to Dr. Parkman's wishes. Although relatively little is known about her, we can be sure that her son inherited much of her determined spirit in coping with the problems of life. Her portrait reveals a face very similar to Parkman's, with a high forehead and a prominent chin. Sickly family members seem to have survived because of the mothering of this extraordinary woman. Parkman looked back on her as a person of affection and devotion who had a "disinterestedness" in her own welfare. An obituary, obviously written by someone who knew her well, described her as "highly gifted with clear insight, practical wisdom, and solid strength of character."[14]

The mother, along with three daughters and a sickly younger son, regarded Frank as brilliant and strong, despite his problems with illness. That he was the object of "brother worship" was not unlikely, as indicated in a later chapter on Parkman's relationships with women. Family admiration and support for Frank's occasional risk taking gave him satisfaction in exhibiting his mental and physical superiority.

Insights into the development of his personality are revealed in his boyhood experiments with chemistry when he managed to concoct "explosions" that burned him.[15] He had, he wrote, a "tenacious eagerness" and "vehement liking of pursuits." His boyhood "Star Theater" theatrical productions, combined with "shows" of chemical oddities and the transmission of electrical shocks to other children, reveal his exhibitionism.[16]

It is clear that many of his activities in childhood and early youth are characterized by attempts to outdo others, to outstrip them, and finally to achieve superiority over them. Evidence for these characteristics in his personality is abundant in his journals, personal correspondence, and autobiographical writings: his college fiction, *The Oregon Trail*, and a novel, *Vassal Morton*, published in 1856. The novel's hero is clearly Parkman con-

quering every physical challenge for the benefit of impressionable on-
lookers, including a pretty girl who resembles a young woman mentioned
in his journals.

Parkman never forgot to tell of his experiences of hunting and trapping small animals on his grandfather's farm. As a teenager he was caught
up with the prospect of reliving, and then writing about, the romantic life
of the colonial frontier. His enchantment with this theme, at the age of
fifteen or sixteen, was (as he wrote in the third person) "a new passion . . .
which, but half gratified, still holds force. He became enamored to the
woods . . . thoughts were always on the forests. . . . his waking and sleeping dreams, filled with vague cravings impossible to satisfy."

Parkman fulfilled his dreams by embarking on his vigorous woodland
expeditions. He had, he tells us, a "fondness for hardships." The experience of "sleeping on the earth without a blanket. . . . would harden him
into an athlete."[17] As discussed by Sigmund Freud in his theory of dreams
as wish fulfillment, it is possible that Parkman's frequent dreams reveal
"unconscious" wishful impulses that influenced his daytime behavior. This
kind of unconscious wish could force its way into his consciousness to gain
control of his power of movement.[18]

The Parkman family papers demonstrate that he had applause for his
role as a woodsman-explorer. There is a clear element of bravado in his
early letters to his parents. He wanted to impress them, and they were delighted with his accomplishments.[19] His family also had an understanding
of compassion for his illness. Indeed, the Parkmans had so many illnesses
that they were a microcosm of a vast, Victorian sickroom. At one time or
another, the Parkmans suffered from a host of ailments: temperatures,
coughs, aches, painful headaches, despondency, and defective eyesight.
The family was often disturbed by Dr. Parkman's severe depressions, which
cast a shadow over the household.

Certainly, the constant concern with illness in Parkman's home during
his boyhood had its impact upon him with his subsequent hypochondria
and complaints of chronic illness. Some relief from the sickroom atmosphere was afforded by Dr. Parkman's frequent and extensive travels, from
which he returned laden with gifts and stories that captivated young Frank.
If we read between the lines of family letters, there is an intimacy between
Frank and his father, in shared talk of headaches, travel, and diary writing.[20] In the warm, caring, but unfortunately sickly family atmosphere,
there was frequent talk about Frank becoming a lawyer, a career considered befitting his station in life. This family pressure on Frank to choose a
professional career reached its apex when as a Harvard student he an-

nounced to his parents that he preferred historical research and writing. This was a time when Frank wrote about his ambition to develop literary projects tuned to his "observations." Parkman's parents did not wish to stifle his literary ambitions. For the moment a conflict was left unresolved.

The father and mother, however, might have anticipated that Frank, the college student, would soon be afflicted with a nervous "disorder." Why not follow Dr. Parkman's solution for this kind of illness? Not unexpectedly, Frank's father and mother encouraged him to seek relief by embarking on a European tour. This sojourn, as described in Frank's journals, was anything but restful; it was, in fact, a frenzied series of excursions, mostly in Italy and Sicily. In writing from Rome to his parents on 5 April 1844, he spoke of his attempt to "thrash the enemy," his first reference to his tendency to personalize his struggle with his illness, now identified as his "enemy."[21] He also spoke of his intention to consult Dr. Pierre-Charles-Alexandre Louis, chief physician at l'Hotel-Dieu in Paris, known for his success is treating acute and chronic maladies. Parkman had a partial recovery by following a spartan diet and by depriving himself of one of his favorite beverages, Italian wine.

After returning to Boston to complete his B.A. degree and to begin law school study, Frank had what amounts to a complete mental and physical recuperation. In his journals and correspondence and in the early biographical accounts written by those who knew him, we learn of his arduous physical conditioning program in preparation for the Oregon Trail trip. He went so far as to hire a circus rider to train him in riding bareback and in jumping off and on a horse at full gallop. This hazardous stunt is still performed today by professional riders for motion pictures, but it is usually attempted after concealed steel grips are bolted to parts of a saddle and horn. Parkman, at least on the Oregon Trail (according to Frederic Remington's drawings, which had Parkman's approval as illustrations), had only a conventional, western-type saddle.[22] Thus, in describing his daring feats of horsemanship on the Oregon Trail, he was probably not exaggerating. The youthful Parkman of 1846, who left Independence for points West, was a prime physical specimen—tough, well-conditioned, and prepared to challenge dangers on the western Indian frontier.

The hardened young explorer on the Oregon Trail, however, encountered more than he bargained for. Weakened by the hot glare of the sun and his dependence upon contaminated food and water, he came close to a complete collapse near the end of his journey.

After his immediate return, however, Parkman found temporary relief from his weakness and blindness and overcame his crippling inability to concentrate. Within months, he began a gradual recovery, possibly related to his increasing interest in the single young women of Beacon Hill. In fact, he was able to complete *The Oregon Trail* and to begin the composition and writing of *Pontiac*. This was also a period when, drawing back from the tempestuous feelings aroused in him by a "Miss B," he chose the calmer happiness of a marriage with Catherine Bigelow, the daughter of a prominent Boston physician.

For a time it appeared that Parkman left the "enemy" behind him. His mother wrote that the prospect of marriage caused a transformation in the life of the young historian. The impending marriage, she reported, "makes Frank so happy & gives him something to think about . . . no reading in evenings or writing at present." [23] In his letters, however, he made little of his engagement other than that "an occurrence of some interest to myself . . . has just taken place." [24] Nor is his marriage in 1850 referred to in personal correspondence, although it must have been a topic of great interest among the gossips of old Beacon Hill society. Here was a "good connection" between two prosperous, patrician families—the Parkmans and the Bigelows. Indeed, the Parkmans were pleased that "father" was "quite satisfied" and thought the marriage "a great thing" for his son. After the event we find, nevertheless, a tone of restlessness on the part of the young husband as he neared the "tag end" of his "honeymoon." [25]

He and his wife, Kate, occupied a new home, "small, snug and comfortable," in the Boston suburb of Milton. Here he began a rigorous writing schedule to complete the chapters in *Pontiac*, but before long there were signs of recurring illness. Because of his partial blindness, he managed to keep at his task by "catching the knack of dictating," which he found, he said, "as easy as lying." Despite this new technique of composing, he was often without a competent amanuensis. Although Kate gave him assistance, as evidenced by her girlish handwriting in dictated letters, she was not always supportive of his work. He reported that she read the introductory chapter on Indians in *Pontiac* and pronounced it "uncommonly stupid." [26] While Parkman made light of her criticism, it is evident that he felt the bite of her words. His correspondence reveals that he turned away from his wife to pour out his heart to a relative, Mary Eliot Dwight Parkman (wife of a cousin, Samuel Parkman). He seems, moreover, not to have been a happy father. After the birth of a daughter, Grace, we find him annoyed with "a young heiress yawling in the next room," and again with "infantile music in the next room." [27]

Following the publication of *Pontiac* in 1852, in an epistle to Mary Eliot Dwight Parkman, he railed about "oppression," "protracted disaster," and "doom that lies before me."[28] With an uncanny sense of portending unhappiness he anticipated deaths in his family. A son, Francis, died in 1857 at two from scarlet fever, and his sorrowing wife followed her son to the grave after the birth of another daughter in 1858.[29] The magnitude of these losses was more than Parkman could bear. It was as if he had capitulated to a vicious attack by a demon malady that left him paralyzed by depression, fear, and pain. His elaborate descriptions of physical and mental torment are depicted in a heroic stance. Parkman stressed his valiant struggle to survive and overcome his illness.[30] This subject became a main theme in his correspondence in the late 1850s. Even when his health was moderately good, he foresaw assaults of his ever-present "enemy."

In these years Parkman's anxieties were made more painful by his concerns about improving what he called his "pecuniary condition." He was concerned about escalating expenses connected with a possible second marriage. Parkman, according to estate records, should have had few misgivings about the state of his finances. As a senior heir of the Parkman family, he, like the other Parkmans, enjoyed an ample inheritance. In the Parkman tradition, he did not make a display of opulence or extravagance. In fact, household and estate records suggest a certain penuriousness. Frank learned to keep detailed account books, still preserved among his papers at the Massachusetts Historical Society. Here he recorded all expenditures, however minor. There are entries of even small coins, less than a dollar. Such faithful record keeping did have its rewards. In his mature years he kept accounts for the real estate he owned, especially a store that gave him, he said, "a fairly good income."[31] He owned two personal homes (a large two-story frame house on a wooded land on Jamaica Pond, and a town house at 50 Chestnut Street on Beacon Hill), a cabin at Rangely Lakes in Maine, and a small island on the coast near Portsmouth, New Hampshire, where he planned to build another cabin.[32] There are scattered references to Parkman's hired help—Irish maids, other servants, gardeners, and secretaries. He always lived comfortably.

Parkman's habit of record keeping enabled him to have a command of his finances at all times. For instance, when he had a dispute about fraudulent charges made in copying research documents, he had payment data for every page. In fact, his letters reveal an almost joyful release of stress in demanding a return of expenditures from a librarian-trickster.[33] We can be sure that Parkman never procrastinated in handling monetary details, no matter how time-consuming or tiresome they might be. As his will and account books show, he did not permit his headaches to interfere with stewardship of family business. Curiously, he left no financial legacy for

Harvard College, although he lectured, in letters to the *Boston Daily Advertiser*, on the import of giving to educational institutions. When it came to Frank's own education, there was no stinginess on the part of his father in giving him the best, and he would have done the same for his son, had he lived.

Male members of this Parkman clan had a special role to play in Boston society. Like other distinguished New England families, the Parkmans were part of the patrician class that viewed itself as custodian of culture. Parkman's friend, Charles Eliot Norton, a Harvard professor, and Norton's cousin, Charles W. Eliot, president of Harvard, were, as Henry May has argued, excellent examples of late nineteenth-century transmitters and arbiters of elegant American taste in manners and in education. The Parkmans were the archetypes of this nineteenth-century New England patrician society.

Among the Parkmans there was, as might be expected, a fear of scandal about newspaper stories detailing accounts of the disappearance and murder of Frank's uncle, Dr. George Parkman, a wealthy physician. The uncle was killed, and his body dismembered and burned, by a Harvard chemistry professor after a quarrel over a debt. Frank and his father found it hard to believe that the uncle's behavior was anything less than exemplary, even after the disclosure of his record as a parsimonious and sometimes vindictive moneylender. The Parkman family seems never to have accepted the dark reality of the uncle's unsavory conduct in hounding debtors.[34] Had not Uncle George made generous gifts to Harvard College and other worthy institutions? Moreover, the uncle exemplified the worthy Parkman tradition of making money earn more money. Grandfather Samuel Parkman had already proved this was possible by managing accounts in the merchant trade. The historian, like other members of his family, not only watched the pennies, but also preserved the Parkman wealth in the wills, codicils, and other legal documents that listed real-estate holdings and stock portfolios that were passed from generation to generation.

Since Parkman's "pecuniary condition" was such that he could give all his time to his writing career (except for a brief adventure into a horticultural business), his main cause of stress was the status of his health. As we have seen, the worst crisis came with a collapse in 1858 following his wife's death. At this time an array of maladies combined to form a complex illness that surpassed anything in his family history. His complaints of heart trouble, despondency, sharp headaches (locking his head with pain resembling a tight iron ring), semiblindness, insomnia, water on the knee, and finally rheumatism and arthritis, in order of occurrence, are recorded in his personal writings. What is of particular interest is that he un-hesitatingly described the origin, development, and persistence of his ill-ness in a lengthy, autobiographical letter written in 1864.[35]

Parkman believed that his illness was the result of "mental tension. . . . With a mind over-strained and a body over-taxed, he was burning his candle at both ends." He also believed that although his "derangement" might be his "nervous system," he was not a "nervous" person, and that his difficulties were threefold: "an extreme weakness of sight, disabling him from writing his name except with eyes closed; a condition of the brain prohibiting fixed attention except at occasional and brief intervals, and an exhaustion and total derangement of the nervous system." Parkman's description of his maladies makes it possible to analyze his illness, but first, let us consider the relationship Parkman had with midnineteenth-century physicians.

Jared Sparks, Parkman's mentor at Harvard
who recommended books on Indians
and "the Old French War" for his pupil.
(From a bust by Hiram Powers in 1857;
courtesy The Huntington Library,
San Marino, California.)

DAMN THE LUCK

I, poor devil, am compelled to lay disabled in port, while others are
prosperously voyaging on the high seas. Damn the luck—
Perhaps my turn will come some time.

—LETTER TO EPHRAIM GEORGE SQUIER,
13 MAY 1849

Seventeen-year-old Parkman made this sketch "from the summit of one of the mountains of the Dixville Notch, representing the appearance of the cliffs opposite." (Courtesy Massachusetts Historical Society.)

CHAPTER TWO

THE CONQUEST OF
THE "ENEMY"

PARKMAN HAD THE ADVICE of a number of doctors besides Dr. Louis of Paris. A New York physician, Dr. Samuel M. Elliott, nearly "blinded" him in 1847, when he sought treatment for his eyes after returning from the Oregon Trail. In the early 1850s he became an enthusiast for Brattleboro's water cures and recommended them for his friend Lyman C. Draper, who shared complaints about chronic illness. While in Paris after his wife's death, Parkman sought out the doctor who, he said, "fixed Sumner's head." This specialist, a French-American neurologist, Dr. Charles Edouard Brown-Séquard, gained international fame by treating Senator William G. Sumner after he was caned on the head by a wrathful Southerner. Brown-Séquard believed that physical sexual energy functioned very much like electricity and had to be conserved. He therefore insisted upon continence because of the need to conserve semen.[1]

Brown-Séquard was representative of the physicians of America who treated nervous diseases by urging rest and continence. Parkman thought highly of the French physician and wrote that his advice resulted in improvement: "The muscles which ever since my first lameness, have been very much reduced & weakened, are restored wholly to their natural size & strength, so that when the neuralgic pain subsides, I shall be in a much better condition than before."[2]

Brown-Séquard's prescription for better health was typical of medical literature of the second half of the nineteenth century, which cautioned against masturbation, adultery, and even "excesses" with one's wife. Leading physicians and neurologists of the time in America and in England stressed sexual purity in order to abide in what was regarded as a struggle for survival.

The prince of the American neurologists, Dr. S. Weir Mitchell, became Parkman's physician about 1869–1870. Available evidence suggests that Mitchell's prescriptions and treatments made it possible for Parkman to live with his illness and make a partial conquest of the "enemy."[3] It is even probable that Mitchell steered him away from suicide, which Parkman at one time contemplated.

Mitchell, a seasoned practitioner, had Parkman's respect. He treated a number of other prominent Bostonians who shared his literary, historical, and scientific concerns. His photo-portraits reveal a handsome man with a crowning head of hair, high forehead, and a short beard. He looks out from these photos with an understanding gaze of confidence that must have impressed his patients. A most agreeable man and conversationalist with encyclopedic interests, Mitchell quickly established a cordial relationship with Parkman. From his Philadelphia office Mitchell made numerous trips to treat Parkman and his other "dilapidated" Boston patients. They welcomed this versatile physician, poet, popular novelist, and historian, who wrote on the youth of George Washington and the two Benjamins, Franklin and Rush. Mitchell's patients, who liked to read about medicine as a profession, could study his gracefully written clinical reports, for he produced a plethora of readable medical articles and books. Modern physicians still consult his essay on what is known as "S. Wier Mitchell's disease," also known as erythromelalgia, or red neuralgia, identified by redness of the hands or feet, a disease of the arteries and blood vessels.[4] He is remembered, especially, for his original methods in curing "nervous diseases."[5]

As a physician Mitchell undoubtedly had a strong impact upon Parkman. For instance, Parkman, in his correspondence with the doctor, states that he faithfully followed Mitchell's regimen about diet and rest. Mitchell must have prescribed his "rest cure" (so well known that it attracted the attention of Sigmund Freud) for his historian patient, although Parkman does not refer to the term.

His published case histories indicate that the good doctor had remarkable success curing patients, especially those who, like Parkman, had headaches "and other neurotic symptoms of eyestrain." In an essay of July 1873, entitled "Favorable Influence of Long Rest in Bed on Neuralgia of Locomotor Ataxia," printed in the *American Journal of Medical Science,* and in a book, *Fat and Blood,* published in Philadelphia in 1877, Mitchell stressed the importance of lengthy rest as therapy for the disease. In *Fat and Blood,* Mitchell pinpointed his successful treatment of women afflicted with "nervous exhaustion," showing that without rest, "even the firmest of women lose self-control at last under incessant feebleness." At least one of his female patients grew to like bed so well that she refused to get out after her recovery. Mitchell solved the problem by threatening her with the statement, "If you are not out of bed in five minutes—I'll get in with you." After he started taking off his trousers, she "leaped out of bed" in a rage but apparently cured.[6]

Parkman, however, like most of Mitchell's other patients of both sexes, after eating butter and cream and fattening himself during a long stay in bed, was eager to get up and take on the world. After reading Mitchell's case histories, one has the feeling that many of his patients were putting on weight and "sick" of being in bed.

But Mitchell's agreeable manner, combined with his wide knowledge as a leading physician of his time, impressed his patients, and Parkman was no exception. For those who resisted his entreaties, he could easily resort to the use of a hypnotic trance, although we have no knowledge that he resorted to this technique with Parkman. Mitchell had one more arrow in his quiver to win over his most articulate patients. He gave them copies of his poetry and fiction. He sent several of his novels to Parkman, who absorbed Mitchell's stories about the importance of subordinating sexual gratification for good health, family affection, and achievement. William Dean Howells, whose novels Parkman also read, had similar themes. In his plots, "seeds of righteousness" could be protected by "disciplined fathers and mothers" from one generation to another.[7]

Howell's characters were convinced that "the natural man is a wild beast" because of his rash behavior in sexual matters.[8] The true savages were those wild beasts of the forest with their multiple mates and promiscuous behavior. Although Parkman does not dwell on this point, in his descriptions of Indians on the Oregon Trail, he portrays Indian sexual mores as part of the savage life of the frontier.

G. Stanley Hall and Theodore Roosevelt, Parkman's later contemporaries, were also concerned with "civilized" conduct as opposed to the lifestyles of savages. A gentleman practiced resolution, self-control, and steeled himself for his role in life.[9] Silas Mitchell's autobiographical novel, *Dr. North and His Friends,* clearly designates the kind of restraint a gentleman had to follow under the norms of "civilized" morality in relations with the delicate, sexually attractive heroine, Sybil.[10] Mitchell's novels are packed with characters demanding the most precise standards of gentility.

AS KAREN HORNEY HAS ARGUED in her essays on the development of self, the individual is often dominated by his view of what he "should" do.[11] Parkman had the self-control to fashion a lifestyle to head

off attacks from his "enemy." With advice from Mitchell, his primary physician in later life, he coped with his infirmities by taking walks (some of
them ten miles or more) with the use of canes or a crutch, by spates of rest,
by gardening and going into a horticultural business, by taking trips to
Paris and London, and by following a prescribed diet. Eventually he was
able to complete his entire series of books. He did not exaggerate when he
wrote to Mitchell that "you have done more for me than anybody else." [12]
In Parkman's relationship with Mitchell one can sense that the doctor became, for his patient, a benign father figure who led him on to recovery.

The magnitude of Parkman's victory over illness is revealed in his accounts of how menacing his "enemy" really was. "No impediment on earth
is so formidable as the prostration of chronic disease," he wrote, "but time
and good courage work wonders." [13] In his attempts to foil attacks from
his illness, Parkman seems to have encountered the rest-cure remedy even
before he came directly under the care of Mitchell in the 1870s. In his correspondence there is mention of Dr. Bigelow, very probably his father-in-
law, a well-known Harvard professor of medicine who advocated rest and
natural recuperative powers rather than medical treatment. Parkman also
had advice from the doctor's son, Dr. Henry Jacob Bigelow, a leading
Boston surgeon, who made similar recommendations.

We can be confident that Mitchell's advice brought about a betterment
in Parkman's health, in both body and mind. After 1870 the "inflammation
of the eyes," the pain, "closely resembling the tension of an iron band, secured round the head and contracted with extreme force," and the "universal turmoil of the nervous system," all seem to have disappeared. Even his
insomnia, accompanied by a "headlong current of thought" in his "brain,
the irritated organ," became less of a problem. He paced himself to avoid
the kind of "exertion" that proved "too costly." [14]

THE SYPHILIS ISSUE

When Mitchell prescribed rest and a diet of "Hoff's Malt extract—arsenic—fat, butter, etc.—meat once a day and a little of it," Parkman wrote
that he "faithfully followed" the doctor's course of therapy. In just over
one year he gained ten pounds. But after he left off the malt and arsenic, he
had an "unpleasant turn of the head." He then began to eat more meat,
butter, fat, and cream, and had hopes for improvement. [15] This kind of report about eating to put on weight is repeated in other correspondence
with Mitchell, who also seems to have prescribed arsenic as a tonic for
Parkman's complaints about his nerves. Yet Mitchell also recommended ar-

senic for other patients who actually had syphilis. In fact, arsenic was a well-known medication for this disease in the nineteenth century and early decades of the next century.[16]

In the 1960s an arsenic prescription for Parkman was found in his desk preserved at the Colonial Society of Massachusetts, and as a result there has been speculation about whether or not Parkman might have had syphilis.[17] Mitchell's experience as a surgeon in the Civil War gave him firsthand knowledge about the disease, and he knew the symptoms when he saw them. Mitchell, however, if we read his correspondence with Parkman, treated him for nervous disorders.

I have found no mention or suggestion in Parkman's papers that would indicate that he had syphilis. My conclusion is that Mitchell prescribed arsenic as a dietary tonic for Parkman in the 1870s. There is nevertheless a possibility that Parkman might have contracted the disease on the frontier in 1846 when he was welcomed by Sioux leaders, who extended every kind of hospitality along with the company of their daughters. But Parkman leads us to believe that he would have spurned sexual favors from Sioux women. Given his Bostonian stance as a gentleman, it is improbable that he would have had sexual relations with Indian women. If he had temptations, Parkman never revealed them. At the same time, however, Parkman traveled widely by himself in the United States and in Europe and could have been exposed to the disease. The burden of historical proof is practically impossible. Yet, after consulting with medical historians, my conclusion is that Parkman did not have syphilis. This is borne out by the fact that Parkman in his mature years did not have the symptoms of advanced stages of the disease, such as those observed in the tragic case of Lord Randolph Churchill and other historic victims.[18]

ANALYSIS

Parkman, as we have seen, was nevertheless plagued by other health problems. There can be little doubt that he was a sick man in his early maturity, particularly during his apprenticeship as a writer. Seven modern physicians and two psychologists who examined his life story, after I presented evidence from Parkman's diaries and autobiographical accounts, agreed that stress was a cause of Parkman's flight into illness. His symptoms are indicative of a complex underlying neurosis. Unconsciously, he created for himself what is called a "struggle situation."[19] He may well have been dissatisfied with his "selfhood" and wanted to see himself in another way. As a consequence, he forced himself to play the role of a vigorous, aggressive man of action. Looking back, in 1864, he wrote about the "abnormal" "conditions" of his "nervous system," stating that he had "no other thought than crushing them by force," which resulted, he himself concluded, in "a state of mental tension."[20]

Parkman seems to have had a bipolar personality. At one pole was control over personal behavior involving finances and adherence to Beacon Hill proprieties. The other pole, easily seen in his early youth and manhood, involved risk-taking, adventure, Canada, the Indians, the prairies, and the Oregon Trail. The bipolar axis required, on the one hand, "correct" behavior, gentility, and tight control over funds. And on the other side, there were the opposing elements of spontaneity and love of nature and adventure. The result was a continual inner struggle to keep a balance and to cope with an imbalance that could bring on feelings of instability. This ongoing struggle became a keynote of his life. By adherence to it, he maintained an intact selfhood. He might be an invalid, but his life was a noble endeavor to forge self-restraint. Like Theodore Roosevelt, Parkman pictured himself as an advocate of the strenuous life.

In his writings Parkman saw major historical figures in a fanciful way as masculine leaders who challenged nature. We can argue that a person who has such heroic fantasies wishes to improve on the life that he or she sees. Parkman did this by diverting his fantasies into his writings. His inner battle to master his enemy can be seen as a powerful creative force, bursting forth in eloquent prose.

Parkman's fierce contests with his illness can help us to comprehend his preoccupation with perfectionism and his impatience with those who failed to live up to his expectations. His penchant for excellence in what he saw as the vigorous, masculine life is omnipresent in his novel, *Vassal Morton,* and is often projected into his *History.* For Parkman, the writer, there was a great personal satisfaction in reliving the exploits of valorous individuals.

As Erik Erikson argues, it is possible for people who identify with the world around themselves to have a sense of knowing where they are going, a feeling of well-being with worthwhile work goals.[21] Parkman had less anxiety about his work and health after his "dark years" in the late 1850s. His interests broadened, as numerous letters to the *Boston Daily Advertiser* indicate. Certainly his vigorous part in opposing woman's suffrage in a public debate occupied much energy and time. Meanwhile, good reviews of *Pontiac* affirmed his confidence in planned literary goals. With compensatory activities such as writing a novel, taking daily walks, and gardening, he gained more control over his life.

Parkman had learned to live with an unhealthy condition of body and mind, but his continual self-discipline did not entirely free him from painful headaches. A setback took place in December 1863, after his proposal for a second marriage was rejected by Ida Agassiz, the attractive daughter of the New England scientist Louis Agassiz. Parkman had hoped, with the improvement of his "health and pecuniary condition," that Ida would accept a proposal for marriage. News of her engagement to a younger man, a Civil War hero and wealthy banker, was a disaster for Parkman, who had "no tolerable sleep for a month." He bitterly complained to his cousin that the "inevitable effect upon my head was very bad,"[22] yet Parkman found that the shock of disappointment and the "pain" was not as "serious" as he had feared. He appears to have reconciled himself with the celibate life that was ahead, but he still lived for years to come with the loss of Ida.

By 1869–1870, after he first met Dr. Mitchell, he was able to plunge ahead with a vigorous research and writing regimen. In his fantasies, he cast himself in a glamorous role and sought the kind of self-sufficiency that psychoanalysts have analyzed clinically. Sparkling commentaries by critics of each new volume bolstered Parkman's self-esteem. His letters to newspapers in the 1860s and 1870s demonstrate that he regarded himself as an intellectual leader who could give the nation advice on war and peace, education, and leadership. He went so far as to take on a whole phalanx of reformers who stood for woman's suffrage and woman's rights. Parkman's behavior showed that he wanted his voice heard. As an "invalid," he had not fought in the Civil War, but his pen had become, as he hinted, a substitute for his sword.

As psychoanalyst Heinz Kohut has written, some individuals create an almost narcissistic armor, a "crust" of resistance about their inner conflicts. Dr. Mitchell understood Parkman's narcissism. When Parkman worked, he felt validated. Mitchell penetrated this "crust" with his genial manner and rest cure prescriptions, though these techniques are now considered sorely dated. He seems to have detected Parkman's "struggle situation," helping him to deal with wounded self-esteem. Most important, by following Mitchell's advice, Parkman almost entirely deflected attacks from his "enemy" and carried on his work without serious interruption. His unmarried sister, Lizzie, who became his lifetime companion, was a protective figure who looked after his every need.

Despite what has been said about Parkman's neurosis and "struggle situation," it is difficult to make a full diagnosis without doctor's records. Two modern physicians, however, after studying Parkman's complaints, offer further insight into the complexity of his illness. In 1951 Dr. Louis

Casamajor argued that there was a neurotic element in Parkman's anxiety about his eyes as well as in his heart trouble and arthritis. Many of Parkman's symptoms were common ones, including a "tight band around his head." He concludes that if Parkman had genuine eye problems they were "a peg around which was hung a mixed neurosis."[23] These conclusions were later partly contested by Dr. Edward C. Atwater, who acknowledges that although Parkman's illness is difficult to diagnose, he actually did suffer from chronic diarrhea, arthritis, and hydrarthrosis (water effusion into joint cavities), and at times suffered from photophobia (sensitivity to light). Atwater argues that Parkman's "demon in the head" may have been related to his chronic arthritis.[24]

Parkman's anxiety about his sight was undoubtedly linked to his struggle to achieve success as a writer. His stressful approach to his work was, as his letters reveal, partly based upon his need to please his parents and partly upon yearning for approval from society. In an early letter to Charles Eliot Norton, he spoke of the incentive he received from "spectators" who admired his pluck in carrying on in the face of illness. His letters in early manhood give one the impression that his stress was in some degree rooted in the fear of failure. He had a deep-seated desire for external sources of approval. When his wife mocked him, he needed reassurance from people who mattered most. He was especially concerned about critics of *Pontiac*, and there is the suggestion in his letters that he considered trying to arrange favorable critiques that could balance caustic appraisals from England. When one particularly hostile British review arrived accusing him of writing about natural sunset scenes for the sake of showing off his literary skills, he responded by making cuts in rambling nature scenes for a second edition of his book. But other notices counterbalanced attacks, especially when the reviewers on occasion sympathetically dwelled on his fight to overcome illness. When he at last surmounted the handicap of partial blindness, he compared himself with William H. Prescott, a historian role model, who at least had reasonably good sight in one eye.[25]

This comparison is carried further in Parkman's use of a "gridiron," a device to alleviate eye strain. This writing guide, fashioned out of wood and wire, enabled him to control his pencil when he wrote in semidarkness. Prescott had a similar device, called the noctograph, a grid crossed with brass wires. Like Prescott, Parkman hired copyists to make transcripts of documents in foreign archives, and he followed Prescott's system of privately printing his first historical volumes.

Considerable evidence suggests that the younger Parkman lived in the shadow of the older Prescott and, like him, felt a strong compulsion to overcome the formidable obstacle of illness to make a mark in the world. The advancement of his "highest interest" was his ambition, he wrote, "irrespective of happiness or suffering."[26]

YEARS OF PRODUCTIVITY

A less ambitious author, one who was not committed to maintaining such a vainglorious self-image, might not have persisted in completing his or her literary plans. Parkman's later writings enlarge upon the whole Anglo-Indian conflict that was first told in *Pontiac*. By 1865, when the Civil War reached its climax, he triumphed over his own "enemy" to the extent that he finished *Pioneers of France in the New World,* a romantic but documented account of exploration and settlement, which set a stage for subsequent studies. In the twenty-seven years following the Civil War, by conserving his energy and by avoiding much of the anxiety and stress that characterized his apprenticeship years, Parkman completed his elaborate series. He seems to have had, in these years, confidence about his work. He no longer had an anxiety for public approval and felt strong enough to take on protagonists in the suffrage movement. Undisturbed by their attacks (he seems to have enjoyed the fight if one reads his letters), he brought into publication *The Jesuits in North America* (1867); *The Discovery of the Great West* (1869, revised in 1878); a two-volume revision of *Pontiac* (*The Conspiracy of Pontiac and the Indian War After the Conquest of Canada,* 1870), deleting a number of panoramic descriptions of scenery and sunsets and adding the story of infecting Indians with smallpox; *The Old Régime in Canada* (1874), a pioneer work in social history; *Count Frontenac and New France Under Louis XIV* (1877); two volumes on *Montcalm and Wolfe* (1884); a revision of the *Pioneers* in 1885 after a visit to Florida; and two volumes of *A Half-Century of Conflict* in 1892, only a year before his death.

It is no easy task to pinpoint environmental, ethnohistorical, economic, political, social, or institutional history in Parkman's works because they were woven into the heart of a story episode, often by a narrator persona who is Parkman himself. The critic who seeks the familiar subheadings of the professional historian must stop to observe how an episode, one framed with historic circumstances, unravels itself.

IN *MONTCALM AND WOLFE* PARKMAN REACHED the pinnacle of his technique by giving his readers arresting portrayals of human character in the affectionate domestic side of Montcalm and the poetic sentiment of Wolfe. Such skill in narrative technique is especially evident in *A Half-Century of Conflict*, a complex but carefully designed narration of Anglo-French rivalries that led to the outbreak of the French and Indian War. Parkman left the completion of this work to the final years of his career because of its complexity and because it did not lend itself to a theme that could be built around leading figures. *A Half-Century* fills the chronological gap between *Frontenac* and *Montcalm and Wolfe*. Among other problems that Parkman had to deal with in this work was linking a wilderness narrative to the distant but significant factor of European power politics. This topic as well as others, such as "the Fur Trade," are skillfully brought into the fabric of his narrative.

While he was writing, Parkman was also revising to incorporate new material into previously written books. The fresh data enabled him to revise details, but he seldom changed his basic interpretations. A good example is the case of *Pontiac*. Nineteen years after the book appeared in print, the British Museum acquired the rich collection of Bouquet and Haldimand Papers. This acquisition enabled Parkman to complete his revision of *Pontiac* for a new edition of 1870, eliminating some chapters and adding others.[27] But his conspiracy emplotment theme was never altered, with its denigrating portrait of Indian people. So it was with Parkman's other historical works. They, too, were unchanged in basic interpretation (i.e., the intrepid, valiant character of LaSalle). At the same time, details were modified as narratives in each volume were brought up-to-date by rewriting and adding new citations. Parkman was always concerned with his reputation, and, like George Bancroft, whom he used as a model during his apprenticeship, he continued to revise, especially when he felt vulnerable to criticism. In the Parkman collection at the Houghton Library of Harvard University, there is a corpus of his revised volumes filled with pasted, handwritten changes that were used by printers for new editions. This penchant for improvement, not unrelated to his illness and "struggle situation," continued throughout life, long after he had at last achieved a position of eminence. He made literally thousands of changes on his pages.[28]

AFTER THE CIVIL WAR, Parkman gradually accepted the life of a gentleman writer looked after by his attentive sister, Lizzie, whom he said was "a beau ideal of sisterhood." A devoted father, he took pleasure in the company of his two daughters, who lived near his home on Beacon Hill with an aunt and their grandparents. Parkman relished the fame his writing gave him in the postwar decades. A man who enjoyed good company, he belonged to a number of Boston's clubs, including the St. Botolph Club (which Parkman helped to organize),[29] the Union Club, the Saturday Club, and "The Club," social organizations of men interested in politics, literature, and art. Meetings of these groups brought him into contact with prominent Bostonians, and at his and his sister's home at 50 Chestnut Street, Beacon Hill, he entertained a circle of friends. One of these, the journalist Edwin L. Godkin, described Parkman as an active conversationalist, well informed on public affairs.

A mugwump in his politics, Parkman was vitally interested in questions arousing public concern at the time. In letters to the press, he wrote on a variety of topics and supported Carl Shurz's enlightened policies toward the Indians. In an 1869 article in the New York *Nation,* he criticized American higher education, pointing to the need for "well-established and wisely conducted" universities in a nation where material success tended to be overvalued.[30] Parkman's criticism of higher education stemmed from his essays attacking coonskin democracy and demagoguery in politics. He believed America needed the leadership of an educated elite, "a palladium of democracy." Not surprisingly, Parkman concluded there was a "failure" of universal manhood suffrage, and he strongly opposed woman's suffrage.

In spite of this controversy, Parkman's later life appears to have been a contented one. The pleasures of his later Boston years were interspersed with trips abroad, to Canada, and visits to the Midwest and Florida. Such travel enabled him to establish friendships with foreign scholars like Abbé Henri-Raymond Casgrain of Quebec, an authority on Canadian history, and Pierre Margry, the French archivist. During his later years, his sister Lizzie was his constant companion. She went with him on daily boat rides on Jamaica Pond, where he had an opportunity to row. Without such exercise his health deteriorated. In the summer, they lived at Jamaica Pond in his house, and in the winters at their home on Chestnut Street on Beacon Hill.

Parkman regretfully left the trees that guarded his home on the Pond: huge sixty-foot elms, Scottish maples, and the garden with its flowers, vegetables, and plants. He loved his hemlocks, the lords of the eastern forests and mountains, often mentioned in his books. Those on Jamaica Pond gave him much pleasure. The Chestnut Street house was, however, conveniently located for winter days of research and writing, and the Boston Common, only a block away, was a favorite place for him.

For years, the Common had been an area where he occasionally met friends while walking. His figure was remembered by those who saw him as he marched quickly along Charles Street in a peculiar gait supported by two canes. Stopping every few minutes to rest against a fence, he would again resume his rapid progress. "I remember," wrote Francis Underwood, a founding father of the *Atlantic,* "very well meeting you a good many years ago on the Common when you were suffering from a pain like an iron crown. I remember your blue spectacles and your Indian or light ventilating hat, also the cane that seemed indispensable."[31]

Underwood recalled that Parkman had told him he was not "allowed to read even a newspaper." This encounter probably occurred when Parkman was in middle life, according to Underwood's recollection. Significantly, it reveals the intensity of struggle that frustrated the hero-historian in his dark years. Another eyewitness, Henry Cabot Lodge, recalled how, when he was a boy, he encountered a strange figure on Beacon Hill: "A tall, slender figure in a long gray coat, with a fur cap, in winter, drawn down close over his head, he would come walking up Beacon Street moving with great rapidity, a heavy cane in each hand, on which he rested his weight and by which he propelled himself. Going at a tremendous pace, he would suddenly stop as if exhausted and lean against a post or railing. Then in a few minutes he would resume his canes, and push away as if he were running a race." His mother told him the man was Frank Parkman. "What a battle for life," she said, "he was compelled to make."[32]

Although Parkman complained about his health throughout life, he was, as these accounts reveal, not really an invalid, and he lived to within a few weeks of his seventieth birthday. He finally yielded to his old "enemy," after what appears to have been an attack of appendicitis. He died on 8 November 1893.

In a poem composed and read by his friend, Oliver Wendell Holmes, the highlights of Parkman's struggles and successes as a historian-hero were memorialized at a later meeting of the Massachusetts Historical Society. Holmes caught the spirit of an image that would have given Parkman satisfaction:

> He told the red man's story; far and wide
>   He searched the unwritten records of his race;
> He sat a listener at the Sachem's side
>   He traced the hunter through his wildwood chase.
>
> High o'er his head the soaring eagle screamed;
>   The wolf's long howl rang nightly; through the vale
> Tramped the lone bear; the panther's eyeballs gleamed;
>   The bison's gallup thundered on the gale.
>
> . . . .
>
> When our far future's record is unsealed
>   His name will shine among its morning stars.[33]

THE CONQUEST OF THE "ENEMY"

Even though Holmes captured the essence of the portrait that Parkman cultivated throughout his life, there is more to the story of what became the Parkman legend. What do we actually know about Parkman's life and work? To answer this question more completely, we now go back to the beginning of his literary apprenticeship to examine his book-length narrative, *The Oregon Trail*. This book not only had a life of its own, distinct from his historical works, but it also is revealed as being a testing ground for writing autobiographical, novelistic histories.

Dr. S. Weir Mitchell, Parkman's physician,
internationally known for his "Rest Cure."
(Courtesy The Huntington Library, San Marino, California.)

Met waggons. "Whar are ye from? Californy?" "No." "Santy Fee?"
"No." "Trappin?" "No." "Huntin?" "No." "Emigratin?" "No."
"What have ye been doing then, God damn ye?"
(Very loud, as we by this time almost out of hearing.)
—PARKMAN'S JOURNAL, 21 SEPTEMBER 1846

Parkman's fringed buckskin "frock," worn on the Oregon Trail. When Parkman and his cousin and companion Quincy Shaw found that their clothes of "civilization . . . wore out," Indian women, Parkman said, made "us fringed buckskin frocks, and trousers to match, with moccasins in the Sioux pattern." (Parkman to Remington, January 2, 1892; courtesy Daniel Sargent and J. Templeman Coolidge.)

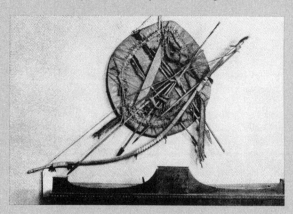

Parkman's Lakota shield, bow, and arrows, relics from the Oregon Trail. These hung on the wall above a secretary in his study at 50 Chestnut St., Boston, and were oftentimes moved in summer months to his home at Jamaica Plain. (Photograph by W. R. Jacobs.)

CHAPTER THREE

THE HERO ON THE
OREGON TRAIL

PARKMAN'S JOURNEY ON THE GREAT PLAINS was a well-planned research scheme to give him first-hand contact with Western Indians. His sojourn on the Oregon Trail had a considerable influence upon all of his later historical writings. Although he appears not to have fully understood that the Sioux, or Lakota, in 1846 had actually been in contact with Europeans for over one hundred years and were integrated into what is now called "the trading-post culture area," Parkman, in a short space of time, did make a series of graphic observations on nineteenth-century Sioux lifestyles. In a sense, he was a beginning investigator into what we now call comparative ethnology.[1]

What he did was to draw conclusions from a somewhat unrepresentative sample of one Lakota Indian culture in order to make interpretations about the behavior of Indian tribes bordering the colonial frontier. Although there were obvious differences between lifestyles of woodland Indians and plains people, it is nevertheless true that there were parallels in subsistence patterns, tribal systems of governance, trading patterns, technology, the diffusion of technology, the impact of white culture, and intertribal relations. At the same time there are flaws in Parkman's portrayal of Indian ways because many of his generalizations are based upon fleeting observations of his Lakota Indian hosts, and he tended to extrapolate from one sample.[2] Other Lakota peoples, for instance, were not entirely dependent upon the bison and had maize and garden produce as a part of their diet. What is nevertheless significant in this part of Parkman's research into Indian cultures is that he undertook the kind of fieldwork that became so popular with later students of native American cultures. We can further state that many of his portrayals of Indians have the ring of authenticity because of his early contacts with the Lakota.

The written version of his summer's experience, based upon journal notes and a good memory, went through a number of alterations before it appeared in book form. What follows is a brief account of how Parkman fashioned his narrative to achieve a series of episodic images of life on the prairies in the summer of 1846.

Parkman's itinerary took him over the eastern third of the Oregon Trail and over a large part of the Santa Fe Trail. His travel gave him exposure to vast areas of the Great Plains and gave him contacts with several Indian peoples. Besides, he saw traders, emigrants traveling to Oregon and California, soldiers, adventurers, and Mountain men. Except for the month he spent in the company with the Oglallah Sioux, or Lakota, he was in the company of his cousin, Quincy Adams Shaw, and his guides, the mountaineers Henry Chatillon and Deslauriers.

Parkman left Boston in late March 1846. After visiting New York and Philadelphia, he traveled overland to Pittsburgh, where he boarded a river steamer for the trip down the Ohio. After stops in Cincinnati and Louisville, the steamer arrived at St. Louis in mid-April.

While waiting for his steamer, the *Radnor*, to sail from St. Louis, Parkman visited Cahokia, the first French settlement in this area, and other historic sights in the vicinity, taking notes on what he saw. The *Radnor* left St. Louis (a starting point for those going west) at the end of April and cruised for five days up the Missouri River to Independence, Missouri, the "jumping-off place" for Parkman and his group.

From Independence, Parkman's party traveled by wagon and horseback to Fort Laramie. There are frequent references in his journals to the difficulties of travel across the plains: broken axles, a wagon sticking in the thick prairie mud, vagrant horses, thunderstorms, swarms of insects, and the annoyance of losing the trail. He was particularly impressd with the size and monotony of the prairies.

Six weeks after leaving Independence, in the middle of June, Parkman and his party arrived at Fort Laramie. They spent a week at the outpost among the Indians, fur traders, and emigrants. Parkman wrote critically of the high prices charged for goods at the fort (perhaps overlooking the reality of high freight charges paid by traders). After another week, Parkman moved south along the eastern ridge of the Rocky Mountains into northern Colorado. Here, early in July, he joined a band of Sioux in their wanderings following buffalo along the slopes of the Rockies. In spite of the occasional coldness with which Parkman comments on emigrants or Indians, clearly he was passionately interested in the life he was able to observe on this journey.

At the beginning of August, Parkman left his Sioux hosts and rejoined his friends and guides at Fort Laramie. Leaving the fort on August 4, the small party struck southward toward the Arkansas River and the Santa Fe Trail, arriving there at Bent's Fort just over two weeks later. Parkman learned about the outbreak of the Mexican War as they neared Arkansas; as they rode eastward, they passed transports of military equipment and soldiers. The eastward journey along the banks of the Arkansas and overland to Westport, Missouri, took another five weeks. They reached this outpost late in September.

Parkman had spent three and a half weeks with his Oglallah hosts, participating in as many of their activities as his poor health and inexperience would allow. He shared their food and living conditions, rode their horses on expeditions, and studied their crafts. His journal notes many details of their life, which he used in his later histories: hunting, social life, personal quarrels and intertribal vendettas, teepee building, and village leadership. Everything connected with Indians was of interest to him.

His letters, journals, and the completed book all convey the impression that he had at last satisfied his appetite for the taste of raw frontier life. These records will always be of interest because of Parkman's attitudes toward the others he met along the trail. Critics justifiably have marked him as a Boston snob who looked down on the westward-moving pioneers with patrician disdain. It has been said that Parkman's background prevented him from understanding the significance of a great westward movement passing before his very eyes. Samuel Morison, a modern counterpart of Boston's old patrician class, seems to have understood Parkman completely when he said that the nineteenth-century westward movement was simply "not his dish."[3]

Nevertheless, his "field trip" to study Indians would pay off handsomely, and his memories of living close to the land, having first-hand contact with Indians, gave him an identification with subject matter that no other historian of his time had. Having been exposed to frontier history in the making, he gained an appreciation of the total American experience from colonial times up to his own day. Although he never escaped from his New England heritage, he did not return to his former status as a writer almost completely bound by provincial tastes and ideals. The sophomoric writings about the blood and thunder published in the *Knicker-*

bocker Magazine in his college days pale next to his later historical works, and *The Oregon Trail* was written out of the authenticity of his own experience.

The first of Parkman's major writings, *The Oregon Trail* has many of the distinguishing characteristics of his later historical works. Like them, it was the product of intentional design, which enabled him to create a background with a framework of nature. It can be read for the story alone because, like the volumes of his *History,* it has the literary structure of a good novel, with plots and episodes yielding a maximum of suspense.[4] Parkman wanted to be widely read, and he knew how to avoid dullness and tell a good story.

If Parkman gave us a vivid narration to hold our interest, he also gave us a valuable original report of life on the Great Plains. From *The Oregon Trail,* posterity has his picture of the prairie life that survived there in the 1840s before it was altered further by encroaching white civilization. Before our eyes he fashions the image of undulating waves of grasslands inhabited by Indians, buffalo, antelope, birds, snakes, lizards, and insects. At the same time, the picture is animated by invasion of the frontier settlers on their way to the Pacific Coast and a number of individual characters wandering over the land: hunters, trappers, and deserters from military service. The image dims when one takes from his pages the backdrop of the prairie, the smell of fresh grass, the hum of insects, the snorting of horses and buffalo, the sweating, shouting actors, some dancing at campfire with fluttering trophies, others on horseback galloping to deliver the fatal blow to a wounded buffalo. Without such images, the reader's sympathy, curiosity, and concern are all but lost. Yet Parkman did not see his narrative as a perfunctory account of events; rather, he gave us the drama of daily existence and survival amid the pulsating life of a changing prairie environment.

Even the description of a river takes on excitement: "The Missouri is constantly changing its course—wearing away its banks on one side, while it forms new ones on the other. Its channel is continually shifting. Islands are formed, and then washed away; and while the old forests on one side are undermined and swept off, a young growth springs up from the new soil on the other. With all these changes, the water is so charged with mud and sand that, in spring, it is perfectly opaque. . . ."[5] The Missouri River is thus not static but a dynamic, moving entity with its own past. By emphasizing the developing quality of the river, Parkman caught something of its essence.

RE-CREATING THE OREGON TRAIL EXPERIENCE

Parkman's journals show us his process of re-creation, from the quick jottings in his journal to the panoramic scenes that unfold in his book. For instance, his journal notes on 1 August 1846 record a Sioux Indian village seen from the vantage point of a hill overlooking a wide vista of activity:

> Climbed a steep hill—on the left, the mts. and the black pine forest—far down, the bare hills and threading the valley below came the long, struggling procession of Inds.
>
> They soon camped in a grassy nook, where crowded together—dogs and horses, men, women, and children—the sight was most picturesque. The men sat smoking—the women worked at the lodges—the children and the young men climbed the steep rocks, or straggled among the pine-covered hills around the place. Droves of horses were driven to water—girls with spoons and buffalo paunches went down to a deep dell for water. Heat intense—sat down in a shady rock and watched the scene. Climbed at sunset a high hill and looked over mts. and pine forests. All night, the Inds. were playing at a great gambling game.[6]

This is an incisive passage, but in Parkman's memory were additional particulars to give the reader a full sense of being part of the scene. As the hero-narrator in the story, Parkman falls back on specific words and phrases to create an atmosphere of dramatic intensity. There is wild "confusion" among his hosts. By using such adjectives as "disorderly," "savage," and "listless," he introduces, as he did in later historical works, value judgments into the narrative. The expanded treatment of the Indian procession and encampment becomes an episode polished and revised for later editions:

> I rode to the top of a hill whence I could look down on the savage procession as it passed beneath my feet, and, far on the left, could see its thin and broken line, visible only at intervals, stretching away for miles among the mountains. On the farthest ridge, horsemen were still descending like mere specks in the distance.
>
> I remained on the hill till all had passed, and then descending followed after them. A little farther on I found a very small meadow, set deeply among steep mountains; and here the whole village had encamped. The little spot was crowded with the confused and disorderly host. Some of the lodges were already set up, or the squaws perhaps were busy in drawing the heavy coverings of skin over the bare poles. Others were as yet mere skeletons, while others still, poles, covering, and all, lay scattered in disorder on the ground among buffalo-robes, bales of meat,

domestic utensils, harness, and weapons. Squaws were screaming to one another, horses rearing and plunging, dogs yelping, eager to be disburdened of their loads, while the fluttering of feathers and the gleam of savage ornaments added liveliness to the scene. The small children ran about amid the crowd, while many of the boys were scrambling among the overhanging rocks, and standing with their little bows in their hands, looking down upon the restless throng. In contrast with the general confusion, a circle of old men and warriors sat in the midst, smoking in profound indifference and tranquility. The disorder at length subsided. The horses were driven away to feed along the adjacent valley, and the camp assumed an air of listless repose. It was scarcely past noon; a vast white canopy of smoke from a burning forest to the eastward overhung the place, and partially obscured the rays of the sun; yet the heat was almost insupportable. The lodges stood crowded together without order in the narrow space. Each was a hot-house, within which the lazy proprietor lay sleeping. The camp was silent as death. Nothing stirred except now and then an old woman passing from lodge to lodge. The girls and young men sat together in groups, under the pine-trees upon the surrounding heights. The dogs lay panting on the ground, too languid even to growl at the white man. At the entrance of the meadow, there was a cold spring among the rocks, completely overshadowed by tall trees and dense undergrowth. In this cool and shady retreat a number of girls were assembled, sitting together on rocks and fallen logs, discussing the latest gossip of the village, or laughing and throwing water with their hands at the intruding Meneaska. The minutes seemed lengthened into hours. I lay for a long time under a tree studying the Ogillallah tongue, with the aid of my friend the Panther. When we were both tired of this, I lay down by the side of a deep, clear pool, formed by the water of the spring. A shoal of little fishes of about a pin's length were playing in it, sporting together, as it seemed, very amicably; but on closer observation I saw that they were engaged in cannibal warfare among themselves. Now and then one of the smallest would fall a victim, and immediately disappear down the maw of his conqueror. Every moment, however, the tyrant of the pool, a goggle-eyed monster about three inches long, would slowly emerge with quivering fins and tail from under the shelving bank. The small fry at this would suspend their hostilities, and scatter in a panic at the appearance of overwhelming force.

"Soft-hearted philanthropists," thought I, "may sigh long for their peaceful millennium; for, from minnows to men, life is incessant war."

Evening approached at last; the crests of the mountains were still bright in sunshine, while our deep glen was completely shadowed. I left the camp, and climbed a neighborhing hill. The sun was still glaring through the stiff pines on the ridge of the western mountain. In a moment he was gone, and, as the landscape darkened, I turned again towards the village. As I descended, the howling of wolves and the barking of foxes came up out of the dim woods from far and near. The camp was glowing with a multitude of fires, and alive with dusky naked figures, whose tall shadows flitted, weird and ghost-like, among the surrounding crags.

I found a circle of smokers seated in their usual place; that is, on the ground before the lodge of a certain warrior who seemed to be generally known for his social qualities. I sat down to smoke a parting pipe with my savage friends. That day was the first of August on which I had promised to meet Shaw at Fort Laramie. The fort was less than two days' journey distant, and that my friend need not suffer anxiety on my account, I resolved to push forward as rapidly as possible to the place of meeting. I went to look after the Hail-Storm, and having found him I offered him a handful of hawks-bells and a paper of vermilion, on condition that he would guide me in the morning through the mountains.

The Hail-Storm ejaculated "How!" and accepted the gift. Nothing more was said on either side; the matter was settled, and I lay down to sleep in Kongra-Tonga's lodge.[7]

Comparison of the journal entry of 1 August and this expanded version reveals important differences. Although the journal entry is abbreviated and, on the whole, a meagre account of what happened to Parkman on that interesting first day of August, Parkman's staccato journal notes have a sharpness of style that gives the reader a feeling of immediacy. Fortunately, the feeling of immediacy is not lost in the longer account, which demonstrates that Parkman's memory unlocked a wealth of factual detail giving the day's events roundness and depth. We can expect that the expanded version is reasonably accurate, for Parkman's preserved papers show that in writing his *History* he relied upon his remarkable memory for much factual detail gleaned from published materials and bound copies of documents.

In the above expanded version of his experiences on 1 August 1846, Parkman, with the sure hand of a painter, creates a sensory image of life among the Sioux at the end of a day's march. His art in vivification is especially revealed in the feeling of space given the reader by a description of the distant Indian procession as "a thin and broken line" "stretching for miles" "like mere specks." Vivid, colorful language describes the animated Indian encampment scene: "squaws were screaming," "horses rearing," and "dogs yelping" amid the unloading of supplies and "the fluttering of feathers and the gleam of savage ornaments." One can almost hear the noise and confusion of women, horses, and dogs and can almost see feathers flutter and savage ornaments gleam. Parkman then appeals to our sense of smell: old men and warriors "smoking" their pipes. And finally he exposes the reader to the intense August heat that made each lodge a "hot-house" in the partly obscured "rays of the sun."

Among the incidents not mentioned in the journal is the brief description Parkman gives of his pause at the edge of a pool of water. We are told of minnows darting to and fro, some of them gobbled up as they innocently pass the hiding place of a monster fish hiding under a hollow bank. The haunting scene of the larger fish gorging himself upon the tiny minnows, an image of the survival of the fittest, occurs in various forms throughout *The Oregon Trail* and is revived again in historical volumes in wilderness scenes ornamenting the pages of *Pontiac* and the *Pioneers*. In *The Oregon Trail* Parkman time and again dwells on the pulsating wildlife of the prairie, the checkered snakes, the prairie dogs, the antelope, and the grazing buffalo, with nearby "ruffian-like wolves" searching for their weakest victim like "conscious felons."

Before leaving this discussion of a comparison of the journal and book versions of I August, we should note that while the book version contains a number of incidents and episodes not mentioned in the journal, the journal entry does mention an Indian gambling game that occupied the warriors far into the night. His design of the book made it necessary for Indian gambling games to be treated in an earlier portion of the narrative. Hence, launching into another description of the subject would burden the reader with repetition and interfere with the flow of his story.

SPECIFIC CHANGES

The specific changes made in transforming the journal of the Oregon Trail into a book can be summarized and classified into three groups. First, many small exaggerations are introduced, concerning such matters as the distance traveled in a day, the severity of the weather, the desolation of the countryside, the treacherousness of river currents; the aim in such cases is quite obviously to smooth the flow of the story. A day's journey of five miles (in the journal) becomes a journey of "six or seven miles." In the journals only a brief reference is made to the character of the Missouri River, but in the book Parkman devoted a paragraph to emphasizing the dangers of navigating the river.

Another category of exaggeration must be noted here. *The Oregon Trail* gives us insight on Parkman's biased interpretations, which are later resounded in his *History*. Not only were critical judgments and biases transferred from the journal to the book, but also they were often blown up to larger dimensions in the process. The "piratical-looking Mexicans" at Independence, Missouri, (journal) became "slavish-looking Spaniards gazing stupidly out from beneath their broad hats" in the book. His criticisms of his British companions (notably Romaine), the Mormons, and others who displeased him are given a greater prominence in the book. There are occasional derogatory references to Indians in the journal, but these became more frequent in the book. In the book, but not in the journal, he commonly calls the Indians "snake-eyed." On one occasion he even allowed himself to describe the pleasure he might have had in shooting a shrunken, ugly old warrior out of a tree because he made such a tempting target. This passage appeared in the *Knickerbocker Magazine* version of the book but was deleted from other editions.[8] Some of the bloody accounts of buffalo killings, a few of them almost sadistic in tone, alluding to the comparable pleasure of killing "human antagonists," were modified for his final edition. The mature Parkman seems to have outgrown his youthful enthusiasm for shooting every wild animal that came within range of his beloved rifle, "Satan," and in his *History*, he protested against the senseless slaughter of Canadian beaver.

There is still another kind of exaggeration involved in writing *The Oregon Trail*. The colloquial language that Parkman sometimes blurted out in the journal suggests that portions of the book were bland narrative tinctured with Victorian rose water. If Parkman himself did not dilute his story, his college friend, Charles Eliot Norton, who helped him prepare the *Knickerbocker Magazine* versions for publication, may have blue-penciled occasional colloquialisms. For instance, we read in the journal that Colonel William Russell was "drunk as a pigeon." In the book this becomes a description of Russell: "With one hand he sawed the air, and with the other clutched firmly a brown whiskey-jug." The argument can be made that Parkman, in deciding on revisions, concluded that an expanded version, with softened language, was more appropriate for his reading audience.[9]

What further basic types of alterations did he make? A second kind of change—and this point has already been referred to—is that chronological changes are made. A typical example: Parkman gathers incidents from several uneventful days, with some minor rearrangement of events, and presents them as belonging to one day of exciting life on the Great Plains.

Third—and this point has also been noted—brief entries in the journals are enlarged from memory, often in order to heighten a melodramatic impact. For instance, in the journal Parkman made a few brief references to difficulties encountered in fording streams with wagons: "Great trouble at a stream. Waggon stuck." In *The Oregon Trail*, however, fully two pages are devoted to one such episode, in which all the details of broken axles, mired wheels, panicked horses, and desperate men are impressively portrayed.

Some of Parkman's changes resulted in an occasional awkwardness or inconsistency in the narrative; for instance, gaps of several days occur. When incidents from the journals were omitted, it was usually because they formed a jarring element in the new setting of *The Oregon Trail*. In the journal, for example, Parkman records a story told by Henry Chatillon during the trip on the *Radnor* of an Oglallah chief who drank, treated his people with great cruelty, and practiced a form of despotism rare among Plains Indian leaders. This journal entry was almost certainly omitted from *The Oregon Trail* because its interpolation would have disrupted the flow of his river narrative and would have anticipated the stories of rivalry and internecine conflict among the Indians exploited so skillfully at a later point in the book. Some of Parkman's omissions, however, such as his description of explorations around the St. Louis area, are not so easy to account for.

The wording in *The Oregon Trail* was frequently taken over from the journals, but details were added and a great deal of polishing took place, even in the first serial publication in the *Knickerbocker Magazine*. The book that emerged at this stage was a far more literary piece than the rough journal had been, and Parkman, who wanted his narratives to achieve a worldwide reputation, continued to rework his text. From his correspondence we know he wanted to show the arrogant English literary world that a Yankee could write a good book. Parkman's work of revision spanned a period of some forty-five years, from the publication in the *Knickerbocker* to the Remington edition of 1892. The later editions benefited particularly from the polishing they received at the hands of an increasingly experienced writer.

In the 1849 edition published by Putnam, a number of details were changed.[10] In both the *Knickerbocker* and the 1849 edition, chapters were introduced with short quotations of poetry. For the 1849 edition Parkman moved some of these quotations from one chapter to another, while other chapters received new headings. A quotation from Byron's *Childe Harold*, for example, was moved forward from the third to the second chapter, and the fragment from *Harold the Dauntless* in the *Knickerbocker* version vanished entirely. A bit of William Cullen Bryant's work appeared at the beginning of chapter three. Most of the poetic introductions of the other chapters went unchanged into the 1849 edition, except for minor corrections in spelling and punctuation, but by the time of the Remington edition, all of the poetry had been deleted.

THE HERO ON THE OREGON TRAIL

The most important revisions were made for the fourth edition (1872). Several changes in the text itself were made on this occasion, and the final Remington edition, from which the present edition is drawn, is similar to the fourth edition except for very minor changes (i.e., modernization of spelling, punctuation, and correction of typographical errors) and the inclusion of the Remington illustrations, which proved an ideal complement to Parkman's text.

For the 1872 edition, Parkman condensed his narrative, omitting many superfluous remarks and most references to his illness. Indeed, each of the editions had reduced the space given to his health. The statement in the *Knickerbocker* that "I suffered not a little from pain and weakness, the latter of which would have forced me to take an uncomfortable refuge in the cart, but for the aid of my former friend, the whiskey," was reduced in the 1849 edition to "I suffered not a little from pain and weakness" and was eliminated altogether in later editions. Similarly, he deleted remarks on his traveling companions of the first leg of the ride and reduced the number of descriptions of unimportant events. The result of all this was that Parkman's narrative gained greatly in continuity, clarity, and coherence. This was done by manipulating time sequence, by exaggeration of certain details, and by enhancing his image as bold young traveler-explorer.

Parkman's revisions gave his book a more impersonal tone. In addition to deleting references to his health, he removed a number of other personal references. For example, the fact that he tried to shave off a month's growth of beard with a dull razor was not considered worthy of inclusion in the Remington edition. In this late edition, references to "the reader" became more frequent, while the earlier conversational style was toned down. Parkman was striving for the appearance of greater objectivity.

Occasionally an incident was elaborated on in the course of the various revisions. Such elaborations usually dealt with the character or life of the Indian. Parkman greatly expanded his account of the austere life lived by the Sioux.

Even the title underwent change. In the 1849 edition it was *The California and Oregon Trail: being Sketches of Prairie and Rocky Mountain Life.* Parkman disapproved of this title, considering the use of the word *California* "a publisher's trick" for the sake of publicity. The 1852 (Putnam) printing and the 1872 edition by Little, Brown and Company and all subsequent editions bore the title, *The Oregon Trail,* including the subtitle: *Sketches of Prairie and Rocky Mountain Life.* By the time of the 1872 edition (which Parkman and his publishers called the fourth edition, a work that was reprinted through 1882), Parkman had made the fundamental alterations that

FRANCIS PARKMAN

he wanted to make, although, as has been noted, additional minor changes were made for the 1892 Remington edition.[11] A comparison of the *Knicker-bocker* version, the 1849 edition, and the Remington edition illustrates the kind of minute changes that Parkman made over the years. For example, he made small changes in wording, spelling, and punctuation in his text. Here are examples of changes that can be traced through the three versions of the book:

Knickerbocker	1849	Remington	Page Number
Delorier	Delorier	Deslauriers	(12)
Sioux, Dahcotah	Dahcotah	Dakota	(94, 98)
Montalon	Montalon	Monthalon	(104)
———	Beckwith	Beckworth	(133)
———	Minnicongew	Minneconjou	(139)
Jean Gras	Jean Gras	Gingras	(147)
Moran	Moran	Morin	(147)
La Boute	La Bonte	La Bonte	(152)
Mahto-Takouka	Mahto-Tatonka	Mahto-Tatonka	(157)
Borque	Le Bouté	Le Borgne	(206)
Shienne	Shienne	Cheyenne	(206)
Cimoneau	Cimoneau	Simoneau	(102)
pantaloons	pantaloons	trousers	(11)
erected	erected	pitched	(24)
rushing past	rushing past	rushing by	(48)
toward	toward	towards	(49)
shrubbery	shrubbery	bushes	(92)
Travaux	*travaux, travail*	*traineaux, travois*	(112, 125)
summit	summit	top	(152)
semblances	semblances	signs	(153)
declivities	declivities	descent	(172)

Parkman's difficulty with spelling appears to have been largely limited to foreign words and names, as seen above, the only Anglo-Saxon name that was changed being Beckworth. One name that should have been changed is Vaskiss (102), which is probably Parkman's phonetic spelling of the Spanish name Vazquez, or Vasquez.

At the beginning of his writing career he had described small groups of people, animals, or things as "a dozen" or "half a dozen," but in the

Remington text he substituted more appropriate terms. This can be noticed at the very beginning of *The Oregon Trail*, where "a party of Kansas Indians" replaces "half a dozen Kansas Indians" (p. 2), and "a group of Indians" is substituted for "half a dozen Indians" (p. 3). His changes in punctuation were designed to conform with current usage. For example, quotation marks became double rather than single. Finally, Parkman made a number of changes in the spelling of proper names.

The arduous process of refinement to which *The Oregon Trail* was subjected has few counterparts in American historiography. With each edition the style was smoother, the narrative more logical, the tone more objective, the images more appropriate. Yet much of this was designed to alter the journal account of what happened. The changes made it more difficult to identify those alterations in the narrative that tended to distort the record and reveal Parkman's biased interpretations. Here, then, was a novelistic, creative narrative, a literary work produced by a gifted young writer.

In a sense, *The Oregon Trail* was a practice run in literary preparation, a part of Parkman's autobiographical record where he could design and recast episodes, still keeping the essentials of his story. We see also a certain cruelty in his character. As a youth he might write chapters for the *Knickerbocker* in which he took a kind of insidious pleasure in contemplating the shooting of an old Indian out of a tree. He also went so far as equating the joy of killing buffalo with the thrill of killing enemy soldiers in battlefield combat. These portraits of himself, after his early apprenticeship, were muted and seldom came to light in later years.

We cannot be sure that Parkman made changes in order to avoid offending the sensitivity of his readers. Still, the bloodletting, especially in hunting, remained. These overtones of violence in *The Oregon Trail* tell us much about the mature Parkman, whose later volumes are tinged with the exciting ferocity of wilderness war.

Remington's illustrations, carefully drawn to represent the bold, explorer image of Parkman the young man, fittingly accompanied the text in stressing the adventurous role a youthful explorer had in pitting himself against the physical dangers of a raw frontier.[12] This, of course, is exactly the kind of portrait that Parkman wanted. He looked back, all his mature life, on his exploratory experience on the prairie. It was a role he could live again in narrating the story of Indians and European pioneers in the New World. First, however, the story had to be told in miniature, encapsulated into the exciting events leading up to Pontiac's "conspiracy." Here was a major challenge for the hero-researcher.

"The Indians giving a Talk to Colonel Bouquet in a Conference at a Council Fire, near his Camp on the Banks of the Muskingum in North America in Octr 1764." (From an eighteenth-century engraving; courtesy The Huntington Library, San Marino, California.)

PART TWO

THE HISTORIAN AS HERO-RESEARCHER

"The Indians delivering up the English Captives to Colonel Bouquet near his Camp at the Forks of the Muskingum in North America in Novr. 1764." (From an eighteenth-century engraving; courtesy The Huntington Library, San Marino, California.)

Before the end of the sophomore year my various schemes had crystallized into a plan of writing the story of what was thus known as the 'Old French War' . . . here, as it seemed to me, the forest drama was more stirring and the forest stage more thronged with appropriate actors than in any other passage in our history. It was not until some years later that I enlarged the plan to include the whole course of the American conflict between France and England in North America; or, in other words, the history of the American forest. . . . My theme fascinated me, and I was haunted by wilderness images day and night.

—LETTER TO MARTIN BRIMMER, 14 NOVEMBER 1886.

Colonel Henry Bouquet,
whom Parkman said was a "jewel of an officer."
(From a painting, after an early engraving;
courtesy The Huntington Library,
San Marino, California.)

CHAPTER FOUR

PONTIAC: THE STRUGGLE TO RE-CREATE FRONTIER HISTORY

WE HAVE SEEN HOW PARKMAN, working out his method of study, spent a summer among the Western Sioux tribes of the prairies. When it came time for him to write a book on Pontiac and "the Old French War," the youthful Parkman knew more about Indians than any other historian of his day. Not only had he read all the personal narratives, all the military journals, the notebooks and reports of missionaries, the letters of pioneers and government officials, but he had also visited the Iroquois of his own day living on reservations in New York. Having pored over every available record and spent a summer on the Oregon Trail frontier, he was now prepared to undertake a formidable task, a reconstruction of events leading up to the Indian war of 1763 led by Chief Pontiac.

If we read his journals and letters, we learn that this is exactly what he planned to do: he would make the effort to recreate the past and bring those days of Indian frontier-woodland life back to the pages of history. Herein is the main reason why *Pontiac,* despite its faults, became one of the most significant books on Indians ever written.

Pontiac was an influential book on Indians in its own day because it clarified and reinforced stereotypes of Indians that the American public had derived over the years from James Fenimore Cooper's Leatherstocking Tales. Cooper's impact on Parkman was such that we might even argue that *Pontiac* was a storyteller's historical version of Cooper's novels. There is no question that Parkman was so caught up in his theme, especially the Indian aspect, that he had nightmarish dreams. In one of his autobiographical letters he confessed that "I was haunted by wilderness images day and night."[1] He made peace with himself, he tells us, by fleshing out the images on the written page. He "resolved to write a history of the Indian war under Pontiac, as offering peculiar opportunities for exhibiting forest life and Indian character."[2]

THE SPECTER OF COOPER

Anyone who studies Parkman's early life can see the ghost of James Fenimore Cooper hovering around the youthful historian. Charles H. Farnham, Parkman's first biographer, his friend and secretary, said that Cooper had an enormous impact upon Parkman in his formative years. One has the impression from Farnham that Cooper and his stories gave the central thrust to Parkman's literary dreams.[3] The argument can be made that *Pontiac* did follow the unoriginal theme of the forest and the Indian so clearly exploited by Cooper, but Parkman's treatment was more specific and exacting.[4] His *Pontiac* raised the level of conflict between civilization and savagery from the level of fantasy to that of historical and dramatic tragedy. Cooper's works provided an audience for the kind of history Parkman wrote. In fact, Parkman's histories were as exciting reading as any of Cooper's volumes, partly because he copied a literary trick of Cooper's, that of giving the reader action in language as vivid as the action itself.[5]

In order to transform Cooper's fantasy wilderness scenes into historical tragedy, Parkman had to immerse himself into the sources far more than Cooper ever did. Moreover, Parkman had the formidable task of making his Indians recognizable as individuals who belonged to a particular tribe and culture. Cooper's Indians were not, for Parkman, authentic tribal people since Cooper had little or no understanding of ethnology. Fortunately for the youthful Parkman, his "Injuns on the brain" case of mind gave him the enthusiasm and drive to embark on an extensive program of ethnological studies. Parkman's autobiographical novel, *Vassal Morton,* tells us that Augustin Thierry's volume on the *History of the Conquest of England by the Normans* gave him a spur to undertake such a challenging project. Vassal, Parkman wrote, was fascinated by Thierry's account of "movements of various races" and "soon began to find an absorbing interest in tracing distinctions, moral, intellectual, and physical, of different races, as shown by their history, their mythologies, their languages, their legends, their primitive art, literature, and way of life." Indeed, Vassal decided to devote his entire life to such studies. He could indulge himself in travel, "over rocks, deserts, and mountains," to become "intimate with the most savage and disgusting barbarians." Such an all-encompassing challenge would "call into a life all his energies of body and mind."[6]

While reading Thierry in the 1840s, Parkman also devoured all the works on history and ethnology that came his way. These included "almost all the works on Indians," he said, "from Lafitau and the Jesuits down to the autobiography of Blackhawk." At the same time, he seems to have been continually reading and rereading volumes of Cooper. In Europe, his journals tell us that he had a copy of the *Pioneers* on hand for a breath of "fresh air," while he was touring Italy. He was emerging from a kind of intellectual cocoon, but he still, as Farnham tells us, was "so identified with the novelist's red heroes that he dreamed of them, talked of them more than anything else," even, on occasion, "whooping and jumping about imitating calls of wild animals in Indian fashion."[7]

COOPER AS A FICTIONAL HISTORIAN

One can imagine how impressed Frank Parkman was to find that there were actual localities where some of Cooper's scenes had taken place. At Glen's Falls, New York, he could still see the "foam and fury" of cascading water and rock caverns as described by Cooper, although the romance of the place was smothered for the angry and disappointed Parkman by an ugly bridge spanning a majestic cataract.

Cooper was able to draw convincing scenarios because of his remarkable penetration of historic sources, a technique that Parkman emulated. Cooper, for example, had based a major turning point in his vivid account of the surrender of Fort William Henry in *The Last of the Mohicans* upon a vitally important message by letter. Parkman seized upon the same missive to create a tense confrontation in *Montcalm and Wolfe*. Actually written on 4 August 1757, the letter was sent at the request of Fort Edward's commandant to inform the besieged forces at Fort William Henry that no rescuing forces would be sent. A sergeant in the Connecticut Rangers carried the message, but Indians accompanying the Marquis de Montcalm's army killed the unfortunate soldier, stripped his body, and sent his clothing to a French officer. Carefully folded in the vest was the letter. It reached Montcalm, who must have read it with satisfaction. As a dramatic and practical gesture, Montcalm sent his aid, Bougainville, with the note to the entrance of the fort under a flag of truce: "I am sending to you the letter because of the generosity I profess toward those against whom I am obliged to make war."[8]

Montcalm's message stated: "The General [General Daniel Webb] thought proper to give you . . . intelligence, that in case he should be so unfortunate from delays of the Militia not to have it in his power to give you timely assistance, you might be able to make the best terms that were left in your power."[9] After the defenders had reached the end of their resources on August 9, a capitulation was signed. A massacre of defenseless prisoners followed. The Indian allies, many of them drunken warriors eager to kill, butchered survivors in a crass violation of the capitulation agreement. To his credit, Montcalm "ran thither immediately" and did all by "prayers, threats, caresses, consultation with chiefs, interposition of officers and interpreter's to end the killing."[10] Survivors, including Colonel Monro, eventually reached Fort Edward, and others were purchased from Indians by French officers in Canada. The prisoners saved only a portion of their possessions from the ravages of the Indians, but the French allowed Monro to keep his official papers. Among these was the August 4 letter and Montcalm's communication to Monro. Eventually these manuscripts came into the hands of the fourth earl of Loudoun, John Campbell, later commander-in-chief of the British colonial forces in America. They remained in the Loudoun family until 1923, when they were placed on the open market and purchased by Henry E. Huntington. The original message to Fort William Henry, carried by the colonial ranger who lost his life attempting to deliver it, is now in the Huntington Library Loudoun Collection. It is folded to the size of a large postage stamp.[11]

However, before being turned over to the earl of Loudoun, the letter was copied and summarized by the French. The first accurate rendering of the letter appeared in *Montcalm and Wolfe,* based upon the copied version in the journal of Bougainville, Montcalm's aide, but as we have noted, Parkman undoubtedly first read about the letter in the narrative of the fall of Fort William Henry in *The Last of the Mohicans.* While Cooper dramatizes the episode, his narrative is reasonably accurate. In *The Last of the Mohicans,* Cooper brings Montcalm face to face with Colonel Monro at Fort William Henry on August 7. When the French general hands Monro the letter, Monro exclaims, "The man [General Webb at Fort Edward] has betrayed me . . . he has brought dishonor to the door of one where disgrace was never before known to dwell, and shame has he heaped heavily upon my gray hairs."[12]

One can imagine the youthful Parkman's excitement when he found the exchange of letters was based upon genuine correspondence. Further, the massacre of Fort William Henry prisoners was, as Cooper concluded, due to the timidity of General Webb, who might have marched through the forest and pushed back Montcalm's forces if he had possessed the courage to do so. Cooper told the story first, but Parkman enlarged upon it and gave it historical narration. Here also were subplots about Montcalm trying to control the Indians amid the wild confusion of Indians brutalizing prisoners. If Parkman had a view of Indians as savage warriors, he first saw such an image in Cooper.

In his review of Cooper's works in 1852, Parkman gave him praise he bestowed on few writers: "His genius drew aliment from the soil where God had planted it, and rose to a vigorous growth, rough and gnarled, but strong as a mountain cedar. His volumes are a faithful mirror of that rude transatlantic nature which to European eyes appears so strange and new." [13] Cooper was for Parkman the "most marked and original" of all American writers, and one who had gained recognition for American literature. Of all his volumes, *The Last of the Mohicans* had the most vivid descriptions of "scenery and action." In Parkman's opinion, Uncas the Mohican did not resemble a genuine Indian, but Magua, the villain, was a truthful portrait, particularly in his falling in love with Cora. "It is well known that Indians, in real life as well as in novels, display a peculiar partiality for white women . . . Cora was the very person to fascinate an Indian." [14] Having made this interesting statement, Parkman went on to tell us that Italian men preferred light-complexioned women, and Swedish men regarded "a brunette with the highest esteem." [15] Thus he concludes his digression on sexual preferences.

Justifying the realism of Cooper's Indians, Parkman elaborated in his review on Cooper's portraitures: "The character of Hawkeye or Leatherstocking is, in the Mohicans as elsewhere, clearly and admirably drawn [despite the frontiersman's] excessive and ill-timed loquacity." Parkman especially admired Cooper's animated account of the battle at Glen's Falls better than anything of the kind in the novels of Sir Walter Scott. Parkman in this instance seems to have reverted to his boyhood love of the forest, which put mist in his eyes. He is actually talking about his own projected *History* in this review.

> The scenery of the fight, the foaming cataract, the little islet with its stout-hearted defenders, the precipices and the dark pine woods, adds greatly to the effect. The scene is conjured before the reader's eyes, not as a vision or a picture, but like the tangible presence of rock, river, and forest. His very senses seem conspiring to deceive him. He seems to feel against his cheek the wind and spray of the cataract, and hear its sullen roar, amid the yells of the assailants and the sharp crack of the answering rifle. The scene of the strife is pointed out to travelers as if this fictitious combat were a real event in history. . . . Nay, if the lapse of a few years has not enlightened his understanding, the guide would as soon doubt the reality of the battle of Saratoga, as that of Hawkeye's fight with the Mingos. [16]

Parkman as a young man had been to Glen's Falls and had relived Hawk-eye's harrowing battle with the Mingos. This was exactly the dramatic fabric that could be incorporated into historic narration. Today Cooper's battle scene seems stale and artificial, especially when compared with Parkman's stirring account of the "Heroes of the Long Saut," a similar scene of strife in *The Old Régime*.[17] Cooper's stories, which Mark Twain called "broken twig" tales[18] because so many characters betrayed their presence in the forest by stepping on twigs, were not humorous to Parkman. He admired their verisimilitude, their accuracy in portraying the past: "Their virtue consists in their fidelity, in the strength with which they impress themselves upon the mind, and the strange tenacity with which they cling to the memory."[19] The clinging to the memory is, as any Parkman reader knows, a singular feature of his style. He learned, possibly from Cooper, and then experimenting in *The Oregon Trail*, to appeal to all senses of the reader to create the illusion of reality.

In style, Parkman complimented his predecessor in woodland-wilderness narratives with the observation that Cooper wrote "with manly directness" and with "pith and substance."[20] In addition, Cooper's narrative was filled "with powerful interest." *The Last of the Mohicans*, Parkman rhapsodized, "has the genuine game flavor; it exhales the odors of the pinewoods and the freshness of the mountain wind. Its dark and rugged scenery rises distinctly on the eye as the images of the painter's canvas, or rather as the reflection of nature herself. But it is not as the mere rendering of the material forms, that these wood paintings are the most highly to be esteemed. They are instinct with life, with the very spirit of the wilderness; they breathe the sombre poetry of solitude and danger."[21] Parkman perceived how Cooper could be placed into a historic context in terms of his own picturization of the wilderness frontier, still retaining a "genuine game flavor." What was especially needed was another kind of portrayal of Indians, and this could be accomplished by study of all available works in ethnology and by actual observation of Indians in the area of the Oregon Trail. This kind of study had been beyond Cooper. Parkman would fill the gap, but one cannot help observing that the treacherous, fictional Magua in *The Last of the Mohicans* has many of the character traits of Pontiac, the conspirator.

HISTORICAL MODELS AND CRITICS

Cooper, in a sense, was a historical model for the kind of novelistic history Parkman wrote, as were François de Chateaubriand and Sir Walter Scott, whose books are on his youthful reading lists. William H. Prescott's histories gave him an example of what could be done in giving a romantic flair to Spanish conquest history; but there were more specific historical models that he could consult for his literary framework of historical narration. For instance, he pored over George Bancroft's volumes relating to early American history, paragraph by paragraph. Bancroft gave him a sense of historic proportion in judging the amount of space for LaSalle's wanderings. Even the eulogy that Bancroft composed for LaSalle has visible similarities to Parkman's. Here was a minature framework for *Pontiac*, which became a preliminary survey of the Anglo-French-Indian story of rivalry and conflict from first contact to 1763. Thomas Mante, an eighteenth-century British officer who fought under Colonel John Bradstreet in Pontiac's War, left a *History of the Late War . . . (1772)*, which had an accurate blow-by-blow account of all important military operations between 1755 and 1764 with accounts of Indian participation.[22] Parkman's copy of the book and the copy he borrowed from the Harvard College Library when he was a student are both speckled with his marginalia. Perhaps Mante's *History* was, as he wrote a friend, "clumsily written," but it was nevertheless the most significant work on the "Old French War" that fell into his hands.[23] This one volume, with its detailed maps and charts, was undoubtedly the source for Parkman's chronological table of events for *Pontiac* and later for *Montcalm and Wolfe*. He also read and reread *The Jesuit Relations* and Father Joseph-François Lafitau's *Moeurs des sauvages* (Paris, 1724).[24] Such authors as Mante, Bancroft, and Lafitau are representative of the kind of historical writers who prepared Parkman for beginning his first major work. He was not quite the self-starter that he has been portrayed.

Certainly the training in use of documentary material he received from Jared Sparks was equally important in Parkman's formative years. Parkman had known Sparks before entering college. Sparks, a former Unitarian minister, had been a close associate of Parkman's father and a visitor at the old Parkman home on Bowdoin Square. One suspects they had long talks on the nature of "historical evidence" or the rules for "historical composition," titles that Sparks used for two of his lectures. And Sparks introduced Parkman to Lyman C. Draper, collector of pioneer recollections and French documents, an enthusiast who shared Parkman's fascination with early American history.

From what may have been an unexpected source, Parkman was fortunate to receive constructive advice on the progress of his work. In a long handwritten critique of *Pontiac*, written in 1851 when the first edition appeared in print, Theodore Parker, friend of the youthful Parkman (Parkman had traveled with Parker and his family in Italy) and leading Unitarian clergyman of his day, challenged Parkman's portrayal of Indian character. "You evidently have a fondness for the Indian—not a romantic fondness, but one that has been tempered by the sight of fact," Parker wrote.[25] "Yet," Parker continued, "I do not think you do the Indian quite justice; you side rather too strongly with the white man and against the red. I think you bring out the vices of the Indian into more prominence than those of the European—which were yet less excusable. The treachery which you censure in the Indian was to him no more a violation of any sentiment or idea that he felt or knew than it was to a Briton to fight with powder and balls. This treachery is not specific to Indians."[26] The weakness in Parkman's portrayal of Indians, pinpointed by Parker, was representative of the sources Parkman used. Parker, a wide-ranging reader with a retentive memory, pointed out that whites were often guilty of "treachery & cruelty" in history and that even the title of the work, *The History of the Conspiracy of Pontiac,* was erroneous because "Pontiac & his scheme are not the central object about which the rest is grouped." Moreover, Parker asserted that the book did not appraise the impact of Pontiac's death on Indian affairs. Further, Parkman was "unjust" to Quakers, steadfast friends of the Indians. Although Parkman was skillful in drawing portraits of Wolfe and Montcalm, other individuals were neglected; even Pontiac's "picture" was "not adequate to his important place in history." And when Parkman gave descriptions of places, or mentioned trees, he spoke only of trees, "leaving us to grasp whether they were pines or palms, bushes or cork-trees."[27]

Certainly, criticism of this kind was of enormous benefit to the youthful writer. As one biographer has argued, Parkman jam-packed his narrative with background events because he was at the beginning of a major literary project, unsure that he would be able to tell the whole story in future books.[28] Parkman did accept the criticism gracefully but still retained his hostility toward Quakers. He had no use for historic Quaker pacifism. It has a negative image in all his books. He did in other ways benefit from Parker's suggestions. On persons and places he did not fall back on blurred images, and henceforth specific identifications of plants and natural surroundings punctuate his books. Parkman's reputation as an environmental historian may be tied to Parker's letter, especially if we consider how Parkman in future books used environmental background to create mood and to modify the tone of his narrative.

COMPLEXITIES IN RESURRECTING THE PONTIAC STORY

In resurrecting the Pontiac saga of the Old French War, Parkman made a wide examination of sources to select the detail that would fit smoothly into a dramatic narrative of frontier warfare. He had to link the Pontiac story to his overview of the entire Anglo-French struggle for the conquest of Canada, and as a result his space was limited. He could choose certain materials and ignore others. For instance, he had his own ideas about Indian culture and deliberately chose to sidetrack the body of literature of his day questioning cultural absolutism and recognizing moral values in so-called primitive societies. These societies, including those of the American Indians, were perceived as having institutional structures of their own integrity.[29] Such concepts are found in the writings of a number of early anthropologists, including Lewis H. Morgan and Adolph Bandelier, with whom Parkman corresponded.

Yet the work of these writers is sometimes equivocal. Morgan's Indians, like Parkman's, are still savages. Morgan adopted a law of human progress in which he argued that progress was "essentially geometrical," that is, "slowest in time in the first period, and most rapid in the last," as humans underwent evolutionary cultural changes from barbarism to civilization. There were certain key elements of progress, such as the patriarchal family, which could be identified with "Upper-Status Barbarism."[30] The Iroquois were well along in these evolutionary stages and on the "threshold" of civilization.[31] They had institutions that could be recognized as germs of the modern state. Both Parkman and Morgan concluded that the Iroquois had a higher type of culture. For Morgan, the Iroquois were neither noble nor ignoble. Nevertheless, he had a particular possessive feeling for the Iroquois, almost as if they were "his" Indians.[32] Parkman also seems to have had this possessiveness about the Iroquois, which may explain why at times they both dignify these people with ennobling traits. Parkman certainly faced complex problems in sifting truth from fiction in evaluating his sources on Indian people.

Early commentaries on Indian "character" that Parkman used are sometimes equally challenging to evaluate. Margaret T. Hodgen, in her penetrating book, *Early Anthropology in the Sixteenth and Seventeenth Centuries,* maintains that explorers and missionaries had their own reasons for giving posterity ennobling images of Indians. In first contacts, Indians were often pictured as generous, loving, gentle people without guile or treachery.[33] Such traits were held up to Europeans as worthy of imitation.

Further, even the most sympathetic writers, such as Bartolomé de Las Casas (who identified Indians as human beings with human rights), had concepts of Indians as ignorant, "poor and indigent," and "naked," that were not dissimilar from those held by Spaniards of his time. Even Father Joseph-François Lafitau, who chastised his countrymen for picturing Indians as having no feeling for religion, nevertheless gave us portraits of savage behavior among the Iroquois.[34] Lafitau was one of Parkman's main sources in the study of the northeastern Indians.

From his contacts with the Lakota Indians near the Medicine Bow range of the Rockies, from reading voraciously in dozens of sources, and from examining the works of other writers, especially James Fenimore Cooper and Lewis H. Morgan, Parkman formed his statuesque Indian image of the warrior character in his books. Once created, it remained unchanged throughout his works. As the next chapter suggests, however, the image had its ignoble and noble shadows.

The youthful Frederick Jackson Turner,
historian of the frontier, who had been
"brought up on Parkman light wines."
(W. R. Jacobs Photography Collection.)

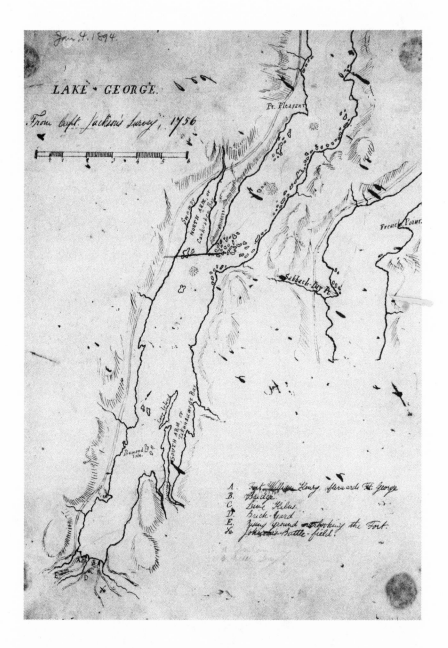

Parkman's hand-drawn map of Lake George in 1756. Parkman also made detailed drawings of Fort William Henry located on the southern bank of the lake when he was writing *Montcalm and Wolfe*. (Courtesy Massachusetts Historical Society.)

I am anxious to obtain as many particulars as possible of Pontiac's life, character and death. . . . He seems to be looked back upon as a hero, by Indians—is it not possible that something might be gathered by personal inquiry among them?

—LETTER TO CHARLES CHRISTOPHER TROWBRIDGE,
7 MARCH 1846

Our reader has just returned to us Mr. Parkman's MS. His opinion, as regards the literary execution of the work, etc. is very favorable,— but he is apprehensive that the work, highly respectable as it is, will not meet with a very rapid or extensive sale.

—LETTER OF REJECTION FROM HARPERS,
1 AUGUST 1850

I have got to the end of the book and killed off Pontiac. The opening chapters however are not yet complete. I have just finished an introductory chapter on Indian tribes, which my wife pronounces uncommonly stupid.

—LETTER TO CHARLES ELIOT NORTON,
22 SEPTEMBER 1850

Parkman in a heroic pose in the 1850s.
(From a print; W. R. Jacobs Photography Collection.)

CHAPTER FIVE

NOBLE-IGNOBLE
INDIAN PORTRAITS

FROM PARKMAN'S EARLIEST WRITINGS, from "The Scalp-Hunter," a *Knickerbocker Magazine* short story of 1845, through the frenzied hunting scenes in *The Oregon Trail* and then the killings in *Pontiac*, violence is omnipresent in Parkman's tapestry of history. It is possible to argue that Parkman's concept of manhood, his idolizing of the ferocious warrior hero, was a projection of his illness, his own "struggle situation" in which he pitted himself in a lifelong war against his enemy. As a semi-invalid, he maintained his self-respect by overcoming the kind of odds that his historical figures overcame in facing the wild interior of North America.

Parkman found savage conflict everywhere in frontier accounts with threats of war, attack, counterattack, murderous assault, and death. His grisly images of man's inhumanity to man become a recurrent motif. Parkman had a seemingly Gothic taste for violence, or rather a Gothic taste for reconstructing bloody, turbulent spectacles. These were highlights of episodes and subepisodes, documented accounts of victims and victors. Some were casualties of history, suffering and dying, according to Parkman, because of their own weaknesses or failings. Others were, he tells us, victims of harsh environmental, wilderness forces. Reader suspense is brought to a gradual increase in intensity because of the threat of impending disaster. Major characters in "The Scalp-Hunter," in *The Oregon Trail*, in *Pontiac*, and later in the *Pioneers, LaSalle,* and *The Jesuits* and other works are often a hair's breadth away from catastrophe, isolated in circumstances of physical danger. All is tuned to the reader's sensibilities. Parkman knew how to entice readers to turn the next page.

There is, in his early writings, and increasingly in later volumes, the ominous presence of fierce Indian warriors. They will, if circumstances permit (as in the suspense surrounding the impending fall of Fort William Henry in *Montcalm and Wolfe*), wipe out whole communities, missions, or poorly defended outposts. The individual is suddenly a cipher, helpless in foreboding surroundings. He finds it hard to escape premonitions of ferocious attack, and this feeling is conveyed to the reader. Lurking in the forest is the villain archetype in Parkman's story, the treacherous Indian barbarian.

Parkman is not the only writer on early American history who stereotyped the Indian men as barbaric warriors when in fact many tribes were relatively peaceful except when fighting as surrogates for France or England in colonial wars. Even Indian women were depicted as brutal characters torturing missionaries. Good evidence supports the argument that Parkman overemphasized the violent side of the Indian personality when actually the wars involving Indians were a result of intercolonial competition between France and England. Both his early and later writings had the kind of coloration of Indians that appeared in Cooper's novels, but his portrayal of Indians went beyond Cooper in its depiction of savagery.

In a modern study of the ignoble savage as a fictional character in American literature, Louis K. Barnett finds parallels in Parkman's depiction of Indians. For instance, the author takes pains to quote Parkman's view of half-blood native Americans as "half Indian, half white man, and half devil."[1] In spite of the fact that Parkman is here recognized as a historian as well as author of *The Oregon Trail,* his portrait of Indians and half-blood French-Indian frontier types is similar to stereotypes found in nineteenth-century romances. Although there is no evidence in his correspondence or journals, he seems to have partially accepted the idea that the "half-breed" was an ignoble character largely because of the nineteenth-century fear of miscegenation. He appears to have believed that marriage between white and nonwhite persons resulted in a fusion of bad qualities of both races.[2]

But it was the full-blood Indian who was usually pictured as the depraved racial type. Like his novelist contemporaries, Parkman consistently portrayed the Indian, as in the case of Pontiac, in dramatic roles. Critics argue that novelists contemporary with Parkman's time relied upon the ignoble Indian villain in their plots because of their general knowledge about avenging Indians' fighting with pioneers using Indian, and therefore barbaric, techniques of warfare. White novelists, imbued with white values, portrayed Indians as savage aggressors and cruel captors of whites. Although the novelists might give lip service to an image of the noble savage, the Indian became ignoble when the fighting began. A. Irving Hallowell,

distinguished anthropologist who surveyed such fictional literature, concluded that such writers generally had no familiarity with Indian culture,
but they were nevertheless sure about the nature of Indian barbarism.[3]

Another eminent anthropologist writing about savagery argued that
there is a key to understanding even a scholar's view of the subject. Clifford
Geertz writes: "Know what he thinks a savage is, and you have the key to
his work. You know what he thinks he himself is, you know in general
what sort of thing he is going to say about whatever tribe he happens to be
studying."[4] This insight elucidates Parkman's conception of Indians. His
social ideas (analyzed in chapters 8 and 9) show that he placed himself
upon an aristocratic pedestal and looked down upon others, that is, races
and classes other than his own, from that perspective. Indians and blacks
were at the bottom of the social pyramid, and Indians were natural barbarians who could not be reclaimed by civilization.

Parkman knew his Indians well enough not to portray them consistently in a ferocious imagery. It is therefore ironic that his ignoble portraitures have certain parallels with nineteenth-century novelists who were
unfamiliar with Indian lifestyles and cultural patterns. There is further
irony in the fact that Parkman's unvarying manner of depicting Indians in
his narratives became increasingly a rigid, closed case. As late as 1892, a year
before his death, while completing *A Half-Century of Conflict*, he wrote
about Indians in the same spirit as that of a fiction writer: "The English
borderers, on their part, regarded the Indians less as men than as vicious
and dangerous wild animals. In fact, the benevolent and philanthropic
view of the American savage is for those who are beyond his reach: it has
never yet been held by any whose wives and children have lived in danger
of his scalping-knife."[5]

In spite of Parkman's wide-ranging research in Indian ethnology and
history, he was willing to accept the eighteenth-century frontiersman's
view of Indians. Parkman was, of course, correct as far as telling us what
"borderers" thought of Indians, but the inference is that this hostile stereotype was the accurate overview of woodland native American people.
After examining his sources, one is impressed with the way Parkman
echoed the special prejudices of certain Canadian missionaries, for he apparently studied all of the available relations left by the Jesuits. At the same
time, Parkman sifted what he accepted, distinguishing for instance between Lafitau's second-hand knowledge about Hurons and Father Jean de
Brébeuf's first-hand experience in actually living with these people. Parkman also waded through the maze of Henry Schoolcraft's writings, as he
said, "taxing to the utmost the patience of those who would extract what is

valuable in it from its oceans of pedantic verbiage."[6] Although he acknowledged that he disagreed with the conclusions of Lewis H. Morgan (very
probably because he thought Morgan sentimental about the grandeur of
the Iroquois Confederacy), he was nevertheless full of praise for the mass
of authentic detail in *League of the Iroquois,* published in 1851, the same year
as *Pontiac.* This was an unfortunate coincidence, preventing Parkman from
consulting *League* for background material in writing an introductory essay on Indian culture in *Pontiac.*[7] Some ten years later when he had had
leisure to digest Morgan's *League,* he published an expanded, ethnological
essay as an introduction to *The Jesuits.*[8] Both of these long treatises in *Pontiac* and *The Jesuits* are basic for understanding Parkman's seeming ambiva-
lence in treating Indians as noble-ignoble people.

For the ignoble imagery Parkman had ample sources to cite. His footnotes tell us that he examined a host of experts, most of them stressing the
barbarism of Indian lifestyles. These included Lewis Cass, William Henry
Harrison, journals and reports of explorers, missionaries, and as we have
noted, the Jesuits, including Fathers Jean de Brébeuf, Isaac Jogues, Jerome
Lalemant[9] and Joseph-François Lafitau. But Lafitau, if we read him critically, will also give one a feeling of respect for the Iroquois league, with
commentaries on the wisdom and strength of Six Nations' leadership. For
the noble savage concept that recognized Iroquois culture in terms of relativism minimizing ethnocentric overtones, Parkman had Morgan's *League.*
Additionally, he consulted Albert Gallatin, leading pioneer anthropologist,
Robert Beverley's sympathetic account of Virginia Indians, John G. Bourke
on the Plains tribes, together with the findings of amateur archeologists,
such as the Canadian journalist, Joseph Tache. Parkman even went so far as
to investigate records of oral interviews with tribal leaders such as Chief
Skeopechi of the Creeks.[10]

ETHNOLOGICAL TREATISES ON WOODLAND
INDIANS

As a result of additional, on-the-spot investigation, Parkman's essays on
woodland tribes in *Pontiac* and expanded in *The Jesuits* evolved into vivid
eyewitness pictorials of Indian cultures in pre-Columbian North America.
In both essays, we see Indians as treacherous, cruel, and barbaric, the kind
of portrayals projected into the narrative. At the same time, however, Parkman gives us believable descriptions of Indian life before the appearance of

Europeans. Some of his paragraphs, particularly his summaries, rank with the best written in his time on woodland Indian cultures.

The Indian culture essay in *Pontiac,* for instance, uses the literary device of taking the reader on a woodland journey through the Indian country. First we see an average woodland Indian community where "each man is his own master. He abhors restraint and owns no other authority than his own capricious will; yet this wild notion of liberty is consistent with certain gradations of rank and influence."[11] Parkman then tells us of sachems and chiefs and the descent from the female line, "so that the brother of the incumbent, or the son of his sister, and not his own son, is the rightful successor to his dignities." Here Parkman, in the early stages of his career, already had a fundamental understanding of kinship systems.

He made the distinction between Indian civil and military authority, but at the same time stated that "both are often united in the same person."[12] The village was "singularly free from wranglings and petty strife though he . . . is inflexible in his adherence to ancient usages and customs." Each community, independent of its local association with tribes, bands, and villages, has distinct class, the emblems of which, whether they be Wolf, Deer, Otter, or Hawk, "In the language of the Algonquians . . . are known by the name of Totems."[13]

Parkman in the 1840s gradually put together his model of an ethnological treatise on the woodland tribes with a focal point on the Iroquois. His annotations tell us how heavily he relied upon Cadwallader Colden's *History of the Five Nations,* extant Moravian and Jesuit missionary records, Schoolcraft's works, and Father Lafitau.[14] If we examine this treatise closely, we can see how Parkman also relied upon historical eyewitness accounts by Samuel de Champlain and French governors, especially Louis de Buade, Count Frontenac, to give his readers a graphic picture of Iroquois towns. Here is the kind of prose that came from the youthful Parkman's pen:

> Along the banks of the Mohawk, among the hills and hollows of the Onondaga, in the forests of the Oneida and the Cayuga, on the romantic shores of Seneca Lake and the rich borders of the Genesee, surrounded by waving maize fields, and encircled from afar by the green margin of forest, stood the ancient strongholds of the confederacy. The clustering dwellings were encompassed by palisades, in single, double, or triple rows, pierced with loopholes, furnished with platforms within, for the convenience of the defenders with magazines of stones to hurl upon the heads of the enemy, and with water conductors to extinguish any fire which might be kindled from without.[15]

Then follows a representation of Six Nation's longhouses and communal life, a composite of eyewitness and ethnological data, a reasonable reconstruction of life in these Iroquois towns:

> The area which these defences enclosed was often several acres in extent, and the dwellings, ranged in order within, were sometimes more than a hundred feet in length. Posts, firmly driven into the ground, with an intervening framework of poles, formed the basis of the structure; and its sides and arched roof were closely covered with layers of bark. Each of the larger dwellings contained several distinct families, whose separate fires were built along the central space while compartments on each side, like the stalls of a stable offered some degree of privacy. Here rude couches were prepared, and the bear and deer skins spread; while above, the ripened ears of maize, suspended in rows, formed a golden tapestry. . . .
> Each passing season had its feasts and dances, often mingling religion and social pasttimes. The young had their frolics and merry-makings; and the old had their no less frequent councils, where conversations and laughter alternated with grave deliberations for the public weal. There were also stated periods marked by the recurrence of momentous ceremonies, in which the whole community took part.

To be sure, Parkman's portrait of the Iroquois is incomplete without discussion of epidemics, for instance, but he gives us impressive detail on such topics as totems, tribal amalgamation, agriculture, and patterns of governance.[16] His reconstruction, even for today's readers, is convincing. The verbal picture of multiple firesides of the extended families, the "rude couches" with deer and bearskin coverings, and the "ripened maize" hanging above forming a "golden tapestry," help form images, almost unforgettable in the reader's mind. And the commentary about the Iroquois young having their "merry-makings," and the old their councils punctuated with laughter as well as "grave deliberations for the public weal," give another side to Iroquois life removed from the imagery of inhuman brutality. Although there are passages to show Iroquois cruelty in this *Pontiac* essay, these people are portrayed as a society that lived, governed, and defended itself with age-old traditions.

A major trait of the Iroquois, Parkman concluded, was their pride. They were a "remarkable people, who with all the ferocity of their race, blended heroic virtues and marked endowments of the intellect."[17] He pointed out that few tribes could match them in prowess, constancy, moral energy, or intellectual vigor."[18] For contrast, Parkman turned to Pierre Charlevoix, who in his *Nouvelle France* argued that the Algonquians were easily converted but became fickle proselytes, while the Huron-Iroquois, though not easily won over by the missionaries, were more faithful converts in the end. The Iroquois tribes also had stability in their subsistence patterns. As farmer-hunters, they were not dependent upon the chase alone. Their method of governance was based upon a "superior social organization," and their cosmology, their religious and social rites and usages, which existed only in the "germ" in other peoples, "attained among them a full and perfect development."[19] The Iroquois, then, in the *Pontiac* ethnological essay, were Parkman's foremost woodland people. In his image of these Indians, Parkman gave us an archetype anticipating later anthropologists who followed the culture-area theory.[20]

The Algonquians, on the other hand, symbolized by the Delaware or Lenape, were forced to "drain the cup of humiliation . . . to assume the name of Women, and forego the use of arms."[21] Parkman goes on to make the argument that the pacific stance of the Delaware was not due to any "inborn love of peace." His conclusion was probably based upon his experience on the Oregon Trail. Here he met remnants of Penn's peaceful allies, the Delaware, forcibly removed from their ancestral home to the plains where they became professional hunters and sometimes guides, "the most adventurous dreaded warriors of the prairies . . . sending out their war parties as far as the Rocky Mountains and into the Mexican territories."[22] The Indians that were to be admired, according to Parkman, were warlike, and he had sources to show their warlike behavior.

TORTURE AND CANNIBALISM

Parkman's most persuasive argument for Indian savagery in *Pontiac* rested on descriptions of torture and cannibalism. For this he relied in part upon a document historically known as the "Pontiac Manuscript," a detailed account of Pontiac's siege of Fort Detroit in the form of a journal that Parkman believed to have been written by a French priest. Sometimes regarded as the state of Michigan's most famous manuscript, the diary has since been attributed to a scrivener, a French Canadian, Robert Navarre. Following his usual methods when confronted with suspect source materials, Parkman collated his copy of the Pontiac journal with other sources and concluded: "As a literary composition, it is quite worthless, being diffuse and encumbered with dull and trivial details; yet this very minuteness affords strong internal evidence of its authenticity. Its general exactness with respect to facts is fully proved by comparing it with contemporary documents."[23] According to the journal, several unfortunate soldiers who were in a party destined to bring relief to the besieged Fort Detroit were captured by Wyandot warriors after an ambush in May 1763, early in the period of the "conspiracy." The fate of these soldiers was confirmed, Parkman wrote, when "naked corpses, gashed with knives and scorched with fire, floated down on the pure waters of the Detroit, where fish came up to nibble at the clotted blood that clung to their ghastly faces."[24]

At this point in the narrative, a long quotation from the Pontiac journal appears. We are told that the prisoners had been tormented by being forced to run through a gauntlet and then "fell dead; after which those who had not fired fell upon the bodies, cut them in pieces, cooked them, and ate them." Others were subjected to different kinds of torment by "cutting their flesh with flints, and piercing them with lances. They would then cut off their feet and hands, and leave them weltering in their blood till they were dead. Others were fastened to stakes, and children employed to burn them with fire. . . . Even the women assisted their husbands in torturing their victims. They slitted them with their knives, and mangled them in various ways."[25]

In the entire work of *Pontiac,* there are no further specific instances of cannibalism detailed, although in *The Jesuits,* written over a decade later when he had occasion to study the matter further, Parkman assured us that cannibalism was practiced. Among the Hurons, he wrote, cannibalism (like torture) was "partly an act of vengeance, and partly a religious rite." Quoting his favorite source on the Hurons, Father Brébeuf's *Relation de Hurons* of 1636, Parkman tells us that while many Hurons turned away from the feast with horror, "others took pleasure in it." ("Il y en a qui en mangent avec plaisir.")[26] This graphic statement with its authoritative footnote implying eyewitness evidence from Father Brébeuf is in Parkman's introductory essay on woodland Indians. Further on in the midst of the narrative, he describes Iroquois barbarity in cutting up prisoners' bodies. The Indians "boiled and devoured them before wretched eyes of survivors . . . they ate men with as much appetite and more pleasure than hunters eat a boar or a stag."[27]

In the descent from Parkman to later historians and anthropologists who wrote about the Iroquois, the subject of cannibalism, or Iroquois anthropophagy, persists as a controversial, even heated, subject. In a 1980 essay "Iroquois Cannibalism, Fact Not Fiction," Canadian scholar Thomas S. Abler, a longtime student of Parkman, concludes that Iroquois cannibalism was a fact of life. Using the same sources Parkman relied upon, Abler mentions thirty-one citations to cannibalism in Reuben Gold Thwaites' edition of *The Jesuit Relations,* along with other eyewitness accounts from French officials, English colonials, and French explorers. Acknowledging merits of cultural relativism and demerits of ethnocentrism and the extreme importance of judging a culture by its own value system, Abler concludes that writings of Iroquois scholars confirm Parkman's portrayal of cannibalism and that "non-literate societies have no monopoly on cruelty." Iroquois torment of prisoners "pales before the cruel injuries and death inflicted by weapons of modern war. It is not that the seventeenth-century Iroquois were inhuman, but rather they were like the rest of us, all too human in their treatment of other men."[28] Their cannibalism was fundamentally ritual in its nature and goals, which were to transfer supernatural powers from the slain to the living, a "ceremonial" cannibalism.

PARKMAN'S INDIANS—SOME CONTRADICTIONS

Modern authorities on the Iroquois and other woodland tribes, as we have observed, differ little from Parkman on Indian cannibalism and torture. As Parkman stated, both were practiced among the Hurons, Miamis, and other eastern tribes.[29] Although Christian priests are not notably reliable sources of detached observation on cannibalism (a subject that could attract donations from sympathetic readers in Europe to convert heathens), Parkman was like other writers who have had to rely upon *The Jesuit Relations* because there are few other accounts on the Iroquois. In Parkman's case, we can be reasonably sure he emphasized Jesuit accounts of torture and cannibalism because they could be used so easily to liven his narrative.

In his most sophisticated ethnological treatise on the Northeastern Indian tribes, the version first developed in *Pontiac* and later expanded in *The Jesuits,* Parkman does not dwell on Indian savagery because he has no plot sequence or suspense element to develop.[30] This introductory essay on Indians provides the reader with some eighty-seven pages describing pre-Columbian lifestyles. He relies on the literary device of taking his readers on a sweeping tour of the Indian country where he gracefully pinpoints cultural uniformities that can be categorized in an overview. Concentrating on the New England Indians and the Huron-Iroquois family, he escorts his readers over a vast territory and gives them an orientation on language families, culture areas, subsistence patterns, housing and architecture, clothing, crafts, marriage and the family, and kin groups, including lineages, clans, and origins of descent. He tells us about Indian government and social controls, violence, raids, wars, religion, medicine, magic, personality, and culture. In his account of totems and clans, Indians' religious attitudes toward animals, Hiawatha, and Iroquois history, Parkman shows breadth and command of his subject. He does all this without putting labels on his subject matter in creating an eloquent portrayal of native lifestyles. His was a convincing and downright interesting device to introduce the reader to interrelationships between woodland Indian culture and early American frontier history.

Yet, as we might expect, Parkman falls short. He argues that Indian people had a lower intelligence, a "savage lethary of mind" that held them back from "improvement."[31] He cites, as evidence, the typical nineteenth-century "scientific" data derived from measuring and comparing skull sizes. The Indian is, he concludes, forever locked into his barbaric past.

At the same time, Parkman's genuine admiration for Indians shines through many of his pages. In *Pontiac,* for example, he makes this expressive statement about Algonquian religious beliefs:

> Some enamoured maiden, scornful of earthly suitors, plights her troth to the graceful manitou of the grove; or bright aerial beings, dwellers of the sky, descend to tantalize the gaze of mortals with evanescent forms of loveliness. . . . To the Indian mind, all nature was instinct with deity. A spirit was embodied in every mountain, lake, and cataract; every bird, beast, or reptile, every tree, shrub, or grass blade was endued with mystic influence; yet this untutored pantheism did not exclude the conception of certain divinities. . . . The sun, too, was a god, and the moon a goddess. Conflicting powers of good and evil divided the universe.[32]

It is difficult to find a more eloquent if brief representation of the woodland Indian's worldview. This passage demonstrates that the young Parkman's talent was such that he could summarize a large corpus of data to give his readers a meaningful view of the natural world of the woodland Indian.[33]

We conclude that in his formative years, from the very beginning of his research, Parkman trained himself to reconcile ethnological and historical data to give us a noble-ignoble picture of Indians in colonial times. His method of reconstructing the past, through ethnological treatises to preface narrative, is useful if we recognize its limitations.[34]

Parkman gave posterity a novelistic history in which Indians were recognized as a people having a tribal social organization with subsistence patterns and methods of warmaking. Indians had a special role in early American history, although often a brutal one, cast as villains and enmeshed in plots and subplots. Pontiac emerges as a powerful, highly intelligent, but treacherous warrior-chief. Nor did Parkman overlook the influential Delaware Prophet, Neolin, a charismatic religious leader. Yet he would ignore other Indians, such as the Ohio chief, Pisquetomen, a peacemaker of the 1750s, who is dismissed by Parkman as one of Christian Frederick Post's "companions." Post was the heroic figure who swayed the Ohio Indians to accept peace, according to Parkman, but Pisquetomen, who was in fact the "hero," as Francis Jennings has demonstrated, was ignored. Parkman in *Pontiac* fleshed out this misrepresentation of an episode and repeated it years later in *Montcalm and Wolfe*.[35]

Parkman's Indians, selectively portrayed in his narrative, are, at first glance, convincing. There are two reasons for this: his narrative has the appearance of authenticity because of his talents as a writer and because he went to such pains to ferret out appropriate details to buttress his case.

There is another element that cannot be discounted. When Parkman was in his apprenticeship in the 1840s and 1850s, the imposing and exciting presence of the great Indian confederacies was clearly remembered. He wrote with passion about Indians that people in his time remembered as fierce and formidable. Pontiac, not Pisquetomen, was that kind of warrior-chief. Parkman's Indians were not the tame people of a later age, conquered and living on distant reservations. His Iroquois were heroic fighters. They conquered an empire of interior woodlands.[36]

Parkman's summer home on his estate at Jamaica Plain, near Boston.
(From Charles H. Farnham, *A Life of Francis Parkman*.)

His complexion was darker than usual with his race, and his features, though by no means regular, had a bold and stern expression. . . . His ordinary attire was that of the primitive savage. . . . Having roused in his warlike listeners their native thirst for blood and vengeance, he next addressed himself to their superstition, and told the . . . tale [of] . . . the Delaware prophet.

—THE CONSPIRACY OF PONTIAC

Parkman's gridiron writing guide, his colored spectacles, and his ink stand. In the upper right is one of Parkman's notebooks, and at the lower right is an account book with a record of his daily expenses. These are placed on Parkman's desk, which held, in one of its secret drawers, a prescription for arsenic. The photograph was taken in the 1950s in his Chestnut Street study before it was dismantled. (Photograph by W. R. Jacobs.)

CHAPTER SIX

PONTIAC'S "CONSPIRACY": A TARNISHED BUT ENDURING IMAGE

IF PONTIAC WAS TO BE PORTRAYED as a dauntless, bold, fearless chief, as the great warrior figure of the Indians, the sources were meager with few records of his speeches and fewer firsthand reports on his appearance, his manner of speech, his bearing as a leader. Parkman, however, overcame this problem by avoiding the trap of focusing on a Pontiac biography. Instead, he gave his readers a lively account of the whole Anglo-French struggle in America as an introduction to a suspenseful narrative of the Indian war of 1763, where, in episode after episode, the shadowy figure of Pontiac emerged as a bold, highly intelligent, warrior-conspirator who, led by an Indian known as the Delaware Prophet, guided a mystical expression of outrage against the whites into an all-out struggle against the English colonies. Here was theatrical history in Parkman style with drama, suspense, and an archplotter and conspirator as hero. The purpose of this chapter, an excursion into historiography and Parkman's sources and interpretations, is to comment on the core of fact on Pontiac's leadership role that the apprentice historian used in giving his readers a history that had many elements of a good novel.

Few Indian wars have generated such historical controversy as Pontiac's War, or Rebellion. Key facts, recorded in Parkman's *The Conspiracy of Pontiac* and other accounts, can be easily summarized.

Early in May 1763, after the French surrender of Fort Detroit to the British, the surrounding Indian people demanded that trade-good prices be lowered and that they be furnished with subsidies, or "presents," of ammunition, food, blankets, tools, and other hardware as they had formerly been able to obtain from both the French and the English. The Indians had also become increasingly resentful of British policies as a consequence of the preachings of the Delaware Prophet, or Neolin, a religious messiah of 1762–1763, and a leader of what we now recognize as a nativistic, millenarian movement.[1] Although it was a militant movement, it was nonetheless religious and was preceded by severe epidemic mortality in the 1750s and early 1760s, resulting in a mindset not unlike that of the Indians in the later Ghost Dance movement, which also had antecedent rapid depopulation. As Parkman tells us, the Prophet of the 1760s preached that by following the "life of their ancestors," the Indians could "soon be restored to their ancient greatness and power, and be enabled to drive out the white men who infested their country."

Pontiac, disciple of the Prophet and war chief of the Ottawa, became the leader of what first had been a religious crusade against the whites. After his scheme to capture Fort Detroit by secret attack was discovered, he launched an open war. By late May and June 1763, British outposts west of Fort Niagara were captured or destroyed by the Indians. The British were all but paralyzed by the organized tribesmen now clearly led by Pontiac. After Colonel Henry Bouquet's forces routed the Indians at the Battle of Bushy Run in August 1763, Indian resistance collapsed. Tribes fighting in the Fort Pitt area were weakened by the ferocity of a smallpox epidemic after blankets used by victims of the disease were given to warriors in response to an order by the British high command. Delawares surrounding the fort appear to have been the main quarry of the besieged British. Pontiac gave up his blockade of Fort Detroit in November, made peace two years later, and then vanished into the forest only to be assassinated by Peoria warriors in the Illinois country.

Debate about Parkman's account of the war in *Pontiac* centers primarily on two factors: the leadership role of Pontiac as an organizer and leader of the Northwestern Indians in war against the whites, and the "conspiracy" designation for the war. In identifying the war as a conspiracy led by Pontiac, largely to build an emplotment and suspense story structure, Parkman tended to warp his narrative; with the "conspiracy" theme, he was obliged to twist the meaning of the religious, mystical side of the movement, what we now call nativistic, or millenarian. In recognition of the recurrence of such movements in Indian history, he did briefly compare the roles of Tecumseh and the prophet of 1812 to those of Pontiac and the Delaware Prophet. But for Parkman all Indians were savages and potential conspirators.

Parkman gave his readers, then, the image of Chief Pontiac as a formidable schemer whose intrigues set the war into motion. The discussion that follows, examining recent scholarship and relevant source materials, suggests that, although Parkman relied upon a conspiratorial framework of plot and counterplot, he was essentially correct in assessing Pontiac's role as an initiator and leader. The racist overtones in Parkman's characterization of Pontiac as a sinister, treacherous chief, however, distort Pontiac's role in a militant, religious movement that erupted into a war for Indian self-determination. It can also be argued that despite the Delaware Prophet's teachings, urging his followers to abandon the white man's tools, to fling "away flint and steel, to abandon firearms," they were, as Parkman wrote, "injunctions . . . too inconvenient to be complied with." Native Americans were too dependent upon guns, powder, metal tools, and even food to seek complete independence. They might seek independence from lethal infections[2] but not from the world market of trade goods.

CONTEMPORARY RECORDS FROM BOTH INDIANS and knowledgeable whites attest to abuses suffered by Indians, sufficient, as Parkman maintains, to cause an outright rebellion against British authority. There is no clear record that Indian outrage exploded into an outburst of sporadic attacks on British outposts in the summer of 1763. On the contrary, circumstantial evidence suggests that Pontiac was the driving force behind the nearly simultaneous assaults.

The title of Parkman's *The Conspiracy of Pontiac* designates the Ottawa chief as the mastermind behind the assaults. In the year 1762, according to Parkman, Pontiac "sent ambassadors to the different nations. They visited the country of the Ohio and its tributaries, passed northward to the region of the upper lakes, and the borders of the river Ottawa; and far southward towards the mouth of the Mississippi. Bearing with them the war belt of wampum, broad and long, as the importance of the message demanded, and the tomahawk stained red, in token of war, they went from camp to camp and village to village."[3] Parkman's authority for this descriptive statement is a letter written by a Sieur D'Abbadie, a newly appointed governor of Louisiana, dated simply "1764," which no one has succeeded in locating since Parkman's time. D'Abbadie arrived in Louisiana from France on 29 June 1763 and was therefore hardly able to give accurate data on Pontiac's war belts sent in the previous year, 1762.[4] It is odd that Parkman relied mainly on a letter written in 1764, two years after Pontiac dispatched wampum ambassadors ranging "from camp to camp and village to village." Since this letter is a major source to confirm his "conspiracy" thesis, Parkman might have furnished us with a complete description of this important epistle along with a statement concerning D'Abbadie's reliability as a source.

In his book on Pontiac's War, Michigan historian Howard H. Peckham argues that "the Indian mind" was unable to comprehend cause and effect problems and that therefore "there was no grand conspiracy or preconcerted plan on his [Pontiac's] part embracing all the western tribes."[5] Peckham contended that the uprising was a war for Indian independence with a local conspiracy at Fort Detroit. According to this synthesis, Pontiac did attempt to bring about a more general uprising, but only after the failure of his first campaign against the British.

THE PONTIAC MANUSCRIPT

The source materials on which to base an evaluation of these opposing points of view by Parkman and Peckham are meager, but Peckham's portrayal of the limitations of the "Indian mind" are simply not borne out by the sources or by modern anthropological studies. Parkman's depiction of the intelligence, character, and positive personality traits of Pontiac are closer to the existing historical evidence and ethnohistorical facts.[6]

The historical foundation on which Parkman built was not easily established. For instance, the Pontiac manuscript that Parkman relied upon for much of his narrative was the work of an unknown author, later identified as a Frenchman, Robert Navarre. In justifying the use of this document, Parkman declared that significant details closely paralleled events described in other manuscripts.[7] The author supposedly learned about Pontiac's speeches and clandestine negotiations preceding the attack on Detroit from French Canadians who were eyewitnesses at Indian council meetings.

Howard H. Peckham in his later study used this same manuscript. Peckham also secured materials from the collections in the William H. Clements Library.[8] Parkman of course had no opportunity to use the Clements Library references, but he did search out parallel sources illustrating, for example, changes in British Indian policy in the early 1760s.

One thing is clear: the evidence shows that by the spring of 1763, the tribesmen along the whole northwestern frontier were ripe for vengeance against the whites. Only a spark ignited by a dynamic Indian leader was needed to start the conflagration.

MODERN SCHOLARSHIP ON THE PONTIAC WAR

In a reexamination of primary materials and secondary works (including Parkman's *Pontiac* and Peckham's book), the Canadian historian Louis Chevrette in a comprehensive biographical sketch states that Pontiac set out "to launch a general uprising" in the spring of 1763.[9] Chevrette asserts that Pontiac "convoked the first of a number of secret councils at the Riviere a l'ecorce on 27 April. About 460 warriors came, including those of his own village." Chevrette mentions other successful efforts by Pontiac to assemble tribes besides the Ottawas: Potawatomies, Hurons, Ojibwas, and Mississaugas. The large secret conference on the banks of the river Ecorces close by Detroit is described in detail in Parkman's *Pontiac*, as are most other episodes mentioned by Chevrette.

Like Parkman, Chevrette reasons that Pontiac, in a secret meeting in Detroit of Lake Superior–area tribes, schemed for a widespread uprising. "The motives for the meeting," writes Chevrette, "are not precisely known, but presumably they were warlike and Pontiac instigated the gathering, for he was in his own territory and he was a war chief."

Parkman only alludes to the earlier conference, but his narrative is basically an expanded version of what Chevrette has to say. Both writers, for example, emphasize the role of an informer, warning the commandant of Fort Detroit that the Indians schemed to take over the fort when they came to parley for peace. Both writers also trace the course of the war in a similar way, including final conferences and other events leading up to Pontiac's death. There are such similarities because both writers depend upon the same sources, particularly the Pontiac manuscript.

In addition to the work of Chevrette (and the book by Peckham written almost four decades earlier), there has been continuing reexamination of Pontiac and his leadership in the Indian war of 1763. Thomas J. Maxwell, in a suggestive essay on "Pontiac Before 1763," explores possible roles that Pontiac had in assuming war-chief primacy among the Detroit Ottawas in the 1740s and 1750s but concludes that only inferences can be made from fragmentary evidence. Michael McConnel, who completed a doctoral dissertation on Indian affairs during the period leading up to Pontiac's War, disagrees with Parkman on Pontiac's role as an Indian leader outside the Detroit area. McConnel contends that Pontiac emerged in 1763 because he was a recognizable chief whose name surfaced only in military reports widely circulated in British officialdom after the summer of that year. Furthermore, after Pontiac moved inland from the Detroit area in the fall of

1763, he became a dangerous military threat far away from British fortifications and almost impossible to track down or control. As a result, McConnel concludes, Pontiac became a symbol of resistance in the perception of the British.[10] This interpretation disagrees with those of Parkman and Chevrette on Pontiac's role as the early leader of a widespread uprising.

It is difficult to prove that Pontiac was as consequential as the British thought he was. If Parkman was at fault, he built on a formidable image of Pontiac, as he appeared in the documentary sources: a powerful, brave, intelligent chief whose impact upon organizing and directing a "conspiracy" went far beyond the Detroit Ottawas and their neighboring allies.

Parkman may have also erred in focusing on one person: the individual hero-figure in Pontiac. This allowed him to spotlight his stage with actions of a major figure without becoming involved in lengthy discussions of Indian factionalism[11] and intertribal rivalries. Yet Parkman did analyze the complexity of grievances that helped to bring about open hostility. His concern was for basic accuracy in a historical narrative. At the same time, his series of events had to be invested with dramatic unity without confusing digressions. These factors may have prevented him from giving more attention to elements behind the Seneca war belts of 1761 and the role of the Wyandotsma, powerful tribal people of the Detroit area. In short, the modern ethnohistorian confronts a tangle of intercultural relations and factionalism that involves issues, individuals, and events. These factors tend to be obscured when the role of one chief is paramount. Nevertheless, it is important to note that the *Pontiac* two-volume history actually discusses or mentions 150 Indian tribes connected in one way or another with the story of Pontiac's "conspiracy."

Modern scholars, if they do as much research as Parkman did, agree with him on one point: Pontiac, by seizing a position of leadership at a critical juncture, was soon recognized by the British as the most prominent war chief on the northern frontier. Miamis, Delawares, Senecas, Wyandots, and Ojibwas all had reasons for hostility against the English, and there was undoubtedly a varied level in the intensity of anger among local tribesmen. This appears to have coincided with widespread resentment. Thus, the total massacre of British forces at Venango may have been a reflection of Seneca rage that represented, as well, a general Indian bitterness against British policies. We can criticize Parkman for brushing out a pattern of local hostility so that he could then more sharply paint the picture of an archconspirator. Parkman delineates in like manner an Indian eyewitness's portrayal of the Venango massacre by the Senecas who forced the commandant to write "a statement of their grievances which had driven them to arms." In a narrative, what could offer better proof that the Iroquoian Senecas had very specific reasons for being outraged by British policies? Parkman, in other words, did allow Indians besides Pontiac to speak for themselves when he found a source that blended into his story.

SECRET PLANS

Parkman, as well as recent scholars, stressed that a plan had been developed by the Senecas, who with some 1,050 fighting men were perhaps the strongest military power in the Iroquois confederacy. Superintendent Sir William Johnson found these people, who had had close contacts with the French for so many years, the most difficult to control of all his Indian allies, but he wisely treated them with the consideration that their fighting strength justified. After the conquest of Canada in 1760, however, the Senecas, as Parkman wrote, like all other woodland Indians of the Northeast, in trading had to confront often arrogant officers who commanded the British forts.[12]

Not surprisingly the Senecas, as Parkman noted, had plotted to take over the British fortifications. In his diary, Indian trader and deputy Indian superintendent George Croghan reported that these tribesmen carefully planned a secret attack on the British forts in 1761. Tribes living in the vicinity of Detroit were to capture the fort, kill the traders, and seize the booty. At the same time, the Miamis, the Delawares, the Shawnees, and all the other tribes living between the Ohio River and Lake Erie were to assault the forts between the frontier of Pennsylvania and the stronghold at Fort Pitt. Scattered villages of the Iroquois in the Ohio region were to spring on Presqu'Isle, Le Boeuf, and Venango. In the interim, lines of communication between German Flats in the Mohawk Valley and Fort Niagara would be severed by fighting men from the Six Nations and Susquehanna tribes. Meanwhile, the Cherokee towns were to be visited by a delegation of some one hundred Iroquois. The Cherokees, who had already been at war with the British from 1759 to 1761, were to be told that an invading French army would join the northern Indians (a belief held by Pontiac, according to Parkman), while the western and southern Indians would clear the remaining frontiers of whites.

Even though this covert strategem was discovered by British agents before it could be put into effect, the strategy is revealing because it shows that the Senecas[13] were willing to fight on the side of their historic enemies, the Cherokees. The details of the plans mentioned by Parkman also help to buttress his thesis that an extensive "conspiracy" under the leadership of Pontiac did take place. Parkman was convinced that the Ottawa chief skillfully wrested leadership of the Indian resistance from the western Senecas, the Six Nations' faction that later joined the uprising against the British.[14] One Seneca group, however, appears to have remained neutral.

Parkman's recognition of Pontiac's leadership is reasonable to accept. Without Pontiac, it is hard to see why the remaining members of the Six Nations would not seize leadership of the war from the Ottawas. The Iroquois were the most formidable of Indian peoples, although they had given up their position as a balance of power between the French and the English. In 1759 they had publicly abandoned their traditional policy of neutrality, giving wholehearted support to the British forces under Sir Jeffrey Amherst.[15] After the conquest of Canada in 1760, most of the chiefs of the Six Nations had been won over by Sir William Johnson. But the Senecas, seldom enthusiastic about the British, became increasingly dissatisfied. They missed the courtship of French emissaries like the Joncaire brothers, the "presents," or gifts, and trading opportunities of Fort Niagara, and were alarmed at the specter of the encroaching Anglo-American frontier.

My own investigation into the sources shows that the Senecas voiced their discontent by informing other tribes that their main reason for hostility was that the British refused to continue a policy of giving them tools, blankets, and ammunition. Other tribes were also desperately short of supplies of powder and lead and made similar complaints and threats. It seems probable that in 1761–1762, the Senecas may really have wished to conceal schemes that their chiefs were discussing with French colonials. One such Seneca chief was the able and violently anti-British Kaiaghshota.[16] It was Captain Donald Campbell, commander of Fort Detroit, and Indian agent George Croghan who discovered the ambitious plans of Seneca headmen. Parkman's narrative details these facts.

While the Senecas, led by Kaiaghshota (called Kiashuta by Parkman), had inflamed the smoldering anger of the Indians, Pontiac, the more able leader, emerged to direct what might have been no more than an explosion of discontent rather than a long and bitterly fought war. Pontiac, as well as the Senecas, is known to have sent messages to the western tribes, even to the Sioux, before his initial attack on Fort Detroit.[17]

I found that the existing sources (as Parkman tells us in his narrative) stressed the activities of Indian Superintendent Sir William Johnson. Once the hostilities began, Sir William did all in his power to prevent the conflagration from spreading to the friendly tribes. The Senecas tried to induce the other members of the Six Nations to join the uprising, but the remaining Iroquois, moved undoubtedly by the astute diplomacy of Johnson entreating them to remain loyal to the British, would not take up Pontiac's hatchet. To show their loyalty, the Mohawks even declared their intention of "living and dying with the English."

Sir William, however, was not able to prevent nine strongholds, among them Forts Le Boeuf, Presqu'Isle, Venango, and Michilmackinac, from falling into the hands of the attacking warriors. Only stubborn bulwarks of the British defense system, Fort Pitt and Fort Detroit, remained. Once the attacks were under way, they were carried on with determination and persistence, strongly suggesting that the Indians were under a leader of Pontiac's caliber. The *Annual Register,* a faithful English chronicler of events in America, commented on the special qualities of the Indian campaign (much in the spirit of Parkman's narrative): "Upon the whole of this war, so far as it has hitherto proceeded, we cannot help observing, that the Indians seem to be animated with a more dark and daring spirit than at any former time. They seemed to have concerted their measures with ability, and to have chosen the times and places of their several attacks with skill."[18]

The fact that all the attacks did not begin at the same time does not mean that the Indians were lacking in an overall plan of assault. Communications in a vast wilderness, interspersed with lakes and mountains, even for native Americans who lived in the forest, were sometimes slow. Moreover, each force of attacking warriors had the difficult task of securing for itself what was a scarce item indeed: ammunition. Another factor adding to the problem of launching a simultaneous assault was the sometimes inferior ability of local chiefs. The Indians at Fort Pitt, for instance, had no leader of Pontiac's caliber. Nevertheless, available evidence, substantiating Parkman, shows that they tried every bluff possible in order to obtain a British evacuation of the fort. Failing that, they fought with tenacity and courage.

PONTIAC'S ROLE

Pontiac, as Parkman recognized him, was an obvious leader of Indians in the Old Northwest by the summer of 1763. After that he emerged as the chief who had to be dealt with. When it came to making peace, the British were well aware that he was the individual who must be consulted for any termination of the war.[19] Parkman's characterization of him as a man who had a thirst for knowledge, carried out agreements, protected messengers, and restored property is echoed in the sources, among others, the testimonies of Major Robert Rogers and Alexander Fraser. Louis Chevrette agrees with Parkman on this point because he, too, has used the same references. Although Pontiac's authority was declared to be "absolute" over other Indians, there is undoubted exaggeration in the assertion.[20] Parkman, who found such statements in his references, was wise enough not to make much of this point in giving his own assessment of Pontiac's role. On the whole there is reasonable probability that an Indian of Pontiac's remarkable talents might well have put into motion a secret plan for rolling back the white invasion of fortification and settlement.

Throughout Indian history and Indian-white history, there has been a singular reluctance to grant Indian people recognition for achievements, a fact that Samuel E. Morison once pointed out. Who can prove that Pontiac was not the mastermind behind the Indian war of 1763? On the contrary, accounts of war belts sent by Pontiac support the assumptions that the war was planned and prepared for and that Pontiac took the leadership away from the Senecas. Pontiac appears to have been shrewd enough to perceive that he could make use of underlying Indian grievances to weld the Indians into a force capable of carrying on a prolonged assault against the enemy.

The uprising that mushroomed among the Indians also had, as Parkman narrated, a mystical side. According to the "Pontiac Manuscript," the Master of Life, speaking to the Indians through Brother Wolf, had urged specific reforms (renunciation of liquor, the taking of only one wife), but his central message was to take possession of the land: "This land where ye dwell I have made for you and not for others. Whence comes it that ye permit the Whites upon your lands? Can ye not live without them? . . . drive them out. . . . Send them back to the lands which I have created for them and let them stay there."[21] The influence of the message from the Master of Life was widespread: certain tribes (Shawnees or Eries—the exact identification is difficult in the "Pontiac Manuscript") declared that "we have also fallen upon the English because the Master of Life by one of our brother Delawares told us to do so,"[22] an indication that their assault on the British may or may not have been because of messages from Pontiac. And it appears that Pontiac himself, later in 1766, denied sending "bad [wampum] belts" to other Indians.[23] It was customary, however, among Indian leaders to disclaim responsibility among whites for unsuccessful warlike acts. What would Pontiac have to gain by admitting guilt for a warlike action at the time of his defeat, when surrounded by enemies? More likely he minimized his position as a leading figure in an unsuccessful Indian revolt, especially in connection with incidents where white prisoners were killed.

The special role that Pontiac had in the Indian war of 1763 is perhaps most clearly described by anthropologist Anthony Wallace in his searching book on *The Death and Rebirth of the Seneca*. After examining the writings of Henry R. Schoolcraft, John Heckewelder, Howard H. Peckham, and other sources, Wallace concludes that Pontiac, as a convert to the teachings of the Delaware Prophet, accepted the teachings of the Master of Life and used the doctrine "as supernatural sanction for his conspiracy."[24]

The Delaware Indians were especially aroused against the whites by the Delaware Prophet, who claimed to have had contact with the "Great Spirit" and who urged the Indians to return to their old way of life. Pontiac was also able to make use of the teachings of the Master of Life. In a speech before representatives of the Ottawas, the Hurons, and other tribes, he asserted that the Master of Life (who apparently put forward no military program in the teachings of the Delaware Prophet) desired that the Indians drive the whites out of their homelands and make war upon them.[25] Thus, he aroused the Indians to a fighting frenzy; even the Illinois warriors attacked the British because of such a message from the Master of Life. The teachings of the Delaware Prophet, already well known to the warriors, were given special interpretation by Pontiac. Much of the tenacity and fury of the Indians in battle may be attributed to religious zeal. Pontiac used the Prophet's teachings to "spirit up"[26] his confederates.

Wallace stresses the powerful influence of the Delaware Prophet's teachings throughout the Indian world of the Northeast where the Prophet's spiritual chart was actually sold (one for each Indian family, the Prophet recommended) at the charge of two doeskins or one buckskin per copy. The Delaware Prophet, like his successor, Handsome Lake of the Senecas, called for a God over both white and Indians and made other references showing his familiarity with Christianity. As Wallace notes, "his code was a syncretism of native and white elements."[27] Yet at the same time his teachings brought rebellion against traditional Christianity and the white man's culture.

In his account of Pontiac's War, Wallace also stresses that a second prophet, a shadowy figure, an Onondaga leader of 1762, preached that the Great Spirit would punish the whites if they persisted in seizing lands in the Indian country. In short, the Indian frontier of the North was alive with religious prophets hostile to white culture. There is no doubt that Pontiac's War had deep religious overtones and was essentially a religious crusade against the white man's culture and religion. Pontiac very quickly saw the possibilities of sparking an Indian rebellion that had already been encouraged by religious prophets. If the Delaware Prophet was "an emotional catalyst"[28] of Indian discontent, Pontiac was the war chief who led an aroused Indian population against the British. Certainly Wallace's account generally supports Parkman's descriptions of the impact of religious leaders. It is unfortunate that Parkman, in tying this movement to an Indian "conspiracy," gave the Prophet and his followers a negative image.

PONTIAC'S "FLYING CAMP" OF WARRIORS

By the fall of 1763, Pontiac's War approached a climax, scarcely three months after the beginnings of the Detroit siege and the capture of Fort Venango and her sister forts in the Ohio country. Pontiac's neighboring allies, Potawatomies, Wyandot-Hurons, Ojibwas, Chippewas, and other tribes had made peace overtures, and Delawares in the south suffered loss of a cadre of warriors, captured by an Iroquois band. Superintendent William Johnson promised rewards to the Iroquois if they brought back Delaware "heads." Johnson was so desperate for complete victory that he would send out these headhunters.[29] Johnson, according to his correspondence with the commander Sir Jeffrey Amherst and London authorities, was embarrassed by the vigor of Indian resistance in the war. He tried to convince the Lords of Trade that he was fighting against a skilled and powerful foe.

The Iroquois tribes, Johnson wrote, were warlike conquerors of many tribes throughout the northwest reaching into the Illinois country. They had "subdued" many tribes of northern and western Indians who fought fiercely against them.[30] These "northern" Indians, Johnson said, were "without any exaggeration . . . the most formidable of any uncivilized body of people in the world." It was the "Ottawa Confederacy" that "begun" the war. "Pondiac" and his "flying camp" and the "Ottawa Confederacy" had committed "acts of hostility." Moreover, the "neighboring French" had "instigated" Indian resistance.[31]

Johnson, in making reports to the Lords of Trade and Plantations in September and November of 1763, could show that these formidable warriors were losing the war. He enthusiastically told of British advances into the Indian country. By late November, only Ottawas and Senecas (and not all of them) held out at Detroit. Pontiac had "under him" a "flying camp" of 300 warriors. But according to Johnson's "enumeration" of fighting men, Pontiac's neighboring allies numbered at least 2,000 warriors, perhaps 2,700 altogether. According to Johnson, then, the Ottawa "league," or "confederacy," was allied to Pontiac and his "flying camp" until he was forced to give up the siege. Besides the Ottawas, Pontiac also had support from other tribes: Wyandot-Hurons, Potawatomies, Chippewas, plus Sacs and Foxes, "Meyomenys," "Folsavoins," and "Puans."[32] Some of these tribes were in "the neighborhood of Detroit," and others lived near Michili-mackinac and on the lower western side of Lake Michigan.[33]

What, then, is "flying camp," the elusive term used by Johnson to describe Pontiac's force of warriors? We may have leads in turning to George Washington, Johnson's contemporary. As military history scholars know, Washington often referred to his "flying camp." In the year 1776, Washington depended on his "flying camp" of militiamen in the first years of the Revolutionary War. He saw the "flying camp" as a mobile army, envisioned at first to comprise 10,000 soldiers. We know from his letters to Congress that the force at one time was at least 3,000 and he moved 2,000 men to join his "head quarters" army surrounding the city of New York. Martha sometimes joined Washington at his "head quarters" camp, but not when he was in the field at his "flying camp." We must assume that there were few amenities at the mobile army "flying camp."[34]

Modern dictionaries support Washington's use of the term. For example, the Oxford dictionary of 1893 describes the "flying camp" as "a little army of horse and foot." And the Webster Merriam unabridged dictionary of 1952 gives the older, historic meaning of "flying camp" as "a body of troops formed for rapid movement from place to place."[35] This latter definition appears to fit Washington's use of the term, and Johnson, as military commander during the French and Indian War, knew his military terminology and used "flying camp" as a term to describe what he believed to be a mobile Indian fighting force "under" Pontiac.[36]

We can argue in this discussion that Sir William Johnson, probably the best-qualified contemporary to evaluate Pontiac's significance as a military leader, gives him the designation of "Chief," having hundreds of Indians "under" him at his "flying camp." What is more, Pontiac is the only war chief named in his 1763 "Enumeration." When Johnson writes about the northern Indians as superb strategists and fighters, he appears to allude to Pontiac. "The Indians," he wrote to the Board of Trade, "are in no wise inferior to us in sagacity and strategem, qualities most essentially necessary in this country . . . as they attack by surprise."[37]

Did the Indian "attacks" originate from Pontiac and his "flying camp"? Although Parkman does not mention the words "flying camp," Johnson's use of the term may well help to buttress Parkman's case that Pontiac was indeed a leader of a considerable force of Indians and that cadres from this "flying camp" may have been used to attack other forts besides Detroit. The eighteenth-century use of the words by Washington and Johnson seems to imply a powerful mobile unit that could be used to force the surrender of outlying enemy fortifications.

There is also the point that Johnson believed, as he stated time and again, that Indian assaults could be made with skill and strategem. This testimony from Johnson runs counter to Peckham's allegation that an Indian chief did not have the mental capacity to lead a "conspiracy" against the English.[38] Whether one accepts the "flying camp" thesis or not, the data furnished by Johnson nevertheless does tend to support Parkman's arguments about Pontiac's skill as an oganizational leader and war chief.

PONTIAC'S "CONSPIRACY"

Was Parkman justified in using the word *conspiracy*? A conspiracy usually refers to a plot carried out by a small group for evil or unlawful ends. From the British point of view, the ends were evil. The Indians, notwithstanding, saw their aspirations as legitimate.

Had the tribesmen lacked grievances, the word *conspiracy* might have been justified. Available evidence shows Pontiac channelized existing grievances and provided leadership for a rebellion that could be more accurately described as a war for Indian self-determination. The American Revolution, though considered by many British leaders at the time as a criminal conspiracy, is usually thought of by Americans as a glorious moment in history.[39] In using the word *conspiracy*, Parkman failed to do justice to American Indian aspirations for independence.[40]

In *Pontiac*, Parkman's coloration of the Indian personality did not stop with the use of a single word; he conjured up a figure of Indian treachery and savagery in molding the character of Pontiac. For Parkman, "all savages, whatever may be their country, their color, or their lineage, are prone to treachery and deceit."[41] What is more, Parkman portrays the great Ottawa chief as a typical savage, one who by his racial heritage was naturally treacherous because "treacheries . . . to his savage mind seemed fair and honorable."[42] Pontiac, in short, "was a thorough savage, and in him stand forth, in strongest light and shadow, the native faults and virtues of the Indian race." It would be difficult to state a more ominous portrayal of the American Indian than Parkman's assertion that Pontiac was capable of "the blackest treachery," or that he was "the Satan of this forest paradise."

We are told that "his complexion was darker than is usual with his race," a hint that this remarkable chief was capable of manifest perfidy. When Pontiac's plot at Fort Detroit was exposed, Parkman's scathing pen at last found its mark in a vivid metaphor: "An entrapped wolf meets no quarter from the huntsman; and a savage, caught in his treachery, has no claim to forbearance." Pontiac's behavior was marked by "blackest treachery."[43]

Even with this characterization of Pontiac, Parkman nevertheless designs at the same time a powerful portrait of a "prime mover of the plot," very necessary for the suspense element in his narrative. It is in this second contrasting figure of Pontiac that the formidable warrior of the wilderness steps forth to command all-out war against the English: "His muscular figure was cast in the mold of remarkable symmetry and vigor"; he "roused in his warlike listeners their native thirst for blood and vengeance"; he "addressed himself to their superstition . . . the Master of Life." To create a feeling for his finer qualities, Parkman compared him with legendary figures of antiquity: "In generous thought and deed, he rivalled the heroes of ancient story." Besides, Parkman tells us anecdotes about Pontiac suggesting "that noble and generous thought was no stranger to the savage hero of this dark forest tragedy."[44]

Thus in the character of Pontiac, Parkman has given us a colorful mosaic of a noble, generous, manly figure who was capable of dark conspiracies and treachery against the white man. Grant that Parkman occasionally shows us that whites as well as Indians were capable of cruel, savage behavior,[45] he still reserves his particular malevolence for the Indians and their leaders. In this book as in others in his series, Parkman dwells at length on Indian atrocities, whereas white outrages against Indians tend to be singled out as understandable responses to Indian attacks.

Despite his rigid stance on Indian savagery, there are parts of *Pontiac,* as we have noted, that offer a more favorable image of tribal people, and certainly the portrait of the chief himself has much truth in it. One cannot help but conclude that Parkman's long study of Lafitau's work[46] and his own contacts with the Sioux gave him a particular sense of what Pontiac must have been like. The portrait is so vivid that it has remained as an image of a formidable chief for generations throughout the English-speaking world.

There is little question that in *Pontiac,* as well as in his other historical works, Parkman bent his sources to capture reader interest.[47] Surely in the characterization of Pontiac as "the Satan of this forest paradise," we have a distorted image. Given this manipulation to conjure up a history of Indian treachery, whitewashing acts of white brutality can be explained as just retribution for evil plots. Parkman deliberately exploited the image of the treacherous savage as an explanation for events.

Yet we find that Parkman in a sense could justify his interpretations because he had proof in contemporary source materials. Parkman's history often reflected a bias in the sources themselves. This bias nevertheless, in certain occasions, appears to have had its advantages in interpreting the extant record. For instance, Parkman appears to have been accurate in appraising extant reports about Iroquois arrogance in their trade relations with other Indians and with Europeans.[48]

In the main, however, Parkman was correct in assessing Pontiac's qualifications as a talented, able Indian leader—the chief capable of planning and carrying out an extensive attack on the British. After 1763, it is clear from white sources as well as from Indian tradition that Pontiac was the major figure in the war.[49]

THE SMALLPOX INCIDENT

In discussing Parkman's account of Pontiac's War, we should be aware of the fact that he uncovered what may have been the first instance of "germ" warfare in American history. In his continuing examination of documentary material after his first edition of *Pontiac* was printed, Parkman was astonished to find a calculated proposal for inoculation of Indians surrounding Fort Pitt with smallpox, the highly infectious viral disease known today as having killed millions of Indians throughout the western hemisphere.[50] The deadly, contagious nature of smallpox was known by the British general Sir Jeffrey Amherst, who, as Parkman noted, had a "blustering arrogance" in his 1763 correspondence with Colonel Henry Bouquet, his commander on the Ohio frontier. According to Parkman, this "despicable enemy" (the Indian) had angered Amherst to such an extent that he made, in a postscript to Bouquet, the following "detestable" suggestion: "Could it not be contrived to send the *Small Pox* among those disaffected tribes of Indians? We must on this occasion use every stratagem in our power to reduce them.—[Signed] J. A." Bouquet replied, also in a postscript: "I will try to inoculate the ——— with some blankets that may fall in their hands, and take care not to get the disease myself. As it is a pity to expose good men against them, I wish we could make use of the Spanish method, to hunt them with English dogs, supported by rangers and some light horse, who would, I think, effectually extirpate or remove that vermin." Amherst rejoined: "You will do well to try to inoculate the Indians by means of blankets, as well as to try every other method that can serve to extirpate this execrable race. I should be very glad if your scheme for hunting them down by dogs could take effect, but England is at too great a distance to think of that at present." Appended to these quotations is Parkman's footnote explaining that Amherst's correspondence is in the manuscripts in the British Museum collection of Bouquet and Haldimand papers.[51]

After exposing General Jeffrey Amherst as a character type of the English military, Parkman went on to state that "there is no direct evidence that Bouquet carried into effect the shameful plan of infecting the Indians, though, a few months after, the small-pox was known to have made havoc among the tribes of the Ohio." Despite his contempt for Amherst, Parkman had admiration for Bouquet, a Swiss mercenary, who "was perfectly capable of dealing with them by other means, worthy of a man and a soldier."[52]

Parkman acknowledged that his evidence for infecting the Indians with smallpox was circumstantial. Since his day, the incident has been pored over by other scholars, but nothing could be added except to confirm the accuracy of Parkman's account. Then, in 1955, a century after the appearance of *Pontiac*, conclusive proof was discovered that at least two blankets were used in May 1763 "to convey the Small-pox to the Indians." The order to replace the blankets, found in the *Papers of Colonel Henry Bouquet*, was endorsed by General Thomas Gage.[53] What is significant about this episode is that it illustrates that Parkman's hunch was correct. Moreover, he had overriding concern about incorporating new evidence into his books. The first edition of *Pontiac* has no mention of the smallpox episode; but in the 1860s, with the aid of booksellers Henry Stevens and his brother Benjamin, Parkman obtained transcripts of documents from the British Museum and the Library of Congress mentioning the use of smallpox to infect the Indians.[54] Later editions of *Pontiac* have expanded chapters on the bitter fighting at Fort Pitt and, with them, the examination of evidence showing that a white commander in the person of Sir Jeffrey Amherst could surpass the Indians' scales of depravity coming out of border warfare. Still, despite the truly heroic effort in research, the basic conspiratorial theme with the treachery of Chief Pontiac remained unchanged.

As has been demonstrated in this chapter, the *Pontiac* volume was based upon a large data base of sources in early American history. Furthermore, Parkman's main themes are echoed by certain modern scholars who have covered the same ground. Yet *Pontiac* is still Parkman's basic novelistic

FRANCIS PARKMAN

work founded upon his own fixed ideas. One cannot help but regret that the mass of accurate factual detail loses much of its validity because of Parkman's insistence upon dramatic unity of events and coloration of historical characters. It is almost as if he searched the sources to justify his design. He might alter details in his revisions, but they did not change basic interpretations and often, as in *The Oregon Trail* and *Pontiac*, were employed to strengthen the fabric of narrative. Underlying Parkman's manner of depicting individuals and their roles in history, whether they be Indian chiefs or generals, were Parkman's literary schemes. These had a powerful impact upon the sometimes exaggerated images of people and events in his future historical writings, as the next chapter suggests.

Abbé Henri-Raymond Casgrain,
Parkman's friend and critic.
(From a photo given "with friendship";
courtesy Massachusetts Historical Society.)

PART THREE

THE HERO AS STORYTELLER

Parkman's Beacon Hill home at 50 Chestnut Street, Boston. His study was on the third floor. In later years he had a chair, attached to pulleys and tackles on the stairs, lifting him from floor to floor. After 1873, Parkman lived here with his sister, Eliza. (Photograph by W. R. Jacobs.)

FATHER ISAAC JOGUES' MARTYRDOM

*By the way, the Jogues papers will facilitate my operation in a matter,
which though episodical, is of such dramatic interest . . . that I am
tempted to give it more space than is consistent with just historic
proportion.*

—PARKMAN TO JOHN G. SHEA,
25 SEPTEMBER 1857

Parkman's study at his Jamaica Pond summer home, near Boston. At the upper right, on top
of the bookcase, are his Lakota Indian shield, bow, and arrows and his powder horn from his
Oregon Trail journey of 1846. Next to his wheelchair, on the left, is his steel safe for protection of valuables. (W. R. Jacobs Photography Collection.)

CHAPTER SEVEN

THE HERO IN THE
WILDERNESS

THE CLOSER WE READ PARKMAN'S *HISTORY*, the more we encounter a personal factor, a sense of being present on the historical scene, observing people in action.[1] With his gifts as a writer, Parkman surrounded his readers with a cargo of data, but facts themselves were of interest because they were part of what an eyewitness saw or believed to be true. In his youth Parkman developed literary skills that enabled him to fuse historical details into imaginative but believable accounts of events.

As he mastered his sources, he gave each of his main characters qualities and personalities that made them appear as recognizable individuals. For instance, Count Frontenac appears as an active governor, with energy, courage, and a certain sense of vanity. Parkman was convinced that such a man would have had his portrait made. Although he was unsuccessful in finding the painting, he did discover at Versailles a portrait of the governor's wife, which he used to describe her distinct characteristics and her appearance when she entered the narrative.

Despite his insistence on molding his lead characters into dramatic personalities (when they may well have been undramatic), Parkman seems to have held back his enthusiastic pen, lest his zeal for a colorful individual not be confirmed in the sources. For example, in shaping the character of Montcalm, Parkman somewhat unexpectedly gave his readers a domestic, affectionate side of the General. When he first read Montcalm's autobiography, he was annoyed to find so many tender family concerns: "Montcalm spends too much time over his wife's child bearing," he wrote a friend. "Still his nervous choppy style gives more the feel of a soldier than of a family man."[2] This kind of detail found its way into his narrative. In another case, upon discovering new data for a second edition of *Pontiac*

showing that Sir Jeffrey Amherst had been responsible for infecting Indians with smallpox blankets, Parkman's earlier view of Amherst's arrogant
blustering was confirmed. There was no need to change the plot. Amherst
was exactly the kind of villain the story needed.

In other character studies, Parkman ferreted out minute details to give
his readers insight into individuals. He went so far as to locate information
about Champlain's child bride, who wanted to leave her husband to become a nun, and he used this sidelight on Champlain's twelve-year-old
bride to provide a fascinating view of the explorer's personal life.

Although such character building in historical narratives makes it easy
to make analogies between his work and other literary forms, especially
novels, Parkman believed himself to be a historian. He dedicated himself
to the task of reconstructing another age peopled with individuals who left
a record. He took on, he wrote, "the task of rekindling, calling out of the
dust the soul and body of it and making it a breathing reality."[3] This "reality" was at least in part due to the manner in which Parkman's leading
characters became authors themselves in recounting their role in historic
episodes.

One way of determining more precisely how Parkman practiced his art
is to examine closely the episode in his writings. To understand how it was
developed as a method of historical storytelling, we must return to the
youthful Francis Parkman and his experiences that he told and retold in
autobiographical writings.

There is an incident in Parkman's youth that revealed much about risk
taking and how the excitement of endangering his life was disguised in
autobiographical fiction. In a letter of 1841, writing to his father, he described his climb to New Hampshire's Crawford Notch, where he and his
party were "saluted . . . with a storm of sleet and snow." He went on to tell
of shooting "partridges and pigeons" and fishing. "I am now," he writes, "at
the Notch of Franconia, having visited the Flume and other curiosities."[4]

From this letter, it is obvious that Frank, as he was called, was living
the life of the woodsman and hunter, furnishing himself with food in the
fashion of the New Hampshire Rangers of the Old French War. His journals, no doubt kept from his parents' examination at this time, have particulars about a dangerous adventure in the Flume Gorge at Franconia. The
Gorge today is largely as it was then, an impressive chasm of several hundred feet in length with perpendicular rock walls, wet with spray and mist.

What Parkman intentionally left out of his letter to his parents (he al-
ternated in writing to his father and mother while on summer trips), was

that he made a hazardous ascent of a rock slide in the Gorge. He actually climbed a huge landslide of boulders, part of an avalanche that had previously smothered a pioneer family, the Willeys, but miraculously left their house untouched.

Today the area is largely overgrown with saplings and understory plants, and new slides have erased the place where Parkman climbed. The ascent is now made by paths carved out of rock for the purpose, but Frank had no such aids. His journals tell us that he laboriously worked his way up a ravine of the slide to the point where he was confronting precipitous walls of decaying granite penetrated by constant sprays and mists of water. He found he could not turn back. The only way out was to continue climbing. Proceeding slowly, by digging his fingers into loose walls and by opening his jackknife with his teeth, he carved out footholds. "Down went stones and pebbles," he wrote, "clattering hundreds of feet below . . . giving me grateful indication of my inevitable fate in case my head should swim or my courage fail." Inch by inch he moved upward, finally reaching the summit, where he looked down upon the hazardous scene below. Loosening a large stone, he pushed it over the edge of the Gorge and heard it thundering below until it came to the end of its journey with a "tremendous crash." [5]

Later, after returning to his inn, the Crawford House, according to his journals, he calmly recounted his experience to a husky young guide, Tom Crawford, and a pretty young woman, Pamela Prentice, of Keene, New Hampshire, visiting the Notch country with her father. Not only was Pamela impressed (she thought his experience should appear in print), but Tom Crawford, known for his strength and agility, "expressed astonishment" at Frank Parkman's climb to safety.

What Parkman accomplished here, despite his seeming reluctance to boast, was to impress his listeners with his adventure. He tells us that another climber had concluded that the ascent of the ravine, at least where Parkman made the climb, was an almost impossible feat. We know the pride and satisfaction Parkman had in recounting the exploit because it later appeared as an episode in *Vassal Morton*. The following dialogue occurs between Vassal, the hero (who is, of course, Parkman himself), and the father of the heroine (recognizable as Pamela Prentice):

"'Crawford was boasting last year, that he could outwrestle any man in New England. I challenged him, and threw him on his back.'

'You! Crawford is twice as heavy and strong as you are.'

'I am stronger than I seem,' replied Morton, with great complacency."

The father of the heroine then casts his eye on Morton and sees that, "though his frame was light, and his shoulders not broad, yet his compact proportions, deep chest, and muscular limbs, showed the highest degree of bodily vigor."[6]

There can be little doubt that Frank fantasized about overcoming the powerful Tom Crawford in the presence of Pamela, cast as the heroine in the novel. For his lady love, Vassal exhibits his chivalry as well as "bodily vigor" to descend a dangerous chasm to pluck a sweetbriar blossom. The difference in this account, compared with that in the journal, is that instead of climbing up, the hero figure goes down. The author retells a similar story: "A fragment of stone loosened under his foot" falls "with a splintering crash upon rocks below, followed by a shower of pebbles and gravel, rattling among the trees."[7]

This very personal episode of Frank Parkman's life, the story of man overcoming one of nature's challenges, appeared earlier in his tale of "The Scalp-Hunter" of 1845. Here an old white hunter pursued an Indian, one of the St. Francis Abenakis, whom Parkman portrayed as a treacherous murderer of New England frontier settlers. Hot on the trail of his prey, the hunter dashed into the stony bed of the Saco River at the Notch of the White Mountains and found himself in "piles of rock and stone strewn by an ancient avalanche over the narrow valley . . . close to the place where the unfortunate Willeys afterward met their fate."

As the Indian frantically ascended the rocky bed, the hunter fell behind. The account of the old man's perilous climb shows how Parkman practiced his craft by borrowing language from his journals:

Journal of 1841	"The Scalp-Hunter," 1845
In the bottom of this gulf a little stream comes down from a spring above and renders the precipitous rock as slippery as clay.	A little stream that trickled down the narrow and steep passage-way, and spread itself over the smooth rocks, made the foothold very precarious.
Still I kept on until I came to a precipice about forty feet high and not far from perpendicular.	A smooth rock, nearly perpendicular, soon arrested his progress.
To ascend was perilous . . . to descend . . . was impossible . . . the other method . . . was my only chance.[8]	To ascend was perilous enough; to descend was impossible.[9]

THE HERO IN THE WILDERNESS

Already expert in building suspense in a story based upon personal experience, Parkman, then writing under the name of Jonathan Carver, actually kept his editor awake at night, reading *Knickerbocker* proofs. Little did G. Gaylord Clark, the editor, know that his unknown author had actually climbed those "slimy rocks."

The Indian warrior, as Clark finally discovered in the story, escaped his relentless pursuer at a place in the ravine "where its sides were less precipitous than elsewhere." Meanwhile, the hunter, with his intended victim out of sight, climbed up the core of the avalanche, finally reaching the top of a flat rock only eight feet across. His fingers "worn to the bone," his body aching with the strain of physical exertion, he threw himself across the rock. Beyond this resting place towered a precipice, "sixty feet high, perpendicular, smooth and wet." On either side were still higher escarpments. Any attempt to climb them would mean certain disaster.

The old man was trapped. His enemy, the warrior, returned to exult over the fate of his pursuer. After two days of waiting came a cloudburst of rain: "In a few moments [it] filled every gully and ravine with foaming waters, and drift-logs driving down into the valley. The old man was swept from his place in an instant, but the watchful Indian found him next morning wedged under a rock; and a week after, his gray hairs were fluttering in the wind from the top of a cabin in the Indian village of St. Francis, by the side of the St. Lawrence." [10] This tale of "The Scalp-Hunter," one of Parkman's earliest published pieces of fiction, tells us much about him as a writer. With a whimsical exaggeration he tells us it is a "semi-historical sketch" taken from oral testimony of old women of the St. Francis tribe whose tongues had been loosened by a bottle of rum. The story, a product of his imagination, illustrates Parkman's preoccupation with Indians, the French and Indian War, and the natural wilderness. Even more revealing is how he adeptly uses his own harrowing experience as a rock climber to make an episode into an exciting short story.

At the same time that we read and reexamine slightly modified accounts of the climb, we discover, many years later, an echo of it in a prelude to the battle on the Plains of Abraham in Parkman's epic, *Montcalm and Wolfe*. General Wolfe, weak from a feverish illness, had scarcely the strength to lead his men up "a great ravine choked with trees; and in its depths ran a little brook . . . which, swollen by the late rains, fell splashing in the stillness over a rock. Wolfe said to an officer near him: 'You can try it, but I don't think you'll get up.' He himself, however, found strength to drag himself up with the rest. The narrow slanting path on the face of the heights had been made impassable by trenches and abattis." [11]

The ravine-climbing episode, modified in *Montcalm and Wolfe,* tells us much about Parkman, his self-image, and the projection of that image into his writings. The original incident, as related in his journals, gives us insight into his risk taking, a kind of bravura further illustrated by his preparation for the Oregon Trail adventure by jumping on and off a horse at full gallop.[12] Parkman's narcissism becomes apparent when we consider that he endangered himself, and occasionally members of his party, by deliberately entering dangerous Indian territories. One of these was the Pawnee country, as he tells repeatedly in his journals and in *The Oregon Trail.*[13]

Beginning with *The Oregon Trail,* we have seen in a previous chapter how Parkman told the story of his experiences by developing or enlarging on episodes that were integral but separable from his continuous narrative. He fashioned a series of occurrences that were smoothly incorporated into the larger, more comprehensive episodes. The beginning chapters in *The Oregon Trail*—"The Frontier," "Breaking the Ice," "Fort Leavenworth," "'Jumping Off,'" and "The 'Big Blue'"—set the scene for a whole new series of episodic events: "The Buffalo," "Scenes at Fort Laramie," and "The War Parties." Gradually the hero-author emerges as he narrates his extraordinary feats of hunting and physical endurance and courage while "Hunting Indians," carrying on a "Mountain Hunt," and making a "Passage of the Mountains" and "The Lonely Journey."

Hunting episodes in the book are typical of Parkman's manner of showing how he managed to overcome potential hazards. An example is his account of a furious mountain buffalo hunt. Parkman, mounted on a mule, followed his guide, who rode a yellow horse. "I set spurs to the mule," he wrote, "who soon far outran her plebian rival."

> When we had galloped a mile or more, a large rabbit, by ill-luck, sprang up just under the feet of the mule, which bounded violently aside in full career. Weakened as I was, I was flung forcibly to the ground, and my rifle, falling close to my head, went off with the shock. Its sharp, spiteful report rang for some moments in my ear. Being slightly stunned, I lay for an instant motionless. . . . Soon recovering myself, I rose, picked up the rifle, and anxiously examined it. It was badly injured. The stock was cracked, and the main screw broken, so that the lock had to be tied in its place with a string; yet happily it was not rendered totally unserviceable. I wiped it out, reloaded it, and handing it to Reynal, who meanwhile had caught the mule and led her up to me, I mounted again. No sooner had I done so than the brute began to rear and plunge with extreme violence; but now being prepared for her, and free from incumberance, I soon reduced her to submission. Then, taking the rifle again from Reynal, we galloped as before.

We were now free of the mountains and riding far out on the broad prairie. The buffalo were still some two miles in advance of us.[14]

Then follow accounts of killing buffalo, deer, and antelope, and of return to temporary haven in a Sioux Indian camp. This single incident, one of many that appear in *The Oregon Trail*, portrays youthful Parkman, though weakened by illness, as a hunter-horseman: fearless, courageous, and master of all the natural or man-made problems he confronted. We see here a pattern that emerges in Parkman's later historical works, which is evident in *Pontiac* and all later volumes, but less visible in *The Old Régime* and in *A Half-Century*. *The Old Régime*, a socioeconomic and cultural history, and *A Half-Century*, a complex narration of intercolonial events linking frontier history of the late seventeenth century to the eighteenth, gave Parkman less opportunity to dwell on exploits of major figures. But exploits are there, in both volumes, vividly portrayed.

The episodic nature of Parkman's entire *History* was due in part to the fact that he was forced to work piecemeal, fighting a battle against his "enemy" to live long enough to complete his series. Although, as we have noted, Parkman did make continual revisions of his work, he did not plan to forge his volumes, as Henry Adams had suggested, into one masterwork. Close examination of Parkman's volumes reveals that Adams's plan would not have been suitable for Parkman because his multivolumed *History, France and England in North America*, was designed as an epic struggle told through biography, that is, by means of connected scenes of action in the lives of individuals.

Although he did not espouse a great-man theory, Parkman undoubtedly had a special feeling about the accomplishments of his central figures. They were, for him, so significant in their times that he could cast them in a mold to reveal the spirit of an age. Their particular image was often Parkman's mirror of himself. At the same time, he consciously relied on his own experiences and observations, as illustrated in "The Scalp-Hunter." He had been there, and he had himself, like Wolfe, climbed dangerous, slippery ravines.

Let us turn to *Pontiac* again to look at Parkman's technique of reconstructing wilderness events. Here we see expert use of circumstantial evidence. An example is the panorama he created when Ohio Indians surrendered to Colonel Henry Bouquet, one of Parkman's heroes, a Swiss mercenary, "a jewel of an officer,"[15] a most favorable contrast to other army leaders. Bouquet, and his men with "steady valor," outfought the Indians at the wilderness battle of Bushy Run in the year 1763.[16] Now the tribesmen, in October 1764, were forced to surrender prisoners and give up the fight. "Bouquet was in the heart of the enemy's country. Their villages, except some remote settlements . . . all lay within a few days' march . . . they were confounded by the hordes of invaders." Methodically, Bouquet led his army through the woods "down the Muskingum, until he reached a spot where the broad meadows, which bordered the river, would supply abundant grazing for cattle and horses; while the terraces above, shaded by forest trees, offered a convenient site for encampment." [17]

After messengers from the army and Indian chiefs had arranged the council place "under a canopy of branches":

> . . . the glittering array of troops was drawn out on the meadow in front, in such a manner as to produce the most imposing effect on the minds of the Indians . . . a spectacle equally new and astounding. The perfect order and silence of the far-extended lines; the ridges of bayonettes flashing in the sun; the fluttering tartans of the Highland regulars; the bright red uniform of the Royal Americans; the darker garb and duller trappings of the Pennsylvania troops, and the bands of Virginia backwoodsmen, who, in fringed hunting-frocks and Indian moccasins, stood leaning carelessly on their rifles—all these combined to form a scene of military pomp and power not soon to be forgotten.

Parkman's imaginative reconstruction of the scene, the meadow, the nearby forest trees, the glittering array of troops, exemplifies his method of creating an illusion of eyewitness reality. He used his device first in early fiction tales and in *The Oregon Trail* and learned to fit it into a historical context. Here the technique, to be effective, was more complicated, involving the congealing of earlier plots and narratives. He also had to call on a research base of facts on such topics as the color and design of military paraphernalia, the exact geographical location of the army route, and the physical detail of the site, including trees, meadows, and river banks.

The colorful imagery in the episode brings the reader to a culminating confrontation, the treaty conference terminating the conflict between Indians and whites during Pontiac's War. Moreover, the council scene sets in motion a whole new series of subepisodes and events, [18] giving Parkman a chance to launch into a panegyric on the wonders of nature, clearly an autobiographical fragment showing the reader that he, the author, was a hero of his own life in tasting the challenge of existence in a wild, natural world.

Parkman then continued his narration through an interlocking sequence of events coming out of the treaty negotiations. This is the time in

1764 when Indians freed their prisoners, mainly white women and children, who had been captives for as long as three years. We can easily follow the narrative because each occurrence is labeled on the title page (Parkman made such instructions for printers on handwritten manuscript copies of his books).[19] We begin with "Bouquet in the Indian Country," as the army passed through "woods damp, still and cool . . . an open meadow, rich with herbage, and girdled by a zone of forest; gladdened by the notes of birds, and enlivened, it may be, by grazing herds of deer." Then we go on to the next page, again labeled with the new unit of action, "Terror of the Enemy," that is, as Parkman read the minds of the Indians, their thoughts of "escape by flight."[20] Thereafter is the account of "The Council," "Speech of the Delaware Orator," a "Reply of Bouquet," and "Embassy to the Showanoes, a Speech of an Indian Orator," another "Reply of Bouquet," then a longer section of "Scenes at the English Camp," and finally a reconstruction of the women "Prisoners of the Indians" who had lived "The Forest Life."

At the grand moment when the prisoners were delivered—"the meeting of husbands with wives, and fathers with children, the reunion of broken families"—there was also a group of prisoners reluctant to face their relatives:

> There were young women . . . who had become the partners of Indian husbands; and who now, with all their hybrid offspring, were led reluctantly into the presence of fathers or brothers whose images were almost blotted from their memory. They stood agitated and bewildered . . . and the shame of their real or fancied disgrace; while their Indian lords looked on . . . standing in the midst of their enemies, imperturbable as statues of bronze. These women were compelled to return with their children to the settlements; yet they all did so with reluctance, and several afterwards made their escape, eagerly hastening back to their warrior husbands, and the tolls and vicissitudes of an Indian wigwam.[21]

Some of these women, Parkman found, were wives of frontiersmen and carried in their arms children born in captivity. Others, like the woman named Mary Jemison, captured by the Senecas, "escaped into the woods with her half-breed children." What could explain the behavior of the captives, especially those who expressed "an attachment to Indian life"? Why would captives actually resist their own rescue? Some, Parkman wrote, "sat sullen and scowling, angry that they were forced to abandon the wild license for the irksome restraints of society." They looked back "with a fond longing to inhospitable deserts." Parkman tells us in no uncertain terms: The very trial of living among "Beasts, and Nature herself" may stimulate those of "a sound and healthful mind."

> To him who had once tasted the reckless independence, the haughty self-reliance, the sense of irresponsible freedom, which the forest life engenders, civilization thenceforth seems flat and stale. Its pleasures are insipid, its pursuits wearysome, its conventionalities, duties, and mutual dependence alike tedious and disgusting. The entrapped wanderer grows fierce and restless, and pants for breathing-room. His path, it is true, was choked with difficulties, but his body and soul were hardened to meet them. . . . The wilderness, rough, harsh, and inexorable, has charms more potent in their seductive influence than all the lures of luxury and sloth. And often he on whom it has cast its magic finds no heart to dissolve the spell, and remains a wanderer and an Ishmaelite to the hour of his death.[22]

Then follows a lengthy footnote quoting the Iroquois historian Cadwallader Colden on French prisoners of Five Nations who would never leave "the Indian manner of living." The former prisoners maintained, in protesting against New York Indian agents' attempts to rescue them, that they enjoyed more liberty and had "greater Plenty than the common inhabitants of New York."

Not only did Parkman have his own autobiographical account to cite on the joys of wilderness life, but he also found evidence in the sources to confirm his views. The frontier existence, with its "reckless independence," its "irresponsible freedom," its "hardening" of the "body and soul" to meet new difficulties, all these helped to bring about a transformation of the men and women exposed to the wilderness. Here is the environmental theme, obviously exaggerated by the youthful Parkman in *Pontiac*, that is carried through the entire series of narratives culminating in *Montcalm and Wolfe*.

Another side of Parkman's depiction of nature appears in his volumes following *The Oregon Trail* and *Pontiac*. In addition to his autobiographical statements arguing that the wilderness life was a powerful factor in molding the character of the pioneer, Parkman, as the years passed, made a deliberate effort to mention explicit plants and animals and climatic factors in order to provide richer images in his recreated scenes. The Unitarian clergyman Theodore Parker, as has been noted, criticized Parkman for neglecting to name particular kinds of plants and trees in the *Pontiac* narrative.

That this advice was well taken and later used we can see in Parkman's journal notes on natural phenomena he observed near and around the

River May (St. John's River) in Florida. Here we find an outpouring of descriptive notations, almost like color photographs, later to be produced in an 1885 revision of the *Pioneers*.

> Tall, lank, bare-stemmed pines. Wire grass . . . below. Sun easily penetrates. Palmetto thickets. Pools of stagnant water. Marshes of bulrushes. Masses of deciduous trees and magnolia—creepers, Spanish moss, sometimes choking the trees like tattered cobwebs, slowly killing them. Liquid amber, maples, live oak . . . large turtles. . . . Numerous leaping fish. . . . Extensive meadows . . . rank vegetation. Morning mists. . . . White cranes abundant; blue and white herons. . . . Large hawks. . . . Maple, ash, gum, cypress, laurel. . . . Palms numerous . . . bright green glistening leaves of yellow water lily.

Parkman even went to the extent of visiting a local Florida menagerie, where he noted a "Rattlesnake—*alive, 7 feet long*," [23] as well as a dangerous "water mocassin, 4 or 5 feet," along with "hooping" cranes, black vultures, an American barn owl, an opossum, a red-tailed hawk, a gray fox and lynx, a live gopher, and its predator, a gopher snake. If he could not see the animals in the wild, he observed them in what was then a local zoo.

Because he had been forced to rely on secondhand accounts for the first edition of the *Pioneers,* this new data enabled him to give his readers one of the most intriguing natural scenes in his entire history. Describing the scene of May 1562 that greeted the eyes of a gallant French pioneer, Jean Ribaut, Parkman takes his lead from references in the explorer's journal, "a quaint old narrative . . . exuberant with delight." He continues: "The tranquil air, the warm sun, woods fresh with young verdure, meadows bright with flowers; the palm, the cypress, the pine, the magnolia; the grazing deer; herons, curlews, bitterns, woodcock, and unknown waterfowl that waded in the ripple of the beach; cedars bearded from crown to root with long gray moss; huge oaks smothering the folds of enormous grapevines; such were the objects that greeted them in their roamings, till their new-discovered land seemed 'the fairest, fruitfulest and pleasantes of al the world.'" [24] As the party moved inland, "morning broke on the fresh, moist meadows hung with mists . . . ranging the woods, they found them full of game, wild turkeys and patridges, bears, and lynxes . . . deer, of unusual size leaped from the underbrush. Cross-bow and arquebuse were brought to the level; but the Huguenot captain, 'moved with the singular fairness and bigness of them,' forbade his men to shoot." [25]

Here we have again a hero-leader, Jean Ribaut, the Huguenot explorer, telling his own story from his journal translated and printed by "one Thomas Hackit" and the Hakluyt Society. Parkman, proud of his distant Huguenot ancestry, could readily identify with journal-keeper Jean Ribaut, who in this vivid travel episode gave us a unique portrait of the early natural landscape of Florida. There is little doubt that the benign mood created here, based in part upon Parkman's observation of the St. Johns' River area, is employed as a contrast to episodes of violence and flux: "Florida Abandoned," "Indian War," "Ambuscade," "Arrival of the Spaniards."[26] As we might expect, there are additional descriptions of the natural scene, but nature's mood could change along with specific actions.

Parkman's extraordinary preparations to gather data for these environmental panoramas of course did not depend wholly upon his personal observations or data he found in Ribaut's journal. He also combed accounts of other visitors to Florida in other decades. There is reasonable certainty that the hoots of owls and gobbles of wild turkeys came from William Bartram's travels. One can even see how Parkman paraphrased Bartram, who wrote of "screams of owls" and a "cheering converse of turkey cocks." Parkman wrote that "owls whooped around" and that there was a "clamor of wild turkeys."[27]

These natural wilderness images are, as we have seen, knitted into the pattern of narrative and surface at appropriate intervals to create a mood or interpretation that illuminates the action taking place. Parkman's experience in exploring and living in the wilderness, even in camping and fishing outings in later life, gave him an imaginative view of what nature's impact was upon man. He found nature to be a place for invigoration and stimulation. As a challenge, as adversity, it tested the strength, the fortitude, the audacity of La Salle and other characters in his *History*. At the same time, as critics have noted, Parkman's natural wilderness was not entirely positive in its impact in giving lessons for self-improvement in courage and in resourcefulness.[28] Parkman's pioneers had opportunities for both personal freedom and license.

In most of Parkman's writings an underlying tension exists between the rival forces representing civilization and nature. Within nature itself, there was also conflict pitting beauty against ugliness, growth against decay, creativity against destructiveness, mirrors of similar clashes within the civilized world.[29] Thus, analogies could be easily made between rot in the forest and decay in the French court of the sixteenth century.

Parkman's wilderness was thus not simply painted scenery. It was often a deliberate attempt to give his readers a picture of what the supreme wilderness was in the eyes of pioneers. He placed his vivid landscape scenes, forest and coastline vistas, burning sunsets, roaring cataracts, and breathtaking views of mountains, meadows, lakes, rivers, and streams, in the narrative to give his story a true woodland flavor. They are remarkably similar to wilderness scenes in Cooper's novels, particularly *The Last of the Mohicans*.

And, like Cooper, he was able to use wilderness to create a mood in his story. The argument can be made that Parkman was even more successful than his mentor, however. Parkman consistently depicted environmental wildness as an ecological conditioner of civilized man. He portrayed the powerful forces of nature as a challenge to the moral strength of his characters, or as elements that destroyed their antique technology.

Close reading of Parkman's text reveals how he deliberately used the natural scene to express his social ideas. For instance, in *A Half-Century of Conflict,* there are scenes of wilderness chaos, anarchy and mayhem, all in a convulsive cycle of growth and decay. Parkman is at his best depicting, in the forests of Maine, the war between woodland seedlings for survival, "rich with the decay of those that had preceded them, crowding, choking and killing each other . . . as they grow, [they] interlock their boughs, and repeat in a season or two the same process of mutual suffocation."[30]

There were lessons of natural selection here to show how such a conflict gave insight into human affairs, even in democracy: "Not one infant tree in a thousand survives to maturity; yet these survivors form an innumerable host, pressed together in struggling confusion . . . as men are said to be in the level sameness of democratic society." The forest growth and decay becomes a negative metaphor to illustrate Parkman's conservative views on suffrage and democracy. On other occasions wilderness of North America is portrayed as continental "savage slumber," the home of "nameless barbarism." In *The Jesuits,* Parkman speaks of the continent before the arrival of the Europeans as "gloomy and meaningless." A clinching point in analyzing Parkman's negative imagery of wilderness is that this wildland is inhabited by the archetype barbarian, the Indian.[31]

Whether or not we accept Parkman's various uses of nature, or wilderness, he nevertheless gave us what he conceived to be a "breathing reality" of the past. His environmental, ethnohistorical and historical images were convincing because he knew the flowers, the trees, the locations, the seasons, the climatic changes, and the animals, birds, and insects, as well as the historical sources. All were blended into animated narrative so wrought that it is, even now, difficult to dissect and analyze. In one grand episode he could describe, as in a painting, the dramatic impact of a marching army as it penetrated the canopy of a forest ecosystem.[32]

Like Cooper, he gave us details of the natural scene by depicting harsh realities of the savage forest on one hand, and on the other by providing a stimulating "far view" on nature. In creating the "far view" Parkman might write as a narrator from a posture of elevation to give us a panoramic sunset to delight the eye before he turned to the ugly spectacle before us of seedlings choking each other in a deadly embrace for survival.

His visual imagery of the land was such that he leaves us with a sense of movement as his narrators take us from one place to another. We move, in Parkman's books, past outposts of settlements, villages, farms, forts, missions, encampments, and then into the wild country of Indian towns with gardens and cornfields dotting the interior woodlands. Parkman's *History* imaginatively illustrates the American penetration of the wilderness with visible signs of environmental changes. He gave us a sense of what it was like when America had its origins in first contacts with the Indians and a vast new land. If we want the best from Parkman, we must acknowledge his sometimes offensive social ideas and racial stereotyping and consider what he left. We may turn away from his anticlericalism, paternalism, social Darwinism, and assumptions of Anglo-Saxon superiority. For him the Indian and the bison, as well as the American forest, were doomed. Parkman, however, was undoubtedly correct about predicting inexorable changes on our frontiers.

When, in middle life, he was writing *The Old Régime,* he took time to spend a summer's afternoon in a virgin forest area, deep in the valley of a small river, the Pimigewasset, in northern New Hampshire. Here he made notes for the composition of one of the most magnificent wilderness portraits that appears in any of his pages.[33] This image, remarkable in its animated, detailed descriptions of food chains, ecosystem circuits of the forest, is at the same time a literary tour de force. In a single sentence, thirty-six lines long, Parkman gives us the product of his talents, based upon a possible combination of Indian pantheism, Lewis H. Morgan, William Bartram, Asa Gray (with whom he corresponded), William C. Bryant (whose poetry he admired), and possibly Milton (whom he had studied and read as youth).

Before beginning this long passage, Parkman introduces it with a view of the Canadian *coureur de bois,* a strange and sometimes "brutally savage," but courageous and reckless, figure: "At least, he is picturesque, and with his red-skin companion serves to animate the forest scenery." Perhaps this bushranger could actually feel, Parkman conjectures, "the charms of the savage nature that had adopted him."

Rude as he was, her voice may not always have been meaningless for one who knew her haunts so well—deep recesses where, veiled in foliage, some wild shy rivulet steals with timid music through breathless caves of verdure; gulfs where feathered crags rise like castle walls, where the noonday sun pierces with keen rays athwart the torrent, and the mossed arms of fallen pines cast wavering shadows on the illumined foam; pools of liquid crystal turned emerald in the reflected green of impending woods; rocks on whose rugged front gleam of sunlit waters dances in quivering light; ancient trees hurled headlong by the storm, to dam the raging stream with their forlorn and savage ruin; or the stern depths of immemorial forests, dim and silent as a cavern, volumned with innumerable trunks, each like an Atlas upholding its world of leaves, and sweating perpetual moisture down its dark and channeled rind,—some strong in youth, some grisly with decrepid age, nightmares of strange distortion, gnarled and knotted with wens and goitres; roots intertwined beneath like serpents petrified in an agony of contorted strife; green and glistening mosses carpeting the rough ground, mantling the rocks, turning pulpy stumps to mounds of verdure, and swathing fallen trunks as, bent in the impotence of rottenness, they lie outstretched over knoll and hollow, like mouldering reptiles of the primeval world, while around, and on and through them, springs the young growth that battens on their decay,—the forest devouring its own dead; or, to turn from its funereal shade to the light and life of the open woodland, the sheen of sparkling lakes, and mountains basking in the glory of the summer noon, flecked by shadows of passing clouds that sail on the snowy wings across the transparent azure.[34]

After exposing his readers to this breathtaking vista of a living forest, Parkman again returns to a favorite topic, the relationships between the Canadian woodsman and his wilderness homeland. It would be, Parkman argues, "false coloring to paint the half-savage *coureur de bois* as a romantic lover of Nature." He lived among the woods because "they emancipated him from restraint." In this instance we have a good illustration of Parkman's upperclass New England view of social class among historic Canadians. He found it difficult to empathize with the *coureur de bois* as a poorly paid transport worker, a social semioutcast hauling heavy loads across portages in cruel weather conditions. Instead, Parkman gave these woodsmen a portraiture that fitted into his scheme of writing.

Perhaps the most relevant aspect of Parkman's work, in perspective, is what it reveals about nineteenth-century attitudes. Parkman was a conservative, aristocratic voice of his time on attitudes toward nature, wilderness,

American Indians, and other subjects. When he fell back upon personal experiences in his descriptions of the natural scene, he soon acquired, with study of natural history, a considerable knowledge of what a good natural historian needed to know.[35] His apprenticeship began with childhood vacations on a Medford farm and college field trips culminating in a summer on the Oregon Trail. Parkman was indeed prescient and farsighted in preparing for his literary career, and although he addressed subjects such as native American and environmental history, he did so from a different perspective than ours today. His descriptions of native-American culture and frontier environmental conditions were removed from our concerns about Indian cultural history and wilderness ecology. He did, however, plead in two essays, almost in the language of John Muir, for the protection of forests from fire and overcutting. Yet he was a man with nineteenth-century Beacon Hill limitations.

We can as well make the inference that much of Parkman's devotion to detail in achieving the illusion of reality was not so much the result of his commitment to tell history as it really happened, as it was instead part of a literary device to grip the attention of the reader. The two objectives are not incompatible, but they are not the same, and one can be had by putting the other aside. There are suggestions in Parkman's correspondence and in his autobiographical statements that his early anxiety about the reception of his books stemmed from his inability to resolve this conflict. One could argue that the persistence of his concern over the clash between truth and interest in writing historical narrative was responsible for a tension that caused eruptions of Parkman's mental illness, his "attacks" from the "enemy."

Pierre Margry, Parisian archivist and Parkman's longtime friend. Largely as a result of Parkman's efforts, the U.S. Congress appropriated $10,000 for the publication of Margry's documents. These enabled Parkman to complete a revision of his LaSalle biography. (Courtesy Massachusetts Historical Society.)

A STORY OF WAR

The story of New France is from the first a story of war; of war—for so her founders believed—with the adversary of mankind itself, war with savage tribes and potent forest commonwealths; war with encroaching powers of heresy and of England.

—INTRODUCTION TO THE *PIONEERS*

Parkman, about 1880,
the hero-historian who had achieved international fame.
From an oil painting by Frederick R. Vinton
of the St. Botolph Club, which Parkman helped to found.
(Photograph by W. R. Jacobs.)

CHAPTER EIGHT

SOME LITERARY DEVICES OF THE HERO-HISTORIAN

ONE OF THE MOST DISCERNING EVALUATIONS of Parkman's work was written by another major American historian, Frederick Jackson Turner.[1] In a long essay-review written shortly after Parkman's death, Turner, an assiduous student of early American frontier history, revealed his interpretations of Parkman's work. It is an appreciative appraisal, as we might expect from Turner, who was a lifelong student of the older historian and who, like Parkman, had a subtle New England bias. Turner's correspondence at the Huntington Library and his review shows that he was familiar with Parkman's life and work.

Turner, for instance, was aware that the youthful Parkman prepared himself for writing *Pontiac* by doing field research among Indians on the Oregon Trail. He found Parkman to be a faithful and "brilliant" writer on what he called "interior" frontiers. On such topics as early American interior fur trading posts and New England pioneer hamlets, Parkman's touch was "firm, true, artistic." Indeed, a hallmark of Parkman's *History* was the portrayal of "ideals of primitive life of the backwoodman Puritan, the traits of the bushrangers and borderers of Pennsylvania and Virginia, and the life of the lawless fur-trader. [But it was] the French gentilhomme, with all his forest diablerie, who is the real hero."[2]

Turner identifies Parkman as a master historical storyteller of hero types among pioneers. Parkman accomplished so much because he was "fortunate in his theme" in writing "a *picturesque story* [my italics] of the American forest," which a "romantic period permitted." Turner went so far as to argue that "the very qualities of Parkman's mind and style" were precisely suited for his theme. Indeed, these very qualities "might have led him astray in other fields." It was actually Parkman's intimate feeling for the frontier wilderness that enabled him to write with "such reality and . . . sympathy" with a touch for "minute details." Other writers might study linguistics, ethnology, and mythology and do so with more scientific training, but, Turner maintained, no other writer would achieve Parkman's skill in creating on the pages images of Indian society. And why was this? It was because, Turner wrote, Parkman was an "even greater artist" than he was a historian.[3] The artistic quality of Parkman's wilderness narrative had the body of fine light wine.[4]

Turner's shrewd assessment of Parkman's talents and their appropriateness for the wilderness theme is borne out in certain of Parkman's published autobiographical letters, which Turner appears to have read. Parkman's own statement of purpose is more clearly set forth in a recently discovered document, his college senior oration, "Romance in America."[5] Here he analyzed several historical themes he might have considered for a lifetime project. Growing up under the shadow of William H. Prescott's histories of Spanish conquest, Parkman shows us that he had time and again given careful thought to finding an appropriate subject for himself. Among the topics he considered was the American Revolution, which he found to be tame, uninteresting, even dull. "The men of New England," he wrote, "heard that they were taxed, called a meeting, and voted resistance." Over "the calm of such proceedings . . . the poet has deep reason to lament." The very battlefields of the Revolution had "no display of chivalry or of headlong passion." Here was "a deliberate effort in favor of an abstract principle. Cool Reason . . . sent the American into the battlefield."[6]

What a bore for the youthful Parkman! He was familiar with the revolutionary movement and war from his studies at Harvard under Jared Sparks and wanted no part of it. By his own admission, Parkman was a confirmed romantic who wanted no other theme than the "fearful romance" of his forest epic.

We have seen in early chapters how Parkman reworked narrative themes in *The Oregon Trail*. There are elements of suspense that are carefully nurtured for reader interest as a spectacle of wilderness happenings unfolds. Here was an experiment at setting up a story narrative describing Indian people, the impact of pioneers on the prairies, the powers of nature in the raw. *The Oregon Trail* was more than a record of his adventures with Indians; it was also a pilot volume trying out literary techniques for narrative dramatic history with a wilderness backdrop that, Turner believed, was ideal for Parkman's talents. While the story elements in *Pontiac, Montcalm and Wolfe*, and other Parkman volumes are dealing with a far dif-

ferent era and place than *The Oregon Trail,* some of the literary techniques
are similar. We can sense a growing sophistication in historical storytelling
if we compare *The Oregon Trail* with Parkman's college writings, many of
them sophomoric by almost any measure.

The Oregon Trail was part of a sequence of historical studies planned
over a lifetime. As Parkman wrote an admiring journalist who in 1887 was
writing a review of his books: "I went to the Rocky Mts with a view of
preparing to write *The Conspiracy of Pontiac.* As to *The Oregon Trail* it is as
much a history as any of the volumes, the condition of things it describes
belonging wholly to the past . . . the best characteristic of my books is, I
think that their subjects were largely studies from real life [plus] a prodigious amount of mousing in libraries and archives." His entire historical
narrative, Parkman wrote, was nearly "cast in the form of one." One volume was still needed to make a "connecting link" between *Frontenac* and
Montcalm and Wolfe. "On this," he said, "I am now engaged."[7] Parkman
referred to the last volume of his *A Half-Century of Conflict.*

In writing this work as well as in revising *Montcalm and Wolfe* and
others of his volumes, Parkman spent many of his last days near Portsmouth, New Hampshire, at his son-in-law's seacoast home, a large, rambling house decorated in the main room with a circular display of colonial
weaponry together with many pieces of Chippendale and Queen Anne
furniture. It was here at the old "Wentworth Mansion"[8] that Barrett Wendell, a neighbor, visited Parkman late on a summer day. The two friends
spoke of fiction, beginning with a book of Harvard stories. Parkman's
"theory" of writing is suggested by his comment that the "stories . . . had
two very reassuring merits: they could not possibly bore you, and they
could not possibly have been written by anybody except a gentleman." According to Wendell, Parkman liked to be amused "and found few things
more amusing than a good rattling story read aloud to him."[9]

We have seen how Parkman in his apprenticeship years used a variety
of techniques to capture the interest of his readers. Almost every climax in
The Oregon Trail spurs us on to further adventure. Sometimes it is only a
suggestion of "stern features" of surrounding mountains that implies a
sense of impending danger preceding a "Passage of the Mountains." Similar but more carefully developed techniques, based upon a plethora of historical evidence, appeared in *Pontiac* as we have noted, but it was in his
later works, particularly in *Montcalm and Wolfe,* where Parkman revealed
his expertise in adopting certain literary devices of the novelist to grip his
readers to the page.

Eliza, or "Lizzie" as Parkman called his sister, could hardly keep her voice from trembling as she read back parts of *Montcalm and Wolfe* after a session of taking dictation from her brother. "There was so much that reminded me of him," she said, "when it came to reading the chapter . . . [describing] Wolfe's death, in spite of having braced myself to coolness in order to read it properly, I fairly broke down and could not finish."[10]

Lizzie probably did not realize that she, like so many other Parkman readers in later years, was exposed to a narrative technique almost involving Parkman himself in a valorous historical role. In this instance, Lizzie, Parkman's constant companion in his later years, knew enough about her brother to see him as the sickly but dauntless figure of Wolfe in a scene of climatic action dramatically bringing to a termination events and developments. All this had been arranged in the narrative to build reader excitement over the outcome of a "rattling" good story.

BUILDING SUSPENSE

We can backtrack in Parkman's pages to find more evidence of how he developed the character of Wolfe seemingly in his own image. In the middle of the second volume of *Montcalm and Wolfe,* the reader learns that the daring James Wolfe, "void of fear" and "reckless of life," is under the watchful eye of the great William Pitt.[11] Some thirty pages later appears a vivid appraisal of young Wolfe's actions at Louisbourg, indicating his desire to move on to Quebec and to carry on "an offensive . . . kind of war" to awe the Indians and "ruin the French." Wolfe then sails for England "to recruit his shattered health for greater conflicts."[12] Finally the simmering story comes to full boil in the early chapters of volume 2 when Wolfe says: "Mr. Pitt may dispose of my slight carcass as he pleases . . . I am ready for any undertaking within the compass of my skill and cunning."[13] Then follows the saga of the Quebec expedition. Montcalm is given somewhat similar treatment except that the suspense is prolonged; the simmering starts in the first part of volume 2.[14] Both generals are brought into the climactic scene of death after the battle on the Plains of Abraham, just outside the old city of Quebec.

The fact that the reader is conscious of two main developments, the rise to prominence of Wolfe and his rival Montcalm, illustrates another aspect of Parkman's craft. Only rarely is the reader completely exposed to all historical threads at one time. As one theme advances, another is left behind, to be caught up and advanced at an auspicious time. Themes and chronology appear to be deliberately manipulated to create interest.

One of Parkman's earlier works, the *Pioneers* (1865), written at the end of his apprenticeship period, also offers excellent illustrations of the deft use of concurrent themes, although the book is divided into two distinct narratives: "The Huguenots in Florida" and "Champlain and his Associates." In the Huguenot narrative, Parkman had an ideal subject for his designs. The villain in this account of early Florida is the Spaniard, who might have been portrayed in a more favorable light if Parkman had had access to more documentary material from Spanish archives.[15]

He begins the story with a vivid report on Spanish adventurers of the American Southwest and then appraises the two rival nations that will fight for the possession of Florida: Spain, "a tyranny of monks and inquisitors" with a commercial despotism linked to a religious and political absolutism; and France, "a discordant and struggling vitality," immersed in religious conflict between priests and psalm-singing Huguenots. It is a violent and dramatic description that brings the reader into the story and asserts a firm claim on his interest. Coligny is introduced as a champion of the Huguenots, and the story of the Florida haven for these persecuted heretics unfolds. For about seventy-five pages, Commandant Jean Ribaut struggles to build Fort Caroline on the River May in the midst of a tropical wilderness. Occasionally we are reminded that Spain, "imminent and terrible,"[16] is watching and waiting. So far, there are two main themes, which the reader follows with ease: the Protestant attempt to establish a colony, and the Catholic rivalry that appears to thwart the project. Developments in Spain lag behind, but in the last paragraph of chapter 6 the lonely Florida colony is disturbed by an unwelcome visitor. Parkman's artistry is exhibited in this eloquent passage: "At half-past eleven on the night of Tuesday, the fourth of September [1565], the crew of Ribaut's flagship, anchored on the still sea outside the bar, saw a huge hulk, grim with the throats of canon, drifting towards them through the gloom; and from its stern rolled on the sluggish air the portentious banner of Spain."[17]

Here we have a familiar technique: ending a chapter with a sudden change of plot, often used in *Pontiac* and *The Oregon Trail*, but not so dramatically as in the *Pioneers*. In this later volume, Parkman does not leave his plot, as many novelists do, to the annoyance of the reader. Instead, Parkman plunges into a new situation to answer questions that have arisen: who is on the ship, and what are the designs of the newcomers? Parkman turns back to tell what has been happening in Spain. Still another flashback accounts for the intrigues of Catherine de Medici in France, for which the reader has been prepared by comments on her "fathomless depths of duplicity."

Chapter 9 in the *Pioneers* relies on the same device of introducing a new situation in a final paragraph. After witnessing the revolting butcheries ordered by the Spaniard, Menendez de Avilés, we are told, to our delight, that in Dominique de Gourgues, "injured humanity found an avenger, and outraged France a champion. Her chivalrous annals may be searched in vain for a deed of more romantic daring than the vengeance of Dominique de Gourgues."[18]

Then follows another recapitulation to bring us up to date on this remarkable soldier who had a rankling hatred of Spain and Spaniards. We are subsequently carried on a new expedition that ends in the Spaniards' bloody atonement for the barbarous slaughter of Frenchmen, perhaps the most dramatic point in the Florida epic.

Some of Parkman's vivid images are forecast in straightforward language; others are anticipated by innuendo. Still others are completely unexpected, a kind of shock treatment unless the reader is familiar with the general history of the period. The climactic scene in the final *Oregon Trail* chapter, "Down the Arkansas," with the arrival at "the Settlements," is low-keyed compared to the deep emotional tensions engendered by scenes depicting the deaths of Montcalm and Wolfe, the surrender of the Ohio Indians in *Pontiac,* or the torment of Father Isaac Jogues in *The Jesuits.* In such scenes we know what is coming. In the Jogues scene, a blow-by-blow account of Indian atrocities culminates in Parkman's comment that it is "needless to specify further tortures," but even more painful details are enumerated to excite the impressionable reader. Finally after two and a half pages, the orgy comes to a climax with the observation that more would be "monotonous and revolting."[19]

Parkman knew the value of authentic blood-and-thunder in stimulating interest, and he did not hesitate to prolong his passages on carnage. His letters suggest that he gave special emphasis to the Jogues saga because of what he called its "dramatic significance." "I am tempted to give it more space than is consistent with just historic proportion," he wrote a friend who had helped him to obtain rare books and manuscripts.[20]

Sometimes brutal and violent scenes were carefully designed to increase powerful emotional shock in the narrative. In the torture of Jogues, for instance, Parkman was able to detail agonizing particulars about a central character. The more exciting the circumstances, the more flashbacks of explanation are set into motion. We see this in the unexpected appearance of an interesting stranger, "Tete Rouge, the volunteer," in the first pages of the twenty-second chapter of *The Oregon Trail,* a name he was given because of his "red curls." This amusing character proves to have a fascinating recent history, which Parkman gives us entertainingly in the brief chapter that follows.

HISTORICAL FLASHBACKS

In similar fashion, we see a dramatic event setting flashbacks into motion on the character of groups of people. In the surrender of the Ohio Indians in *Pontiac,* for instance, Parkman had to give his readers an account of the exemplary qualities that made an Indian warrior a good husband. He had to explain why white women who had been prisoners and then took Indian mates refused to live with their white husbands after they were turned over to British troops.[21]

The technique of moving back and forth in the many incidents in *Pontiac* and in *The Oregon Trail* keeps the story in motion throughout all the Parkman narrations, adding zest with a persistent element of suspense. Close analysis of Parkman's narrative reveals that he often advanced the story action by means of partially explained circumstances. This method enabled Parkman to build one traumatic scene upon another in preparation for grand climaxes. At the final scene, Parkman has still held back his most exciting material. Then he lets the dammed-up cataract of dramatic excitement splash over his pages with powerful imagery and feeling.

We then see Parkman's creative imagination at work: a constant scheming to lock the reader into the narrative through a persistent yet varied air of expectancy. Readers share the unfolding historical events as if they were participants. This reader participation occurs time and again in *The Oregon Trail's* accounts of buffalo hunts, visitations by Indians, and confrontations with immigrants.

During 1846, Lewis Garrard covered much of Parkman's trail on the Great Plains and left an account of his experiences, *Wa-To-Ya and the Taos Trail,* but the book is largely unknown today except to scholars. Compared to Parkman's *Oregon Trail,* Garrard's narrative is tame, unexciting. By contrast, Parkman reaches for the melodramatic touch. For instance, he describes the prairie Delaware people (displaced and removed) as "dreaded warriors."[22] Garrard in the same year described these Indians as friendly hosts and prosperous farmers.[23] This comparison, showing Parkman's tendency to stereotype with racial overtones, was also a factor in creating illusions of peril when in fact there was little prospect of danger.

In his vivid account of Robert Rogers' raid on the St. Francis Indians in *Montcalm and Wolfe,* we share the experience of Rogers and his men in an exciting chase.[24] In this case, Parkman fell back on the attention-holding technique of what Vernon Parrington called "the uncomplicated problem of flight and pursuit."[25] Also, the device of the chase is central to *The Oregon Trail*. One chase follows another, with the hunting of buffalo and the search for remote Indian encampments. Indeed, the narrative becomes so complex that, as Herman Melville noted in his review, it was difficult to follow Parkman and his party "through all their wild rovings." The book did, however, have "the true wild-game flavor. And amazingly tickled will all their palates be, who are so lucky as to read it."[26]

APPEALING TO THE READER'S SENSES

Melville pinpointed one of the haunting qualities of *The Oregon Trail:* its wilderness flavor. He noted images of Indian women "in brass and ver-million" and the romantic figure of Henry Chatillon, "as gallant a gentle-man . . . as ever shot buffalo. For this Henry Chatillon," Melville wrote: "we feel a fresh and unbounded love. He belongs to the class of men, of whom Kit Carson is the model; a class, unique, and not to be transcended in interest by any personages introduced to us by Scott. . . . May his good rifle never miss fire; and where he roves through the prairies, may the buffalo ever abound."[27]

Quincy Shaw, Parkman's friend and cousin and companion on the trail, impressed Melville in a different way: a dashing hunter who slaugh-tered buffalo in execution style, "like our fancy friend, Alp, in Byron's 'Siege of Corinth,'—piling the dead around in semicircles."[28] We can see in the character of Shaw an adventurous search for manhood that was partly satisfied by the joy of the hunt, even though he might be saturated with the blood of his victims. It is an unforgettable portrait, just as is the contrasting picture of Henry Chatillon, the gentleman hunter who killed for his needs rather than for pleasure.

In *The Oregon Trail*, as Melville noted, there was almost an aroma to Indian banquets of delicious roasted buffalo "humped ribs." This was a singular feature of Parkman's style, for he learned, possibly from Cooper and certainly with experimenting in *The Oregon Trail*, to appeal to all senses of the reader to create the illusion of reality. A good illustration is Parkman's elegant historical reconstruction of the site of Fort William Henry in *Montcalm and Wolfe:* "The earthen mounds of Fort William Henry still stand by the brink of Lake George; and seated at the sunset of an August day under the pines that cover them, one gazes on a scene of soft and soothing beauty, where dreamy waters reflect the glories of the mountains and the sky. As it is today, so it was then; all breathed repose and peace. The splash of some leaping trout, or the dipping wing of a passing swallow, alone disturbed the summer calm of that unruffled mirror."[29]

Looking carefully at this passage, one can discern words and phrases offering the reader a clear sense of participation. Parkman brings the spectacle before the reader with the phrase, "one gazes on the scene." He introduces sensual words to highlight the feeling of calmness: "soft," referring to touch, and "soothing" to taste. He gives us contrasting words, "splash" and "dipping," to reinforce what the sentence says. Moreover, he assures us that "as it is today, so it was then; all breathed repose and peace."

The modern investigator, critically reading this passage, however, can immediately detect, in Parkman's recreation of the scene, weaknesses that reveal his novelistic touch. For instance, a summer's visit could not actually tell Parkman exactly what the weather was like in 1757. Moreover, there was anything but peace at the fort when smallpox made it a pesthole. And, as for the cool pines, those trees undoubtedly came to maturity long after 1757, when the fort's officers very probably had troops at work clearing extensive fields with fire so that the post was isolated in the midst of barren ground.

We may conclude from this example that Parkman's reconstructions were detailed approximations, very probable images of the past. We know that he visited the site of every other significant episode in his *History*. In fact, he even revised the *Pioneers* after a tour through the Florida swamplands.[30]

Seemingly Parkman had been everywhere, read everything, and forgotten little that pertained to his story. The result of this kind of investigation was an inventive representation of sensations of sight, touch, smell, and hearing. In the Fort William Henry image, one feels the cool shade of pines (whether they were there or not), sees the panorama of mountains and water, and hears the splash of leaping trout. An educated guess in this case is that Parkman gave us considerable exaggeration, even misrepresentation. But his description is a delight to read.

Elsewhere in Parkman's *History*, particularly in his formative works *The Oregon Trail* and *Pontiac*,[31] panoramic scenes appeal to the reader's senses. It is difficult for the novelist to create believable imagery, but the research involved to achieve an approximation of authentic historical reconstruction is extremely time-consuming and complex. Parkman's tenacity of purpose, his extraordinary dedication to creating this kind of historical past, was not unrelated to his illness and his personal struggle to overcome his physical handicaps. Literally nothing would stand in his way to complete his lifelong work. What he wanted to do, he wrote his Canadian friend and critic, Abbé Henri-Raymond Casgrain, "was to tell things as they really happened."[32]

Historic characters talked, so Parkman gave his readers in *The Oregon Trail* dozens of exchanges of words, sometimes modified from his journal notes. These gave zest to his story. In his historical research, he ransacked documents for authentic give-and-take dialogue in accounts left by eyewitnesses. He was particularly successful in using recorded treaty talk from selected colonial Indian treaties that fit into his emplotment schemes. There was a protocol in treaty negotiations, which the whites followed because of Indian insistence. First came introductory welcoming speeches, then position orations, accompanied by gifts intended to stimulate a congenial mindset for compromise or bargaining. Indian speakers, as a second effort at pinpointing the issues under discussion, took up proposals one by one. Parkman showed, for example, how the tough, shrewd Count Frontenac persistently held his own against well-reasoned contentions of Iroquois orators. It is unfortunate that Parkman tended to neglect peacemaking efforts of Indians recorded in treaties.

In addition to dialogue, his pages abound with quotations from journals, reports, and letters. Yet Parkman was conservative in relying on quotations to tell his story. Unless the quoted material was extraordinarily meaty, he made it brief and adroitly fused it onto his page. Analysis of his quotations reveals that his narrative rides on a skein of documentary record, so that lifelike sequences almost explode when an appropriate time for action arises.

According to the practices of his time, Parkman changed antiquated spelling, capitalization, punctuation, and diction, all of which made his quoted sources more readable. Using his privileges as translator, he modified quotations from early French sources. He also deleted occasional passages without showing omissions, and it can be argued that he thereby altered the source to make it fit more conveniently into his interpretation of events.[33] An obvious weakness in his work, which he appears not to have perceived, was his tendency to pick and choose original material that dovetailed into his theme. At the same time the hallmark of his style was his expert use of the quotation, which gave his writings a recognizable flavor of authenticity. If we find alterations in his use of documents, there are many examples of accurate quotations that I have found in some thirty years of exploring Indian archival materials.

Parkman's novelistic style of writing history was in part an outgrowth of his youthful enthusiasm for the Leatherstocking Tales. He never out-

grew his fascination with fiction. If one examines his reading lists and correspondence over a lifetime, there is evidence to conclude that he spent
almost as much time reading novels as he did researching and writing history. Parkman not only read novels, but he also wrote to authors and complimented and sometimes criticized their work. For instance, after reading
William Dean Howells's *Chance Acquaintance*, Parkman wrote the author
about his "pleasure and admiration" in finding "truth, freshness, subtle
penetration of character."[34] In *The Lady of Aroostook*, which Parkman's sister read aloud to him (he apparently read some novels on his own), he
complimented Howells again on character analysis, especially "truth &
delicacy . . . of feminine analysis" and the fact that the book painted "a
gentleman realistically."[35] On *The Rise of Silas Lapham*, Parkman wrote in a
favorable vein but later chastised the author privately in a conversation.
But in his initial opinion he praised the realism of the book: "It is an admirable portraiture, realistic in the best sense of the word. It must touch the
consciousness of a great many people; and as we descendants of the Puritans are said to be always on the lookout for a moral—it will teach the
much needed lesson that money cannot do everything."[36] Still, Parkman
had serious reservations about the "moral" of the book. He did not like the
idea that a money-oriented, merchant type like Silas Lapham could actually win respectability and recognition in society. Howells recalls in his
book, *Literary Friends and Acquaintances*,[37] that the angry Parkman, despite his infirmities, "walked" from Beacon Hill to Cambridge, a distance
of some five miles, to argue about questions of class recognition in
Boston's upper crust.[38]

Howells, despite this disagreement, became an admirer of Parkman's
works and saw in them the practical meanings one might find in good fiction. In Parkman's volumes, he wrote, "one moral is traced from beginning
to end,—that spiritual and political despotism is so bad for men that no
zeal, or self-devotion or heroism can overcome its evil effects."[39]

Another Parkman correspondent was Henry James, whose novels and
dinner company he enjoyed. "I read next to no novels," Parkman wrote
James in 1885 in a bit of forgetfulness (his library charge lists show dozens of
novels), but his sister, he said, read James's *The Bostonians* to him. He was
full of admiration for James's "masterly analysis . . . that was as sound as a
nut." Concerning one of James's key characters, an ardent feminist, Olive
Chancellor, Parkman (who himself had battled Lucy Stone) wrote, "I have
had the ill luck to know her component parts, and you have combined them
with felicity and truth." Another character, "Miss Birdseye," an elderly
woman suffragist, Parkman called "a masterpiece" in characterization.[40]

One compliment deserves another, and James in a previous letter gave his friend Parkman the praise that few great novelists have ever given a historian: "I have been reading your *Montcalm and Wolfe*. It has fascinated me from the first page to the last. You know, of course, much better than any one else how good it is. . . . The manner in which you have treated the prodigious theme is worthy of the theme itself, and that says everything. It is truly a noble book, my dear Parkman, and you must let me congratulate you with heartiest friendliness, on having given it to the world."[41]

Both James and Howells saw in Parkman's works what Turner had observed: an overwhelming theme. Howells had mentioned a "moral," showing inherent weakness in despotic governments, a concept that may have its origin in Parkman's reading of Edward Gibbon as a college student.

Frederick Jackson Turner recognized the Gibbonesque flavor in Parkman and recommended the New England historian as a literary model for some of his former students. As he wrote to Herbert Eugene Bolton, historian of the American-Spanish borderlands, "You must water your rum and offer it in a small glass to a man who is brought up on Parkman light wines."[42] It is Parkman himself, however, who gives us the best insight on his romantic perspective on education and literature. Sir Walter Scott, Parkman contended, gave him more pleasure and profit "than any other writer." If Scott's influence was "undemocratic," it was nonetheless "an educational force of first value" in traditions of chivalry and in the qualities of a gentleman. "For my part," Parkman declared, "I would rather my sons should take lessons from *Guy Mannering* than from *The Rise of Silas Lapham*."[43]

Parkman's conservative, patrician ideas appear and reappear in his works. They formed the basis of much of his purely ideal scheme of writing as he contrived to arouse, sustain, and shape the unfolding of events.[44] His bias and its impact is the subject of the chapter that follows.

PART FOUR

THE HERO-HISTORIAN'S SOCIAL PERSPECTIVES

Major Robert Rogers, one of Parkman's heroes.
From a print, identical to the one Parkman hung on his study wall.
(Courtesy The Huntington Library, San Marino, California.)

"THE BOTTOM OF SOCIETY" AND
"THAT BRAHMIN CASTE"

It is a matter of common remark, that the most highly educated classes among us are far from being the most efficient either in thought or action. The vigorous life of the nation springs from the deep rich soil at the bottom of society. Its men of greatest influence are those who have studied men before they studied books.

—REVIEW OF THE WRITINGS OF
JAMES FENIMORE COOPER, 1852.

That 'Brahmin caste' . . . has yielded a progeny of gentlemen and scholars from the days of the Puritans.

—BOSTON DAILY ADVERTISER, 1863.

We descendants of the Puritans are said to be always on the lookout for a moral—it will teach the much needed lesson that money cannot do everything.

—LETTER TO WILLIAM DEAN HOWELLS,
6 NOVEMBER 1885.

Father Jean de Brébeuf, "Ajax" of the missions. Parkman acquired this photograph of a Brébeuf bust in a Quebec church through the efforts of Abbé Henri-Raymond Casgrain. It was then framed for Parkman's 50 Chestnut Street study. (Photograph by W. R. Jacobs.)

CHAPTER NINE

THE HERO-HISTORIAN AND THE ARISTOCRATIC MALE TRADITION

ALL THE EVIDENCE IN PARKMAN'S personal record tells us that he emerged from his teens as a physically strong and precocious young man finding his way out of the narrow cocoon of aristocratic Boston of the 1840s. The year 1846 was his turning point in returning from the searing experience of raw life on the Oregon Trail. His complaints of blindness, insomnia, severe head pains, and a variety of other symptoms were so persistent that they can be seen now as the beginnings of his lifelong illness, or neurosis. Notwithstanding these staggering "attacks" of his "enemy," Parkman finished two of his most notable books, *The Oregon Trail* and *Pontiac*.

In the early 1850s Parkman could no longer hold off onslaughts of his adversary and staged a gallant retreat into a fortress of inactivity to hold on to life itself. His letters tell us he was practically paralyzed by stress and anxiety, to the point that he was like a "crate of brittle china." He was literally locked in a sickly body, but there was hope for the kind of men the Parkmans had always been, leaders in their class in New England's history. And Parkman knew his ancestors, and the kind of indomitable Puritan legacy that was his.

Even though engaged in what seemed to be an eternal struggle to overcome adversity, he could with heroic effort achieve his lifelong literary ambitions and at the same time leave a legacy of noble personal achievement.

Despite the severity of his physical maladies, he seems to have overcome most of them except partial blindness and arthritis and could, when the occasion demanded, walk considerable distances, even from Boston to Cambridge, to argue with his old friend William Dean Howells about the need to control brash, newly rich elements of society. Meanwhile, he publicly maintained a posture of the valorous writer-historian, quietly battling the handicaps of blindness, pain, and a crippled body.

It can be argued that Parkman's behavior was idiosyncratic in the sense that he persisted in his literary efforts more to sustain his gallant romantic image than to make his reputation as an able writer-historian. To be sure, the record of his correspondence shows that he was highly motivated to make his mark as a writer, even to the extent of achieving a kind of perfectionism.

One might go so far as to argue that there was even a subtle, subdued braggadocio, almost sly, to prove what the gentle-blooded but handicapped hero-type could accomplish. Parkman himself was that kind of manly figure of the gentleman's class. These kinds of men represented the masculine tradition of achievement as generals in war or as leaders in political, educational, or literary arenas of combat. Parkman thundered on these themes in his essays in the press during the early 1860s.

From Parkman's letters, particularly his very personal correspondence with Mary Dwight Parkman, one can detect a kind of neurotic reverie that he had in sharing, vicariously, the romantic struggles of valorous, aristocratic men of strength and determination who explored and conquered the early West. Their lives, like his, had resolution and consequence. One can imagine Parkman in his Chestnut Street home on Beacon Hill (on the third floor of a townhouse that had a kind of wheelchair elevator to propel him up the stairs), gazing up at the jarring portrait of wide-eyed frontiersman Robert Rogers, his favorite boyhood role model. He could then turn and look on a photo of Father Brébeuf's bust, a likeness of the "Ajax" of the missions. Parkman had these, along with his Dakota Indian shield and bow and arrows and fringed hunting shirt, all from the Oregon Trail, at his elbow as he wrote. The Indian, personified in the "Mohawk warrior," was a savage figure of rocklike strength and courage, a worthy foe of the patrician European soldier-explorer who conquered the land.

From reading his correspondence and pages of his histories, one has the feeling that Parkman, at times, allowed himself to spill out an emotional projection of himself onto favorite characters who he reincarnated in one way or another to bear a clear resemblance to himself. Even more to the point, he had a particular conception of masculine leadership that had an association of force, as in the cases of LaSalle, Count Frontenac, Colonel Henry Bouquet, Robert Rogers, Montcalm, and Wolfe. They fit into his conception that the profession of war was an appropriate expression of male leadership. Parkman accepted elite assumptions that implied that men of "birth and breeding" (a favorite Parkman phrase) had authority over others and that family resources were passed on to future generations of aristocratic power. Such ideas of patrician leadership were current in England and in parts of eastern North America during Parkman's lifetime, and he expressed them continually in his letters to the press and in his historical writings.[1]

There is ample evidence from Parkman's correspondence and published writings to demonstrate that he was a stubborn advocate for the aristocratic male tradition. His concern with the behavior of "gentlemen" as opposed to the vulgar rich of his time appears in his correspondence and in his comments about the fiction he read. If we read his journals and *The Oregon Trail* carefully, particularly the early unrevised versions of the book, we see that he constantly reveals his attitudes of social superiority in references to emigrants on the trail, and more particularly blacks, Indians, or half-blood Canadians and Mexicans.

It is not surprising, therefore, that the youthful Parkman, during his apprenticeship, turned away from progressive social commentators of his day, even though they came from the same New England nineteenth-century upper class that he did. Not unexpectedly, he failed to nurture his early friendship with Theodore Parker, Unitarian clergyman and family friend, who had made a compelling criticism of *Pontiac*. Parker, who pleaded the cause of slaves harassed by the Fugitive Slave Act, and who recognized mounting social problems pertaining to labor, women's rights, and war, was not the kind of role model the young Parkman was likely to accept. In his apprenticeship years he came to oppose almost everything that Parker so vigorously supported. In his historical writings, where he could revive the days of chivalry and the role of gentlemen leaders, Parkman wrote glowingly of the excitement of conspiracy, politics, and warfare, and the deeds of men of gentle birth who led the Western world in occupying the new continent. With his kind of social values, we can anticipate, also, that Parkman, as he tells us in his correspondence, had little in common with two other illustrious New England contemporaries, Ralph Waldo Emerson and David Thoreau.

PARKMAN'S NEGATIVISM

Parkman's outlook on society of his time seems unchanging, from the very early days when evidence of his ideas appeared in letters, notebooks, and early works of fiction. His views became more widely known during his mature years because, during times of attacks of illness, he relaxed by writing letters to the press and magazine articles on controversial subjects. We can turn, therefore, to a discussion of both his letters to the press and magazine articles where one finds clear expression of his thoughts. In his historical works the same ideas often appear, partly muted, because he had less opportunity to editorialize. What follows is a discussion of Parkman's social ideas together with some implications these concepts had upon his legacy as a historian.

Critics have classed Parkman as a Brahmin of Brahmins, a racist writer, who was negative, even reactionary in his societal views. He has been accused, with justification, of being anti-Indian, anticlerical, and antidemocratic. He has been condemned for opposing universal manhood suffrage, women's suffrage, pacifism, and philanthropy.[2]

In his personal correspondence a recurrent theme is his emphasis upon the cultural background in appraising the worth of an individual. A journal entry of 1846, the time of the writing of *The Oregon Trail* notebooks, asks this question: "Is it not true, that the lower you descend in education and social position, the more vicious men become?" His biographical novel, *Vassal Morton,* published ten years later, is additional evidence of his disdain. "Measure the distance from Shakespeare down to that fellow," the hero remarks about a soldier, "and from him to a baboon, and which measurement will be the longer?"[3]

We have already noted Parkman's stress on Indian savagery and his adjectival downgrading of Mexicans ("piratical-looking") and Indians ("snake-eyed"). Yet it should be said that Parkman did esteem manly virtues when he found them, regardless of social position or education. As we have mentioned, he had an almost extravagant admiration for Henry Chatillon, his guide on the prairies. With a quick eye for character evaluation, as his journals disclose, Parkman sketched other humble individuals who possessed attributes of manful distinction. Nor did he, as a youth, overlook "the warm rich cheek and bright glance" of a pretty girl, regardless of her origins. But as we shall note in the chapter that follows, Parkman was a masculine chauvinist in the extreme whenever he set forth his social ideas on women and was rash enough to put them into print.

Parkman's *Oregon Trail* notebooks and the various editions of the book show him to be condescending in his remarks about western traits as he saw them in the 1840s. On his journey westward in 1846 he wrote to his mother from Cincinnati that table manners were outrageous, "such a set of beasts are these western men."[4]

The youthful Parkman disliked the aggressive westerners and their "scraggy-necked" women. Whether on the prairies or in Europe as a young man (and increasingly as he grew older), he preferred the society of gentle-men and gentlewomen or of inferiors who would do his bidding. He was happy, for instance, as a young traveler to be with a Sicilian guide or his Canadian *engages*. His romanticism and elitism tended to blur what might have been meaningful to his otherwise clear vision and intensity of obser-vation. Just as he failed to recognize the significance of cultural changes in the cigar-smoking Iroquois at Onondaga, who later proved to be such val-ued informants for Lewis H. Morgan, Parkman likewise overlooked the importance of the vast westward movement that took place before his very eyes on the Oregon Trail. Perhaps he did prefer the company of his own kind instead of that "rude and intrusive" emigrant, but after all, these people were not much different than the "rude and hardy" Paxton Men in *Pontiac*.[5]

When Parkman fell back on melodramatic techniques to stimulate reader interest, he revealed his bias. Individuals and groups and classes in his books were molded into kinds of opposing forces and stereotypes. "Our side" is the "good man" and "they" are the "flaw."[6] We see these clas-sifications in *The Oregon Trail* and in his later historical works. In his judg-ment of the society in which he lived, Parkman was also severe and looked down on the common man from an aristocratic pedestal.

It is true that Parkman's travels broadened him and softened his sever-ity; the Oregon Trail experience came after a grand tour of Europe, and he returned to France and England a number of times in later life. He came to have a certain respect for the martial spirit of the common people during the Civil War; indeed, in a book review of 1852 he went so far as to argue that "the vigorous life of the nation springs from the deep rich soil at the bottom of society."[7] A key to Parkman's aristocratic stance is found in his attitude toward democracy. Although he believed in a representative gov-ernment, he wanted leadership to rest in the hands of the aristocratic, in-telligent, public-spirited segment of the population. A vigorous, masculine society, free from paternalism or charity and liberated from the tyranny of the uneducated masses, was for him an ideal.[8]

LA SALLE, THE MASCULINE IDEAL

In his historical works there is clear evidence of Parkman's disregard for the importance of individuals from the lower stratum of society. He was adept at describing the aspirations and attitudes of the lower classes as a whole; but there is an absence of recognition for the role of minor associates of his heroes. Parkman could utilize Seth Pomeroy's journal as a source for his narrative, but Pomeroy receives little recognition as a significant individual. He is merely a typical soldier.[9]

LaSalle is a biography that contains recognizable elements of Greek tragedy. A heroic figure of indomitable will strikes out against a circle of enemies and hostile forces of nature. His murder eventually occurs, as Parkman implies, because of "tragic flaws" of character. LaSalle, as Parkman found in examining original accounts, may have been mentally deranged, but Parkman declined to accept this interpretation even though some of LaSalle's critics were convinced that the explorer had lost his mind. After acknowledging such accusations, Parkman went so far as to make this comment about his hero: "It is difficult not to see in all this the chimera of an overwrought brain, no longer able to distinguish between the possible and the impossible."[10] In spite of this statement, Parkman, with obvious empathy for the explorer, went on to portray him as if no doubt existed about his sanity. If LaSalle had tragic flaws, they were largely confined to his arrogant treatment of subordinates and associates.[11]

Despite criticisms of Parkman's personification of LaSalle, Parkman's version persists largely because of his ability to create believable historical personalities on his pages. A recent critic argues convincingly that Parkman's successful portrayal of LaSalle was keyed to a sympathetic understanding of LaSalle's crippling problems.[12]

Parkman's *LaSalle,* concentrating so much on the man as a central force and figure in his narrative, neglects the role of minor figures. As Otis A. Pease pointed out, the author fails to enlighten the reader on why Duplessis attempted to assassinate the explorer.[13] What actually were the grievances of Duplessis and LaSalle's other subordinates? The reader is left in the dark, and the narrative moves on after a vivid description of the wilderness surroundings.[14] In all justice to Parkman we must point out that the sentence on Duplessis was an insertion in his 1878 edition.[15] Parkman's sources for his biography of LaSalle were often in mere fragments of data, so we are perhaps fortunate to know that an attempted assassination even took place.

It is nevertheless true that because the spotlight is clearly on the singular figure of LaSalle, Parkman neglects to explain how LaSalle's character defects had an impact on his men. Able explorer that he was, the plots and intrigues, the desertions, the attempt at assassination, the use of poison in his food, and his final murder—all of this must have been based upon legitimate grievances. To pass these off as jealous attempts to get rid of LaSalle by enemies, fur-trading rivals, creditors who wished to seize his property, and Jesuits who feared him, seems superficial. The worst that Parkman has to say about his hero is that he was ill fitted for business, that he lacked a "sympathetic power" of leadership, and that his personality was a curious combination of pride and shyness.[16] In the last analysis, it was LaSalle's "haughtiness of manner," his "harshness toward those under his command which drew upon him an implacable hatred, and was at last the cause of his death." This, Parkman tells us, was the testimony of his faithful officer, Henri Joutel.[17]

In his eulogy to the explorer, Parkman's identification with his subject is marshaled forth in theatrical prose:

> It is easy to reckon up his defects, but it is not easy to hide from sight the Roman virtues that redeemed them. Beset by a throng of enemies, he stands, like a King of Israel, head and shoulders above them all. He was a tower of the adamant, against whose impregnable front, hardship and danger, the rage of man and of the elements, the southern sun, the northern blast, fatigue, famine, disease, delay, disappointment, and deferred hope emptied their quivers in vain.[18]

One stands back at such adulation, but as my analysis of Parkman's illness confirms, Parkman, the narrator, speaks not only about LaSalle, but also of Parkman himself overcoming his "enemy." Parkman, as narrator, reveals a sympathetic understanding in bringing out the "mythic" qualities in his hero's character. Facts are given to us by the narrator, but there is also a brooding that becomes a kind of poetry suggesting that LaSalle's destiny is beyond his control. Before the explorer is his lurking enemy, the shadowy figure of death. Parkman, in this carefully devised tragedy, gives us a blend of history and patterns of myth.[19]

But let us return to the eulogy because it also helps to silhouette his romantic and aristocratic social ideals that often revealed themselves in his *History*. "That very pride, which Coriolanus-like," he wrote of LaSalle,

> declared itself most sternly in the thickest press of foes, has in it something to challenge admiration. Never, under the impenetrable mail of paladin or crusader, beat a heart of more intrepid mettle than within the stopic panoply that armed the breast of LaSalle. To estimate aright the marvels of his patient fortitude, one must follow on his track through the vast scene of his interminable journeyings—those thousands of weary miles of forest, marsh, and river, where, again and again, in the bitterness of baffled striving, the untiring pilgrim pushed onward towards the goal which he was never to attain.[20]

When Parkman wrote in a letter that his ideal of manhood was "a little medieval," he surely did not exaggerate. LaSalle was a "paladin or crusader" who guided America "to the possession of her richest heritage."[21] We have, in the embattled explorer, a figure whose career is transformed into an arena for prolonged combat between right and wrong, where a "masculine" character pushes the very limits of what it is possible to accomplish.

Throughout the biography the reader is exposed to theatrical situations in which there are grand gestures, an almost simplified moral code, not unlike nineteenth-century melodrama, which also had its conservative values. Out of all emerges an archetype hero.[22] LaSalle, a gentleman "trained amid arts and letters," had a gentleman's qualifications for leadership because he "could stand hardship." With Sieur de Bienville and La Mothe Cadillac, he was a member of a class of men, Parkman tells us in *The Old Régime*, "who discovered the Ohio, explored the Mississippi to its mouth, discovered the Rocky Mountains, and founded Detroit, St. Louis, and New Orleans."[23]

With emphasis upon particular characters, lesser figures tended to be ignored, although some undoubtedly had a modifying force on events and on main actors.[24] Because Parkman gave us history stressing the careers of aristocratic leaders, he tended to limit his narrative to actions at high levels. For instance, in narrating New France's history he gave much space to quarrels between Bishop Laval and governors who resented church encroachment on civil authority.

At the same time, when his narrative design permitted him to do so, Parkman did give attention to the wartime life and hardships of ordinary pioneers in Canada and on several English frontiers. His social views on colonial peoples tended to be concentrated in his introductions or conclusions in his historical volumes. But they were also used to accent a particular event or turn of plot in his narrative. These same ideas, however, are more easily identified in Parkman's corpus of newspaper and magazine articles on social issues of his time.

POLITICS AND EDUCATION

Parkman's aristocratic ideas are clearly visible in his emotional letters to the press during the Civil War and his essays on democracy, women's suffrage, and education. If Parkman was pleased with the valor of Union soldiers during the Civil War, he was nevertheless unwilling to accept the excesses of popular sovereignty after the peace. To him the former slaves brought

"monstrosities of Negro rule" to the South.[25] Meanwhile, universal suffrage caused vice, corruption, and demagoguery at levels of government in
the North. He shuddered at the menace of an untutored plutocracy and an
ignorant proletariat. It would be better to take the latitude, he believed,
lest society be wrecked on the rocks of "debased irresponsible suffrage."[26]
It was nonsense, he said, to accept the fiction of inalienable rights. With
popular rule, American society was bent on an unchecked orgy of materi-
alism; the nation was being transformed into a nation of pleasure hunters.
He lamented "the plight into which our precious system has fallen."[27]

In "The Tale of the Ripe Scholar" of 1869, Parkman set forth his clear-
est solution to the problems.[28] He hinted at the desirability of curtailing
suffrage, but as a contemporary critic responded, "Mr. Parkman does not
feel quite sure universal suffrage will consent to abolish itself."[29] The rul-
ing power of public opinion, Parkman then argued, should include a fair
portion of "the best and maturist thought." A class of thinkers is needed,
he said, "a palladium of democracy," to project its image in public opinion.
This class, the only real hope for society, could be recruited from the
universities.

Another remedy he proposed was a complete overhaul of the popular
educational system. It was one thing to teach a man to read and write; it
was another to stimulate in him a sense of responsibility and development
of powers of reason, analysis, and observation. "Individual aptitudes" of
children should be carefully studied, he wrote. "What is interesting and
fruitful to one is dull and barren for another, and it is a mistake to force a
child to any special course of reading, however excellent, unless it answers
to some native inclination. . . . Nothing can be more wholesome to the
natural boy, than his old friend and benefactor, Robinson Crusoe, followed by Sir Walter Scott."[30] Parkman consistently recommended Washington Irving, followed by Shakespeare and Molière when a boy reached
mature years. Byron, and French romantics like Michelet and Chateaubriand, are found on his own early reading lists.[31]

The public schools did not sufficiently encourage the reading of the
best literature, but instead, he said, gave the average citizen a crude, imper-
fect body of knowledge. This practice put money in the hands of those
who sold sickly pulp magazines and sensational newspapers designed to
satisfy the popular appetite for amusement. The common man (and we
should note that Parkman consistently in these essays spoke of education
of men and boys, not girls and women) learned just enough to savor the
sweetened oratory of political charlatans and to throw men of ability and
integrity out of office. We must teach the teachers, Parkman declared,

and give money to "wisely-established" and "wisely-conducted" colleges and universities.[32] Parkman's will and account books show, however, that he did not wholly follow this good advice despite the fact that he was comfortably well-to-do, affluent by reason of inheritance (and thus never had to abandon his literary work), which brought him a good income during his lifetime.[33]

Parkman, then, hoped for the development of a rational social force strong enough to cope with the natural impulses of men who were scarcely more than improved savages. He pinpointed an intellectual inferiority in the working classes and in the new plutocracy of his day. The people, without the "palladium of democracy," were incapable of self-transcendence and unable to comprehend the needs of society. The duty of forming the social intelligence rested primarily upon the colleges and could be accomplished only after radical changes were made in the common schools.[34]

THE PATRICIAN LEGACY

There is little doubt that the Brahmin world of Boston's Beacon Hill left an indelible imprint in the man and his social perspectives. Because that world was being transformed during his lifetime, Parkman, like his contemporary Henry Adams, was a witness to the abrupt political reversal that brought Irish politics to the State House, heretofore dominated by the well-educated patrician families. If Parkman, the Brahmin, cherished the values of the traditional culture, it is to be expected that he would project them into his books and other writings. Like his modern disciple, the late Samuel E. Morison, Parkman was a patrician to his fingertips who looked backward on the New England cultural legacy as a link to the emerging, growing American nation. Unlike Morison, however, Parkman's conservative views were more sharply silhouetted with nineteenth-century stereotypes and Anglo-Saxonism funneling out of a Puritan heritage.[35]

Parkman's social ideas, tenaciously held during his entire lifetime, were negative, conservative, and based upon a social-Darwinist concept of Anglo-Saxon superiority. Although his views were those of an aristocratic conservative of his time, we should not overlook the positive side of his interpretations. For instance, he anticipated Frederick Jackson Turner in an expression of a frontier theory describing social change. Moreover, he had an appreciation of natural history that gave him the background to describe forest ecosystems and values of wilderness forest lands.

In Parkman's view, he was telling a story as truthfully and as dramatically as it could be told using the evidence he had before him. If he knowingly contrived to give us a fictional representation of the past, he seems not to have been completely aware of the exaggeration and stereotyping that crept into his narrative.[36] From the body of evidence in his writings and the personal record he left, one could conclude that he made a persistent effort to achieve what he thought was the highest degree of excellence. Parkman in this case should speak for himself, as he did in his introduction to the *Pioneers:* "The narrator must seek to imbue himself with the life and spirit of the time. He must study events in their bearings near and remote; in the character, habits, and manners of those who took part in them. He must be, as it were, a sharer or spectator in the action he describes."[37]

Whether or not we are repulsed by certain of Parkman's social ideas, nevertheless we can be attracted to him as a writer who created a novelistic panorama of the past. His talent in providing a spectacular narrative was based, as he said, on sharing "the life and spirit of the time." In one of the most visually vivid paragraphs in his history, replete with stereotypes and romantic portraits of chivalric figures, Parkman revealed his skill in reconstructing lifelike images in the mind. Here, again from the introduction to the *Pioneers*, Parkman summarizes over a century of New France's history:

> The French dominion is a memory of the past; and when we evoke its departed shades, they rise upon us from their graves in strange, romantic guise. Again their ghostly camp-fires seem to burn, and the fitful light is cast around on lord and vassal and black-robed priest, mingled with wild forms of savage warriors, knit in close fellowship on the same stern errand. A boundless vision grows upon us; an untamed continent; vast wastes of forest verdure; mountains silent in primeval sleep; river, lake and glimmering pool; wilderness oceans mingling with the sky. Such was the domain which France conquered for civilization. Plumed helmets gleamed in the shade of its forests, priestly vestments in its dens and fastness of ancient barbarism. Men steeped in antique learning, pale with the close breath of the cloister, there spent the noon and evening of their lives, ruled savage hordes with a mild, parental sway, and stood serene before the direst shapes of death. Men of courtly nurture, heirs to the polish of a far-reaching ancestry, here, with their dauntless hardihood, put to shame the boldest sons of toil.[38]

Let there be no doubt about Parkman's elitist perspective in this passage written by the mature Parkman shortly after the end of his apprenticeship. "The dauntless hardihood" of those "men of nurture," those "heirs to the polish of a far-reaching ancestry," these were the able leaders of France's new world empire. They "put to shame the boldest sons of toil." While this concept of leadership was and has been accepted by generations of readers because the social ideas behind it are phrased in a chivalric manner, there were other of Parkman's ideas that have become particularly controversial. These involved his manner of portraying women and the Catholic church in his *History* and his writings to the press. The following chapter focuses on this aspect of Parkman's legacy.

The Harvard History Club, ca. 1890. The hero-historian and admirers at the home of Robert C. Winthrop, president of the Massachusetts Historical Society, 1889–91. Left to right in the front row are Justin Winsor, the Reverend George Ellis, Robert C. Winthrop, Francis Parkman, and Samuel Green, Massachusetts Historical Society Librarian. Beyond Green is future Harvard librarian William C. Lane, and behind him on the right is William H. Tillinghast, assistant librarian. In the rear, the two dark-bearded gentlemen are historians William H. Siebert, *left*, and Albert Bushnell Hart. (Courtesy Massachusetts Historical Society.)

Parkman at a Canadian Batiscan River camp in 1886 with his friend and future biographer, Charles H. Farnham (not shown in photograph). In reporting to his sister, Eliza, Parkman wrote, "Fishing good. Flies bad. Farnham very pleasant." (Courtesy Massachusetts Historical Society.)

Those who wish the Roman Catholic Church to subvert our school system, control legislation, become a mighty political force, can not do better than to labor day and night for female suffrage.

In politics, the virtues of women would sometimes be as dangerous as their faults.

The right of voting and the duty of fighting should never be divorced. Women though non combative, are abundantly combative when excited. . . . they might vote in majority that the men should fight.

—"THE WOMAN QUESTION," 1879

Parkman with his sister, Eliza, or Lizzie, and his cat
at his Jamaica Plain summer home, ca. 1891–92.
There is a visible swelling of his knees.
Parkman in his very last years increasingly complained of lameness.
(Courtesy Massachusetts Historical Society.)

CHAPTER TEN

THE HERO ON CATHOLICISM AND WOMEN

AS HAS BEEN SEEN IN THE PREVIOUS chapter, the youthful Francis Parkman, sick or well, exhibited, in his letters, notebooks, and in his publications, unbending, conservative, Brahmin social values. Despite his illness, with its periodic "attacks," there is no evidence of his mellowing. Increasingly, as he matured beyond his apprenticeship years, there is evidence of his inflexible negativism, especially in his anticlericalism and hostility to woman suffrage. Overtones of these views, as one might expect, appeared in his historical writings.

Parkman's ideas on women in politics were clearly set forth in what he called the "woman question," an assessment of the woman-suffrage movement. His intense feelings on this subject were partly aroused by his concept of the Roman Catholic Church's influence on women during his time and in early American history.

Parkman's temper, if we believe what his secretary had to say, reached an intensity when it came to talking about the Catholic church and evaluating its dominance over men and women in politics and in history. His feelings on this topic and related subjects may well have been expressions of his mental illness as he extended his own battle to overcome infirmity.

It can be argued that Parkman used his maladies to create a public image of self-respect as a courageous writer overcoming formidable odds. This sense of self-confidence, it can be further contended, came as a result of the strong feminine family support he had in publicly opposing woman suffrage. He had backing at first from his mother and sisters and later from women friends. His wife, from all the fragments that have come down to us, was also supportive but increasingly frustrated by the severity of his illness and his singleminded concerns about writing.

By the time Parkman entered the debate over the "woman question," he was beyond his apprenticeship, already an internationally known historian applauded by admirers as a man with a courageous explorer image and as a talented writer steadfastly committed to completing his historical volumes. Between 1879 and 1887, during the years of the final writing and completion of *Montcalm and Wolfe,* his most widely acclaimed work, Parkman wrote three essays on women and politics, as well as several rejoinders to quiet the tempest of wrath he aroused. The pontifical tone of his writings, some of them widely distributed in pamphlet form, were bound to anger leaders in the women's movement.

Parkman's main premise appears to be this: "If exercise of the suffrage by any individual body of individuals involves detriment to the whole people, then the right to exercise it does not exist."[1] If women were involved in politics, he maintained, their virtues would become their faults. What was particularly dangerous, in Parkman's view, was the potential political power of what he considered the ignorant, lower-class "shanty" Irish Catholic woman of the tenements. Parkman knew this type of woman because she, or her sisters, worked for years as servants in his household. She would enormously increase the strength of evil politicians because of her impulsiveness and lack of a sense of responsibility. If she became a politician herself, she would be, he said, a "Delilah" sharpening her shears for the "Congressional Samson." Parkman hurled polemics at the suffragists because they did nothing to prove their fitness except, he wrote, carp on theories like the notion of abstract rights. They had not supported what he regarded as desirable measures, such as Civil Service reform and free trade. If they obtained the franchise, they would form a large noncombatant class in government and might, in a time of crisis, overwhelm the nation by a frenzy of emotionalism. Let us protect and respect normal womanhood, he concluded, but "let us also protect ourselves from females in politics."[2]

As an apprentice writer in *The Oregon Trail* Parkman had painted humiliating thumbnail sketches of women on the migrant trail. This might be expected, considering his later statements about woman suffrage and his view of the male as the dominant force in society. In his historical works there are few sympathetic portraits of women who influenced public affairs. An example of contempt for female rulers was Parkman's denigrating picturization of Madame de Pompadour in *Montcalm and Wolfe.*[3] His critics overlooked his disdain for influential women in history, but his suffrage articles aroused a tempest. From the West, Parkman wrote his friend Abbé Casgrain, came attacks of "insane wildcats."[4] Joan of Arc was brought into the fray, and St. Paul was cited for authority. Women were declared to be in a state of subjection like the former slaves. Yet Parkman seemed cool in his response, since he expected opponents would "make up in fury what they lacked in logic."[5] Yet he was not amused when critics garbled his words and quotations. He was accused of saying that "three-fourths of a female constituency would sell their charms, and those who had no charms of their own would use those of young girls."[6]

THE ROMAN CHURCH

In the course of his arguments, Parkman roused the anger of a powerful opponent, the Roman Catholic Church. He asserted that the church would derive immense benefits from female suffrage because of the power priests exerted over women, who were, in his opinion, more easily shepherded than the men of the flock.[7] Parkman's hostility toward the Roman Catholic Church was generated by what he believed to be its powerful appeal to the masses. He contended that priests, through their hold on common people, especially women, subverted democracy in Canada in the nineteenth century.[8] "A democracy educated by priests for its own purposes, and controlled by them, is an ugly element in any country. Ignorant as the French Canadian masses are of everything except the little that it suits their spiritual rulers to teach them, they are a standing peril in a free country."[9] What irritated him in particular was what he called the church's manner of pardoning sins. Charles H. Farnham, his friend in later years and first biographer, wrote: "I can see him now get up from his stool and stride about, giving vent in the most forcible terms to his wrath at such an organized system of pardoning everything . . . he shows in his writings a remarkable degree of moderation and self-control."[10] Anticlericalism pervades Parkman's writings, although his early journal notations show praise as well as blame. Perhaps the contradiction is resolved by what Parkman made Vassal Morton say to the priest: "I was born and bred among Protestants. I respect your ancient church for the good she has done in ages past, and for the good men who have held her faith; but I do not believe in her doctrine, nor approve of her practice."[11]

Parkman went to pains to know the church, even to the extent, when he was a young man, of living in a Passionist monastery in Rome. He perceived that supernaturalism was a key to the early history of New France, but when it came to visions, like a remarkable apparition that appeared before Father Brébeuf, he paused in his *History* and said, "To explain such phenomena is the province of psychology, and not of history." [12] He praised Jesuit martyrs, but criticized the order. Any spiritual interpretation that Parkman might have given early Canadian history was precluded by his penchant for secular kinds of evidence. No doubt his training in the law, his Huguenot, Puritan, and subsequent Unitarian heritage, and finally his own agnosticism and Brahmin outlook, tempered by mental illness, were forces that shaped his ideas.

Parkman, however, could have words of praise for individual male Catholics such as the soldier-ethnologist, Captain John G. Bourke, whose writings on western tribes he called "studies from life." In contrast to Abbé Henri-Raymond Casgrain, whose historical writings had distinct themes of Catholic interpretation, Bourke left his religion behind him when, as professional ethnologist and soldier, he wrote about the Apaches and other tribes. In fact, there was much about Bourke's soldiering in the Indian wars that appealed to Parkman. Bourke was, in truth, a kind of hero of the frontier in the tradition of the French Catholic explorers of the Old West. Yet there was, for Parkman, a lurking menace behind the romantic Catholicism of seventeenth-century New France. [13]

In an 1885 article in the *Critic,* he traced the political instability of France and her failure in the New World to the revocation of the Edict of Nantes in 1685. [14] This mad act, Parkman argued, began an era of bigotry and deprived France of "a balance wheel," that is, the stabilizing influence of an energetic Huguenot population. Streams of innovation found no channels for peaceful flow. Instead, liberty of thought finally burst the dams of bigoted tyranny, and a torrent of ruin flooded Europe with the Revolution and Napoleon. The mother country's spiritual absolutism and political tyranny were reflected in miniature in New France and had a lasting impact upon Canada. The Church of Rome was, Parkman said, the nurse and mother of Canada. She was permanent, but the royal authority was transient. With the happy calamity of the conquest of Canada by British arms, Parkman concluded, came a purer and better church, strengthened by the presence of an adverse faith. [15]

Catholic writers have responded to these attacks. A doctoral dissertation, written under the supervision of Jesuit scholars in 1942, devotes more than three hundred pages to Parkman's views, asserting that "Parkman approached his task intellectually limited by a blind spot; he was possessed with a rationalistic contempt for the supernatural." Furthermore, "he used his talents and research to uphold a thesis conceived in prejudice; the superiority of English Protestant civilization over that of French Catholicism." [16] Abbé Casgrain probably best expressed the most charitable Ro-

THE HERO ON CATHOLICISM AND WOMEN

man Catholic position with regard to Parkman when he said the historian judged "everything from a standpoint purely natural and human." [17]

Casgrain was among the Canadian clerics who supported a movement to have Parkman awarded an honorary degree by Laval University. Parkman was flattered to learn of an uproar in the Canadian press caused by his critics, the ultramontane party of the Canadian Church; they successfully defeated the proposal by citing quotations as evidence that Parkman was unfriendly to the Catholic church. As soon as Parkman became aware of the quarrel he wrote to Casgrain urging that Laval University consider its own best interests and not feel committed to any course of action. Noting the violent attacks against him, "that man," "an infidel," who "insulted our country and our religion," and the extreme hostility of one Jules-Paul Tardivel, Parkman thanked Casgrain for publicly defending him. "You need not fear that I shall find anything *'qui puisse me blesser,'* in your kind article," Parkman wrote. "I see in it as in all you have written about me, the hand of a friend, who differs in opinion, but is united in feeling." [18] Though Parkman was later to quarrel with Casgrain over treatment of the Acadians in history, the two longtime rivals resolved their differences in friendship. Casgrain undoubtedly believed that at least some of Parkman's themes of history were sympathetic to what Canadian historians themselves held dear. [19] When Parkman wrote that "my position as a writer is within the French lines," he told us that he was primarily a historian of early Canadian history. [20]

The obvious weaknesses of Parkman's anticlericalism should be compared with his strengths. We can argue that Parkman believed in the importance of religious toleration and the need for a reasonable, even respectful, attitude toward the Catholic church. He had these attitudes at a time when many of his contemporaries reflected the popular prejudice against Catholicism, regarding it as a threat to the Protestant religion, the American democratic system, and even public morality. While it is true that Parkman could not bring himself to the point that he might encourage acceptance of the special doctrines of the church, he saw himself as having a basic nonsectarian posture in his writings and in his personal beliefs. [21] Parkman had no sympathy for either Puritans or Catholics whose aim was indoctrination. And further, he was critical of those who left a record of false piety, which, to him, was hypocritical and self-seeking. At the same time he lionized the early Jesuit missionaries, symbols of the missionary spirit. They achieved fame "because Parkman wrote about them." [22]

Parkman believed he gave his readers an accurate image of the Catholic church of New France. As he told Abbé Casgrain, when he found corruption, he wrote about it. "La vraie histoire du Canada," Parkman argued, could not ignore "fraud, peculation, and adultery," although the church did denounce prevailing vice. But, said Parkman, "Such denunciations never have much effect. They offend nobody and reform nobody."[23]

HISTORIC CATHOLIC WOMEN

Parkman, as we have seen, was able to write positively about certain Catholic leaders in history if they possessed the particular qualities he admired. But on the question of women, particularly the Catholic women he dealt with in his *History*, he seems to have succumbed to the view that women really had no place in public affairs because of their inherent deficiency in the matter of emotionalism. For example, in his correspondence with the suffragist Lucy Stone, he accused her of wanting "calmness" so she could read what he had written "in connection with the context."[24] Seemingly Parkman based his opinion on the weaknesses of women in politics on the contact that he had had with women in his family and a series of Irish maids and house cleaners in the various homes the Parkman family had occupied on Beacon Hill. One should understand, he argued, that common women were not necessarily reformers. And further, he deplored "those rude masses of their sex of whose votes nothing can be foretold except that they will reinforce the ignorant male vote which already puts our institutions to so perilous a strain."[25]

As we read these comments and understand Parkman's fear about Irish Catholic immigrants and their political leaders who were rapidly taking control of Boston politics and the State House, we can see that his real fear was the Catholic woman—in his own day, the Irish-Catholic woman in Massachusetts. A traditionalist and conservative in his attitudes toward nonwhites and women, Parkman never saw either as having a visible place in self-governing society. Nor did they have a legitimate role in the dramas of war and politics that were central to his historical writings. Western European men in history were, for him, the measurement of significance. Not unexpectedly, he found, as we have noted, Madame de Pompadour wanting as a figure in the French court. Catherine de Medici, "with her stately form, her mean spirit, her bad heart, and her fathomless depths of duplicity strove by every subtle art to hold the balance of power" in a court where "corruption and intrigue ran riot." In contrast, the measure of the male-archetype leader, the personification of "the warlike noblesse," was recognizable in the character of Gaspard de Coligny, Admiral of France.[26]

As Catherine's character is formed in pages of the *Pioneers,* we learn that her son, the king, and his queen-mother, Catherine, are "helpless amid the storm of factions which threaten their destruction."[27] Yet she survives, and by "a thousand crafty arts and expedients of the moment, to retain the crown on the head of her weak and vicious son."[28] Charles and his queen-mother are weak, "tame" in their relations with Spain, and find themselves "fast subsiding into the bloody embrace of Spain, for whom, at last, on the bloody eve of St. Bartholomew, he [is] the assassin of his own best subjects," the French Protestants.[29] Here we see the corrupt influence of Catherine upon her son, resulting finally in the horrors of St. Bartholomew's Day Massacre.

Other portraits of women are more favorable, but there are shortcomings that follow in the narrative. The Comptesse de Frontenac might be a "blooming goddess," athletic and skilled as a rider who "passed on horseback before the troops," but she was also "not of tender nature; her temper was imperious, and she had a restless craving for excitement."[30]

When he wrote about the early settlement of Canada, Parkman was confronted with positive achievements of women, whether they be wives of settlers or nuns who established hospitals, convents, and the schools for Indian children. Among the Ursulines, as Parkman tells us in his saga on the Jesuits, were noble women such as Madame de la Peltrie. The traditions of the Ursulines were full of her virtues, her humility, her charity, her acts of mortification. But Parkman goes on to say, her "zeal would have been less ardent and sustained if it had had few spectators . . . the fair devotee thirsted for admiration. The halo of saintship glittered in her eyes like a diamond crown, and she aspired to outshine her sisters in humility."[31] Even Marie de l'Incarnation, whom Protestants may view as a "christian heroine," had at one time been "lost in the vagaries of insane mysticism." Despite the fact that Marie de l'Incarnation and her nuns instructed Indian children, there is real doubt, Parkman tells us, "that their teachings were always wise or useful, since Father Vimont tells us approvingly that they reared their pupils in so chaste a horror of the other sex, that a little girl whom a man had playfully taken by the hand, ran crying to a bowl of water to wash off the unhallowed influence."[32] A true story, no doubt, but Parkman fell back on it along with other anecdotes to modify her achievement as a courageous pioneer, a Mother Superior for a Canadian convent in the wilderness. "A woman to the core," a "stately figure, with features strongly marked and perhaps somewhat masculine," she was a woman to whom he could give a grudging record of accomplishment. She was in truth, a "heroine, admirable, with all her follies and faults."[33] Parkman's preoccupation with what he called her "masculine" qualities impinged upon his final appraisal of her role in history.

Parkman had little to comment on lower-class women who came to the struggling Canadian colony except to say that they had questionable virtue and played a positive role in population growth. Between 1669 and 1673, one thousand "girls" were sent to Canada, where they were sorted out into three groups for a "bazaar" selection process. The "girls" were permitted to reject any suitor after asking a key question: Did he own "a house or a farm?" Most of the young women, he wrote, became pregnant soon thereafter.[34] Having described this "matrimonial market," Parkman then quotes a scathing but questionable criticism of "the mothers of Canada" by Baron La Hontan (who wrote fifteen or twenty years after the women arrived in Canada): "Ships were sent out freighted with girls of indifferent virtue under the direction of a few pious old duennas, who divided them into three classes . . . three harems."[35] Thus, Parkman relied upon his skill as a writer to give us unfavorable character sketches of groups of Canadian women, as well as individuals. As Gerda Lerner argues, history based upon powerful patriarchal assumptions overlooks the fact that women, in history, have been "the majority of humankind."[36]

WOMEN IN PARKMAN'S LIFE

It is ironic that Parkman, a critic of women in history, had great dependence upon upper-class women in his personal life. He himself had an almost "feminine" attitude of sentimentality about Mary Dwight Parkman, his cousin-in-law, who consoled him during his "dark years" of depression in the immediate decade after his return from the Oregon Trail. In a series of very intimate letters he confessed to her that his ambition was such that he would strive to attain his "highest interest, irrespective of happiness or suffering." Though the concept of infirmity dooming him "to a weary death in life" was his prospect, she was able to encourage him because, as Parkman wrote, "You and I have certain vital aims and feelings in common, and I feel that a friendship founded on such sympathies must be enduring."[37] In Mary Dwight Parkman, he found a woman whose talents and abilities were close to his own. She wrote secretly for the *Nation* and in her later life became a close friend of Henry Adams and his wife. The correspondence between Parkman and Mary Dwight, or "Mary," intimate as it was, seems to have been concerned with Parkman's personal problems, his severe illness ("I am . . . like a crate of brittle china") and his frustrations in being rejected as a suitor by the beautiful Ida Agassiz. Though

Parkman (after the death of his wife) had sought the hand of Ida, daughter of the scientist Louis Agassiz, he was astounded when she became engaged to someone else. As he wrote to "Dear Mary" in a letter of 6 December 1863: "The truth is, that for a year or two, my dearest wish has been to make her my wife; but during all that time I have carefully avoided the expression of anything beyond a simple though a very cordial friendship. And, to my astonishment, she seems to have been completely deceived." [38]

What may we make of this expression of Parkman's relation with Ida? Surely, he did not know human nature and certainly women's feelings as well as he thought he did. And with his relations with Mary, he never really confided his strong opinions about manhood suffrage, woman suffrage, abolitionism, and we can be reasonably sure, when we read his letters to her, he knew nothing about her secret unsigned writings in the *Nation*. Further, we might comment that during his "dark years" when he carried all his frustrations to Mary, he seems to have totally bypassed his wife, Catherine, a shadowy figure in his life until her death in 1858. Much of what we really know about her is Parkman's response to a letter from Ellen, Mary's sister, in which he describes his wife as being a person who had "inestimable value to all near her." [39] An argument can be made on Parkman's behalf that he wished to spare his wife's feelings by not complaining, but at the same time there is a recognizable pattern of confusion in Parkman's relationship with the upper-class women in his personal life. If we read the correspondence with Mary carefully, there is another woman, a mysterious "Miss B," whom he thought had been jealous of his relations with Ida Agassiz. In an almost frantic letter to Mary in 1862 he pleaded for help: "B's jealousy centres on Miss Agassiz, and her superlative powers of intrigue will, above all others, be directed to injure me here. Her diplomacy is as hardy as it is subtle and she never shrinks from risks. . . . Will you have the kindness to write a letter to me . . . such a letter as may be shown if the occasion should demand it, and which, coming from you, will refute the most ingeniously devised slander . . . vindicating me." [40]

We don't know the outcome of the Beacon Hill intrigues except that Ida's decision to reject Parkman may have been based in part on the "hardy" diplomacy of Miss B. The incident gives us further background on Parkman's patriarchal attitudes toward women and his floundering in trying to cope with the women of his own class. Mary was probably the original Mrs. Ashland, whose gentle understanding brought forth tears of responsiveness from the hero in Parkman's *Vassal Morton*. After Parkman's wife died, Mary became a kind of sounding board for his conscience in personal matters as he debated the merits and demerits of a second marriage. But to repeat, in his intimate letters to her he scarcely mentioned public questions of the day, even in the midst of the Civil War when he was writing emotional letters to the press pleading for better Northern leadership in battling against the Southern armies.

During his most productive years, the decades in which he produced major volumes of his *History*, Parkman had a restful, tranquil domestic life. Parkman's closest companion through his mature years was Eliza, or Lizzie, his youngest sister, with whom he lived. She is mentioned briefly in many of his letters, especially in his private correspondence, as a loving person, whom, as Parkman wrote of her, "I am always affectionately conscious, though I do not say much."[41] Though he did "not say much" about his enormous indebtedness to Lizzie, it was fortunate that she was aware of his gratitude. Family tradition told the story of how Lizzie, out of her love for "F.," declined a handsome suitor. She remained single the rest of her life. Friends concluded that she had made a sacrifice that her brother, absorbed in his work, did not fully appreciate.[42]

Parkman's correspondence tells us that after his return from Paris in 1859, where he had spent several months sightseeing, relaxing, on the top deck of the omnibus, following the death of his wife, he lived with his mother and sisters Eliza and Mary on Walnut Street in Beacon Hill.[43] Each summer he spent at a big rambling country house near a large pond in Jamaica Plain, a Boston suburb. Except for Lizzie, Parkman's close women relatives gradually disappeared from his life. Carry (or Caroline, his oldest sister and his favorite), married a Montreal Unitarian minister. Mary, another sister, who became an invalid, died in 1866. When his mother died in 1871, Lizzie moved to join him in the Chestnut Street house where he lived for the rest of his life.

There seems to be little question that Parkman from the beginning was idolized by his sisters.[44] He was gifted, handsome, about five feet eleven, big boned, and athletic. Certainly he was a contrast to what appears to have been at times a bland ministerial father, Dr. Francis Parkman. And we can be sure that Parkman, as we reconstruct his personality from his youthful letters, diaries, and his novel, cultivated the image of a dashing, bold, athletic young man.[45]

Charles Farnham details Frank Parkman's preparations for physical conditioning and expert horsemanship almost in terms of preparations for gladiatorial combat. The young Parkman, for his sisters and family, was in fact the manly figure that emerged in many of his later historical portraits. From the Oregon Trail he wrote back to his mother and father, telling them over and over about the enormous challenges of wilderness life and how he survived the hazards of living with Indians on a wild frontier.[46] His brave image, for the women in his family, would forever be preserved.

The remarkable phenomenon of "brother worship" by his sisters gave Parkman a peculiar relationship with them. Lizzie's diary, preserved among the Parkman Papers at the Massachusetts Historical Society, reveals the extent of her devotion to her older brother,[47] whom she called "Frank" all his life. In the early 1860s she spoke of reading "Pickwick" to him and of his being "highly entertained . . . as if he had never read it before." She helped Frank with preparations for a rose show: "F. took four 1st prizes and a large 'gratuity.'" She recorded his daily feelings and aches and pains in the late 1860s and in 1870: his "very good spirits" one day, and the next, after a trip, "Frank's head is almost as bad as before he went away." A special entry was made on Frank's appointment as professor of horticulture in Harvard College's Bussey Institute in 1870 and noted how much "Frank likes the appointment."[48] Parkman's work at the institute was to give occasional lectures to young women interested in raising flowers. From what we know of Parkman, he would find satisfaction in this situation, where upperclass young women were exposed to the kind of education he thought proper for them. Parkman looked forward to teaching horticulture to female students. All in all, he lived within a world of loving and devoted women, with Lizzie sharing every day of his later years in a kind of partnership. More and more, Parkman became dependent upon her. A tall, handsome figure, with a high brow and hair beautifully rolled in a bun, she was indeed an attractive woman as we see her in a photograph at the Jamaica Plain house, with Parkman, holding one of his cats, seated before the fireplace.[49]

In later years, Parkman maintained an affectionate relationship with his daughters, Grace and Katherine. Katherine, or "Kate," married John Templeman Coolidge, who purchased the historic Wentworth Mansion where, as we have noted, Parkman spent months writing *A Half-Century of Conflict*. All of the women within the immediate circle of his life were his champions in his youth and in his maturity. They understood his infirmity and appreciated the significance of the major literary work he was completing. These women, at least by their silence in not opposing him, supported Parkman in his opposition to woman suffrage and did not question the kinds of portraits he made of women in his books. This kind of loyalty was echoed by women who wrote to Parkman approving his stance. Typical of the incoming letters he received was a missive of 10 October 1879, written to Parkman after the sender read his piece on "The Woman Question." "In reading and re-reading your article," Martha Calhoun wrote, "it has seemed to me that the most bigoted suffragist had nothing to refute—could do nothing but if she had a particle of modesty—hide her head."[50] Parkman's circle of female supporters upheld his views on public issues and their reflections in his articles as well as in his books. Yet he still had to cope with the intelligent women of his own class whose publications and opposition often made him appear faintly ridiculous in print.

In his correspondence we detect a tone of cool rage directed against the "wrathful five" who countered his assertions on woman suffrage in the *North American Review*.[51] The five, three of them women, Julia Ward Howe, Lucy Stone, and Elizabeth Cady Stanton, were to become legendary figures in the women's movement of the day. But what angered Parkman was that two of his opponents were men. Wendell Phillips and Thomas Wentworth Higginson were skillful writers who joined the women leaders in countering his assumptions. Parkman took them all on in public debate and even went so far as to attempt a last word in his essay, "The Woman Question Again," printed in the January 1880 issue of the *Review*.[52] There is good reason to believe that he was more famous in his time as an antiwoman suffrage writer than as a historian. According to one authority, Parkman's suffrage articles were reprinted by the thousands and sent all over the United States.[53]

One reason Parkman seems to have been so effective in stating his views is that he could fall back on the romantic, chivalric position that assumed women's dependence and helplessness. He successfully masked a contempt behind an appearance of admiration. In his battle with the opposition, his voice had a distinctly patriarchal tone. He remained rigid in his social views, although he lived in an era of tremendous socioeconomic, cultural, and political turmoil. An explosion of immigration accompanied by a new industrialism had occurred during the Civil War. After Appomattox there was a frenzy of railroad building and large-scale manufacturing and an exploitation of forests, fields, and mines. The lost cause of slavery was carried down along with older ideals of aristocratic leadership. Thus, Parkman's patrician social attitudes were increasingly out-of-date.

There was even a kind of desperation in the manner in which Parkman marshaled his arguments in the "woman question." For instance, prosuffrage advocates in Parkman's time often pointed to the ignorant immigrant vote as a reason for giving Protestant Anglo-Saxon women the franchise. Their votes would counteract those of Catholic immigrants. But Parkman would give no vote to women. He grasped seemingly for any argument that would support his views: women might undermine their virtue in the evil world of politics; immigrant women would make politics even more evil; powerful women might become threatening Delilahs; women would not support the right issues; they were too emotional. In history, the Catholic church with its hold on women was an obstacle to progress; the church was closely identified with a grasping hierarchy and elements of a feudal monarchy.

Yet for all his biases he could write with generosity and grace about Catholic women: "The nuns died but they never complained. Removed from the arena of ecclesiastical strife, too busy for the morbidness of the cloister, too much absorbed in practical benevolence to become prey of illusions, they and their sister community were models of that benign and tender charity of which the Roman Catholic Church is so rich in examples."[54] In almost the same breath, Parkman could add subtle qualifications for his praise with the statement that "in countries intensely Roman Catholic begging is not regarded as an unmixed evil, being supposed to promote two cardinal virtues,—charity in the giver, and humility in the receiver."[55] By using the words "unmixed evil" and "being supposed to promote," Parkman implies that the church promoted the evil of begging at a time when Canada swarmed with beggars and a farm, as Parkman noted, could be had for the asking.[56] Parkman was an artist in giving a double meaning to his text. Still, he could give his readers sympathetic understanding of the Canadian church in a historical reconstruction of a school founded by Bishop Laval. Here he relied upon Catholic custom and liturgy to give his pages beautifully phrased similes: "From the vast meadows of the parish at St. Joachim, which here border the St. Lawrence, there rises like an island a flat low hill, hedged round with forests like the tonsured head of a monk. It was here that Laval planted his school . . . athwart the gaunt arms of ancient pines, the river lies shimmering in the summer haze, the cottages of the *habitants* are strung like beads of a rosary along the meadows of Beaupre."[57] In this same continuing paragraph Parkman enlarges on his image to paint a fascinating picture of birch forests, wild fruits, flowers, torrential waterfalls, rocky solitudes, and "pious influence" that still hung about the "old walls embosomed in woods of St. Joachim."[58]

Such a memorable image of the Catholic church comes from the pen of a nineteenth-century Unitarian. It appears on his pages as a mature writer along with other interpretations that show his social-Darwinist ideals of social progress, all developed when he was still in his apprenticeship. His preoccupation with such themes, orchestrated in several of his volumes, especially in *Pontiac* and in *The Old Régime,* is discussed in the Epilogue.

Sire:

Will your Imperial majesty do me the honor to accept these volumes. They form the beginning of a series designed, when complete, to embrace the whole subject of French discovery and colonization in North America. . . . I venture to hope that, as ruler of France and as a man of letters, this attempt to impress my countrymen with a just sense of what they owe to the heroic virtues of Frenchmen will not be without interest to your eyes.

With profound respect
Your Imperial Majesty's Most Obt. Sevt.

—PARKMAN TO NAPOLEON III, [1869–1870]

John Fiske, historian and Parkman eulogizer.
(Courtesy The Huntington Library,
San Marino, California.)

THE LEGEND OF THE HERO-HISTORIAN

SO MUCH HAS BEEN SAID ABOUT the hero-historian's dedication to completion of his *History* that it is easy to neglect his devotion to growing flowers and experimentation with cross-pollination of lilies. If the youthful and gifted Parkman was highly motivated to achieve fame as a writer, the mature Parkman, at the end of his apprenticeship, had an equal determination to be successful in horticulture. Parkman today would be known as an important horticulturalist if he had never written about history. One could go so far as to argue that his drive for recognition was so strong that he would not tolerate the prospect of falling short of superiority whether it be in writing or in growing flowers. His emerging fame in both fields of accomplishment was such that he became a legend in his own time.

LILIES AND "PURE BLOOD" ROSES

Horticulture, a traditional hobby for gentlemen in Parkman's class, was his favorite pursuit after his first confrontation with debilitating illness. Near the termination of his apprenticeship, in his late twenties, Parkman turned to growing flowers as a therapy. His young wife, perplexed by his strange maladies, suggested, "Frank, with all your getting, get roses."[1] He followed her advice, and within a few years became a well-known rosarian and specialist in importing rare plants from the Orient. He then went into the nursery business, advertising the sale of plants throughout the Boston area. He seems to have enjoyed writing articles on plant experimentation, putting together a book on roses. He also had a role as a professor of horticulture at Harvard's Bussey Institute. Nevertheless, his letters tell us that he constantly battled his malady.

In the early 1860s, when his "enemy" confined him to a wheelchair, he directed Michael, "his man," to prepare a rose garden of forty-by-sixty feet. His friend Henry Sedgwick tells us how carefully Parkman turned over his topsoil of black-and-yellow loam with a mixture of manure and shavings of horse hoofs. Sedgwick recalls that Parkman grew many kinds of flowers, concentrating upon roses, grafting them to a sturdy wild stock. He was also able to bring about hybridization of Japanese lilies in cross-pollination by applying "the pollen of the Lily Golden to the pistils of the Lily Beautiful as soon as they were in a condition to receive it. Conception took place, and the pods swelled, and the seed ripened. . . . Fifty seedlings . . . their stems all mottled like the father plant."[2]

After several years Parkman planted bulbs for blooming. One finally opened and spread a "flower nine and a half inches in diameter, resembling its father in fragrance and form, its mother in color." This was the *Lilium Parkmanni,* distinct from the other forty-nine hybrids, which all put out blooms like those of the female parent.

Parkman's beautiful lily was a source of great pride to him. It came from a collection of Japanese plants that he had acquired about 1860 through a college friend. The group of plants, the first of its kind in America, was sent from Yokohama by the botanist, George Hall. It also included the strikingly colorful double purple form of the Japanese wisteria, which Parkman was able to flower, as well as an attractive treelike shrub, known as the Parkman crab, a crabapple that bore clusters of bright, roselike flowers.[3]

As Parkman wrote in his *Book of Roses* of 1866, success in cultivation would come with "knowledge and skill," especially if one could discriminate among roses of "pure blood," those of "hybrid origin," and others having no "legitimate offspring."[4] Parkman's favorite roses, like the central characters in his books, were aristocrats. He verified Darwin's theories in his flower-raising experiments and in his planting of trees at his Jamaica Plain home of three acres. His "pure blood" roses won hundreds of prizes at flower shows, a factor in his election as president of the Massachusetts Horticultural Society.

In the 1860s he continued research and writing, pacing himself with rest and gardening. Analysis of the records he left behind shows that despite his preoccupation with horticulture, Parkman's mind was on his *History.* Time in the garden was for him thoroughly relaxing, enough so to soften buffeting attacks of his "enemy." One suspects that often, in the periods when he says whirlwind visions captured his mind, he relived his youthful and sometimes dangerous expeditions and his never-ending search for new historical sources of information.

His quest for data included oral interviews with Indians and pioneers, inspection and reinspection of historic sites, and correspondence with anyone who could help him. College friends, historians, librarians, book dealers, antiquarians, anthropologists, scientists, and former teachers at Harvard all helped to throw light in his path. On occasion he was led astray by those who took advantage of his semiblindness or his ignorance of contents in archival collections. But he persevered and by diplomacy or sheer persistence overcame those who attempted to deceive him.

DOOM, DECAY, AND PROGRESS

The youthful Frank Parkman, as has been seen, soon outdistanced his contemporaries in knowledge of his areas of specialization. He also became a knowledgeable student of French literature, drama, and history before he emerged as a writer on the history of New France.[5] He had, there can be little doubt, an uncanny ability to perceive the essence of his research themes and to ferret out the sources. Prefaces in his books tell his reader what he believed he had accomplished. In the 1872 preface to *The Oregon Trail* he stated that the book was "a reflection" of another time, "the image of an irrevocable past." There is more nostalgic tone in his 1892 preface in which he lamented the passage of a "Wild West" whose "savage charms had withered." "If this book can help to keep their memory alive," he added, "it will have done its part."[6]

The theme of recovering the past is, of course, clearly observed in *Pontiac*. In its preface Parkman told his readers that he depicted "the American forest and the American Indian at a period when both received their final doom." After describing the murder of Pontiac, Parkman ends his story with a predictive statement on the future of all Indians: "Neither mound nor tablet marked the burial-place of Pontiac. For a mausoleum, a city has risen above the forest hero; and the race whom he hated with such burning rancor trample with unceasing footsteps over his forgotten grave."[7] Here Parkman links Pontiac's leadership with his death and evokes the idea that obliteration of other Indians is in the future. He leaves us with the fatal and inevitable destiny of the Indian, and, having established that fact, the tragedy of Pontiac and his followers is manifest. Indians were obliterated because they were in the path of progress. Although Parkman did not use the phrase "manifest destiny," just coming into vogue when he was writing the Pontiac volume, he did, notwithstanding, set forth an interpretation of social-Darwinist implications that fully embraced the idea.

In later volumes the idea of progressive change became a part of the structure of narrative. Early Canadian history, Parkman argued, is a drama enacted in "the untamed forests with a distant gleam of courtly splendor and regal pomp of Versailles." It was this "distant gleam" that in time created a "deformity" reflecting the mother country's spiritual and political absolutism, which could be seen as through a "microscope."[8] Progress "doomed" the old regime of Canada as well as the wilderness culture of the Indians.

Like other writers of the 1840s and the 1850s, Parkman fell back on the idea that a given society might be "doomed," "destined," or "fated." He chose the historical year 1763 in *Pontiac* to illustrate a turning point in the progress and triumph of Anglo-Americans: "Could the French have maintained their ground, the ruin of the Indian tribes could have been postponed; but the victory of Quebec was the signal of their swift decline. Thenceforth they were destined to melt and vanish before the advancing waves of Anglo-American power, which now rolled westward unchecked and unopposed. They saw the danger, and led by a great and daring champion, struggled fiercely to avert it."[9]

Although the Indians rose to oppose what was their destiny, which they perceived, they were "doomed." Their fate was so clearly apparent that no circumstances could alter the course of events. Pontiac himself was lost because of his barbarism and treacherous Indian traits. In the same way, the flaws in the culture of old French Canada were such that this society, like that of the Indian, had to be sacrificed to the march of progress. *The Old Régime* concludes with Parkman's sweeping generalization on the benefits of English victories in North America: "A happier calamity never befell a people than the conquest of Canada by British arms."[10]

HISTORIC AND "HEROIC CONSTANCY"

Parkman's conception of progress, set forth in *Pontiac* and later in his other books, is an example of how his apprenticeship period was a foundation for his later literary career. It was in *Pontiac* as well that his main historical characters were first identified as having recognizable traits. LaSalle, for instance, in *Pontiac* stands "forth in history [as] an imperishable monument of heroic constancy."[11] This is precisely the image of the explorer Parkman later developed in his biography. As a figure of "heroic constancy," therefore, LaSalle could not be portrayed as a deranged, insane character.[12]

We can say further that Parkman's principal characters, Sir Jeffrey Amherst in *Pontiac,* arrogant, egotistical commander who ordered Indians infected with smallpox blankets, as well as General Edward Braddock, courageous but "profligate . . . perverse, and a bigot to military rules,"[13] all had a distinct role to play. As in the case of LaSalle, those we first encounter in *Pontiac* act out their historical careers in later volumes. Robert Rogers, a fantasy figure in Parkman's youth, first introduced to readers in *Pontiac,* reappears in *Montcalm and Wolfe* as an exemplary frontier leader.[14]

The additional argument can be made that Parkman's other "actors," Pontiac, Amherst, LaSalle, or Catherine de Medici, were personages who had to conform to a particular kind of theatrical stance wherever they were placed—in a European court or in an intriguing wilderness scene.[15] Parkman, himself, also preserved his role as an author with "constancy." He and his characters were in an inflexible literary situation, a kind of gridlock that set a grand design. To the extent that Parkman governed his own life and reputation so as to cultivate a gallant, brave image of himself, his valorous stance was consciously or unconsciously fabricated. Similarly, when Parkman molded historical characters so they blended into a storylike role, he often gave his readers a manufactured version of history.[16]

NOVELISTIC STRATEGIES

Let us pinpoint a central argument of this book, that Parkman wrote novelistic histories. The contention has been made that his books resemble historical novels dealing with human experience in another age. Furthermore, his narratives are episodic, meaning that they are incomplete variants with heroic themes of violent confrontation. Because of his emphasis, Parkman often missed the larger, flowing streams of history.[17] It is ironic that this one-sidedness, this weakness in Parkman's work, was in fact the result of his undeviating thrust of interpretation. A further irony is that he put enormous effort into sifting sources that, in his view, justified his explanation of events and emplotment schemes.[18]

Yet Parkman did not write historical novels. His narratives, as analyzed in previous chapters, deal with actual events. He did not invent characters, dialogues, or happenings. There is, to be sure, no imaginary "Old French War," nor are there fanciful individuals called Pontiac, LaSalle, and Seth Pomeroy, the last a soldier who left a valuable journal of his percep-

FRANCIS PARKMAN

tions and observations while serving in a campaign against the French at Lake George.[19] The hundreds of other people, the numerous Indians and their tribes, and the many geographical landmarks appearing on Parkman's pages are real. His historical personages lived in earlier ages and were affected by turns of events. For instance, Jeffrey Amherst's role in distributing contagious smallpox blankets to Indians besieging Fort Pitt in 1763 was an extraordinary discovery coming out of Parkman's dogged research, which continued long after the book on Pontiac was first published.

Careers of Parkman's characters, such as that of Amherst, parallel Parkman's accounts of what happened in the sense that they are visible at an authentic time and place. Parkman, we are reminded, had his own purposes in putting individuals into specific roles by placing them on a stage of events in a historical story. We have seen how he manipulated data and time sequence in composing *The Oregon Trail*. The main exaggerations in *Pontiac* came from his "anchoring" his plot around Pontiac as an archconspirator.

We must be mindful that when he skewed the record he did so because his "anchoring" was central to his novelistic strategy. His main literary "anchor" in almost all storytelling was violence, the beginnings and continuation of endless turbulence and furious, often destructive action or force. Thus he put in place brilliant social-history sketches of the British and French colonies so readers could picture the resources of "contestants" in the fighting.[20] Individuals had roles in the war for empire, and their personalities and actions had to be refracted into an active beam of tumultuous imperial rivalry and killing.

There are, therefore, understandable causes for Parkman's distortions and exaggerations. For instance, he gave us portraits of individuals who were primed for the battle. They had to be courageous, daring, even grand and noble, valorous figures of another time. Yet in fact, they were, we have found, not so grand, not so daring, not so courageous, not so noble. Count Frontenac, for instance, has been downgraded by the Canadian scholar, William J. Eccles.[21] Villains, such as the Spaniard Menendez de Avilés, scholars believe, were not as despicable and murderous as Parkman depicted. Moreover, the brave, valorous Huguenot captain, Gaspard de Coligny, "a tower of trust," the counterpart of the unsavory Menendez de Avilés, had shortcomings that Parkman ignored. Still, there is enough in the original sources to make Parkman's story believable.[22]

Since the *Pioneers* was the first book composed by Parkman after his apprenticeship, he seized the opportunity to expand on literary devices already practiced in *The Oregon Trail* and in *Pontiac*. The *Pioneers* also became a useful volume for trying out themes not fully developed in his first two books. One of these, easily recognizable, is the portrayal of progressive forces and people in conflict with decadent societies. To do this, Parkman goes to great lengths to create suspenseful episodes where good triumphs over evil. One feels the atmosphere of hair-raising nineteenth-century melodrama.[23] We may ask, is this history or fiction? It is Parkmanesque novelistic history, extremely exciting to read, however biased or one-sided it may be.

Although he invented natural tropical forest backgrounds for episodes in the *Pioneers*, this and other panoramas were not, as we have seen, cardboard settings. We can feel confident by the record of Parkman's intense research that there actually were beautiful sunsets, roaring waterfalls, bright comets, gleaming rivers and lakes.[24] The overstatement was not so much in the creation of natural woodland settings as in his account of what was taking place. We cannot emphasize enough that Parkman's focus was on violence in forest warfare, often with the most horrendous examples of cruel behavior on the part of explorers, colonists, and Indians. With this kind of lens, his images were particularly distorted because they left out so much ordinary day-to-day peaceful activity. His version was often a shadow of what Parkman knew was taking place.[25]

For instance, a full view of Indian-white efforts at frontier diplomacy, found in the plethora of original Pennsylvania records that Parkman examined, was shaded out of his pages. The data, a voluminous record of Quaker-Indian peacemaking and peacekeeping, appeared in a series of Indian treaties during the period 1740–1760, all convened and held in the midst of the continual war activity that Parkman chronicles.[26]

Parkman would fall back on Indian treaties if he could bring them into his narration of conflict (as in the surrender of Indians in Pontiac's War), but the story of the Quaker-Indian pursuit for peace is representative of the kind of material that Parkman ignored. His chiefs were not negotiators seeking concord between foes; they could not act out their roles as statesmen-diplomats to mitigate abrasive relations with the colonists.

Not only were treaties coming out of important deliberations passed by, but as a result the Indian leaders were also left to oblivion unless, of course, they were caught up in the military events of Parkman's narrative. Some of Parkman's forgotten "heroes" of peacemaking diplomacy are Half King of the Senecas, Connesetago, Pisquetomen, Ohio Mingo leaders, along with King Hagler of the Catawbas, and the Delaware chief and orator, Teedyuscung. Parkman knew that these tribesmen could not easily be squeezed into what is now known as a "conspiracy theory" of Indian history.[27]

What fills the scholar with frustration in reading Parkman is his deliberate neglect—indeed his deliberate mispresentation—of Quakers in joining Indian leaders in the search for diplomatic alternatives to violence. Parkman saw no manhood in pacifist Quakers or their agents, including the skilled and intelligent Conrad Weiser, a veteran diplomat who left a flood of journals on his movements. Despite the fact that Weiser's name also appears in his journals and in hundreds of public documents, Parkman gave him one chance for visibility in *Pontiac* and then in an appendix document that insults his integrity and misrepresents his work.[28] Likewise, Parkman contorts his narrative to represent the Quakers falsely except in one instance when they stood between the Conestoga Mission Indians and armed Paxton Boys to prevent a second massacre of this peaceful people.[29]

Parkman's narrative strategy, then, seldom varied from stories of wars and conflict. He was, I believe, well aware that he was on a narrow path of fact that could easily verge on fabrication. He exposed himself to constant testing, to maintain what he regarded as an equilibrium, so that he could document his story. He was on a kind of treadmill of conflict, writing about struggles in the past and laboring to keep them within bounds of believability. One has the suspicion that these tensions and confrontations were not unrelated to his inner turmoil, his neurotic crises and subsequent "attacks" from his "enemy." Parkman's personal "story," acted out in his study as the heroic historian, undoubtedly intertwined with the stories he was writing about. When his characters were in trouble, he had to see them through the blistering challenges they faced.

In his study his characters took on reality. Here were pictures of woodland heroes on the walls, a Sioux bow, arrows, and a leather shield set high above a bookcase, and his huge desk was piled high with books and bound copies of documents. His study was at once a physical place and a room of the mind, made for himself as well as those who would read his books. This was a reposeful room where Parkman almost seemed to join in flesh and blood with those illustrious historic figures about whom he wrote. In that room, too, were reiterated patterns of action and events that assumed real substance. If an intruder opened the door and ungraciously questioned this state of affairs, cynical doubts would be met with hostility. With the door closed, all was well. Again a Parkmanesque atmosphere in viewing history and historic records prevailed. Within the room Parkman took on the role of a writer who expanded, tightened, or trimmed a story to fit a storyteller's pattern. At the same time he retained his post as a historian, continually documenting, deleting, adding, and revising in a fine-tuning process to achieve credibility. So important were his pictures and Indian relics that Parkman moved them from his Chestnut Street study to his study at Jamaica Plain, where he continued writing during summer months. In the fall they went back to Beacon Hill. The rooms might be changed, but the atmosphere had to be the same.

THE ISSUE OF PERSONAL HEROISM

Perhaps the most difficult problem in understanding Parkman centers on the question of his personal heroism. Was he a writer in the heroic mold, the kind of intellect that Samuel E. Morison and others have admired? Or was Morison fooled by Parkman's lifelong attempts to take on the coloration of such a person? Perhaps. But Morison was not easy to deceive, as those who remember him will agree. More likely, we can accept the fact that there was honesty in Parkman's view of himself. In accepting his infirmity, he was, in many ways, the kind of person he pretended to be. For him, there was no impersonation in being imprisoned in a sickly body. Nor could he be accused of being a weakling. Parkman was, instead, a self-styled literary hero-type who adroitly publicized his own case. In a quiet, subtle way, he told and retold his story of deep suffering to those who would give him sympathy, such as his cousin Mary Dwight Parkman.[30] Even when virtually incapacitated, he had strength to write, in spurts of highly personal correspondence, that he would never give up his strivings for victory over illness. Through Mary and other close relatives and friends the story of "Frank" Parkman's tragedy spread through the Beacon Hill grapevine and on to the wider circle of Boston's literary world.[31]

What makes Parkman's case so fascinating is that he implicated himself with his characters through a mental process of transference by searching out and exploiting materials that would justify creation of his own performances. He had his diaries to jog his memory to mold a self-portraiture of brave penetration into the Oregon Trail Indian country. This was a relatively easy literary exercise for the gifted young author. But he encountered diverse problems promoting self-imagery in *Pontiac* because he had to sort out and identify key characters who might later appear in subsequent volumes. Thus, in *Pontiac* he sketched in brief appearances of LaSalle, Frontenac, Montcalm and Wolfe, all with a special touch of valor. By the time he was writing legendary biographies of these characters, he was on familiar ground.

In books completed after his apprenticeship, he could more fully represent himself in fashioning his "actors." His books thus became a kind of "history of self," largely concerned with historic personages, who like himself had a longing for attainment.

We have seen how Parkman's elaborate treatment of the legendary LaSalle concludes with the statement that America owed him "an enduring memory." Although Parkman defended his seeming bias for the explorer by saying that he gave "both sides of his character,"[32] we can also make the argument that Parkman was incapable of such impartiality because he identified completely with this indomitable figure. LaSalle's enemies even have the appearance of being Parkman's enemies, especially those Jesuits who sought the downfall of a great man.[33]

FASHIONING A SELF-IMAGE

The troubled history of Parkman and his hidden battle with illness is shadowed by a veil of privacy. Our knowledge is based on his autobiographical letters and personal correspondence. This is supplemented by what he and his immediate family told friends. In addition, Parkman occasionally gave interviews to journalists and writers who made it known that they would write about him. The whole story consistently dwells on the theme of tragic heroism. Yet there are openings in the shadowy tale that tell us about another kind of hero who challenges his illness, who from time to time takes on the air of a normal, healthy person.

Sick, blind, and arthritic as he was in middle life, we have seen that he actually managed to "walk" from Boston's Beacon Hill to Cambridge to argue with his friend, William Dean Howells. What is even more amazing is that later, at the age of sixty, he made a six-day, eighty-mile horseback ride in the White Mountains of New Hampshire, to Crawford Notch, through rain and snow. As he wrote his friend Pierre Margry, "the rain turned to snow . . . I reached Wentworth's hotel by evening. He received me with alacrity like an old customer and immediately brought me a good glass of hot whiskey. I got out my trunks, changed my clothes, and, though I'm a grandfather of 60, don't find myself any worse off for the adventure." Three years later he went shooting and fly-fishing in a month of camping in the Canadian wilderness of the Batiscan River, which flows into the St. Lawrence.[34] It seems obvious that Parkman in his sixties was hardly a sick man. Close examination of the many photographs taken of Parkman, from his youth to his last years, reveal a man of health and vigor. A portrait, painted of him in 1880, shows remarkable strength and vitality.

EPILOGUE

Yet he persisted in portraying himself as a semi-invalid. His tale of woe was as important to him as the literary models he developed for his readers. The tragic overtones of his personal story were present when he took up the pen.

Further tangible evidence, moreover, shows that Parkman deliberately, through carefully composed and distributed autobiographical letters, embellished a picture of personal valor strikingly like that of LaSalle. In two long, soul-searching missives, Parkman told posterity about his private war with adversity. He spelled out, in tortuous detail, his story of misery, inflicted upon him by a mysterious illness. His complaints are convincing. They are, one can believe, from the heart with no pretense. His neurosis, it is apparent, made it impossible for him to comprehend that much of his agony was self-inflicted.

But there was logic in this mad world of Parkman's. By identifying his "enemy," he singled out an adversary, and this seems to have given him grim satisfaction, even pleasure. He could now counterattack, even win a series of personal engagements against an implacable foe. He seems at times to have actually enjoyed the combat in fending off "enemy" assaults that insidiously attempted to prevent him from carrying on his work. This "war" with illness had its longest and most severe period beginning in the last years of his apprenticeship in the late 1840s lasting until 1864, the year of the completion of the first autobiographical letter. His books *The Oregon Trail, Pontiac,* and *Pioneers* were completed in this traumatic period of "dark years." [35] From this time on he had the most productive period in writing.

THE AUTOBIOGRAPHY OF 1864 AND THE SEARCH FOR FAME

In his preface to the *Pioneers* Parkman tells us about his eighteen-year period of illness, which made, he wrote, continuous work without rest periods "merely suicidal." [36] At the end of this long period of illness and agonizingly slow progress in writing, he was well enough to compose the first of his miniautobiographies in or about the year 1864. This manuscript was finished at this time, but Parkman mysteriously kept it on his desk for an additional four years before he sent it to the recipient. One can speculate that he delayed, polishing and editing, because of the singular importance of the self-analysis he had made. In the end, he created a readable, plausible story about himself with overtones of objectivity. As his doctor, S. Weir Mitchell, [37] later told him, Parkman knew his own case very well indeed. With the literary dexterity of a physician, Parkman did chronicle a fascinating case history. Writing in the third person, Parkman, the author, took on the posture of an impartial observer looking at the scenes of a tragic medical situation.

There is no internal evidence of the emotional turmoil Parkman must have had in composing his personal story. The completed manuscript is clearly and cleanly written in the hand of an assistant without the sort of revisions sometimes found in letters written by Parkman himself.

He finished a second very similar letter some twenty years later, about 1887, again when he had a recovery period from illness. The 1887 letter, written in the first person, is also a convincing account, but in my judgment does not have the dramatic impact of the earlier manuscript. Since the two letters are nearly identical in content, one can assume that Parkman decided to make sure that posterity would have the personal facts about his illness. One cannot help but believe that Parkman, the historian, thorough researcher that he was, wanted his own life saga well documented. If one letter was lost, the other would probably survive, and if neither were lost, so much the better.

His two manuscripts were undated and had cover letters with brief comments addressed to old friends, George E. Ellis, Unitarian clergyman and historian, and Martin Brimmer, prominent member of the Massachusetts Historical Society.[38] Parkman made it clear in his cover letters (as well as in conversations with the recipients) that the manuscripts were to be held and passed on to those who would acquire his collected papers and research materials. The letters and other materials were later given to the Massachusetts Historical Society. Altogether his papers comprised a mass of correspondence as well as large notebooks containing duplicates of historical documents. Some of the handwritten copies of his books, together with his large map collection (many of them hand-drawn by Parkman with his identification notes) were willed to Harvard College. All the records buttressed what was said in autobiographical statements about Parkman's extensive researches. Parkman nevertheless withheld a few very personal items, such as a cache of letters from the Oregon Trail sent to his family along with his journals, which were later discovered in his study.[39]

There can be little doubt that Parkman had an obsession about preservation of his autobiographical letters. George Ellis, because of his skills as a historian, was exactly the person who could be trusted to pass the first letter on to Parkman's first biographer, another intimate friend, Charles H. Farnham, secretary for Parkman as well as his fishing companion. The legend of Parkman's "nobility" probably began in earnest with Farnham's biography, published some seven years after Parkman's death. Farnham molded his study largely around the tragic events set forth in the letter of 1864 and seems to have been among those present when "the package of posthumous manuscript was opened."[40]

On 21 November 1893, soon after Parkman's death, the Massachusetts Historical Society held a "Special Meeting" to honor his memory and to open Ellis's "closely sealed" package containing the manuscript of Parkman's first letter. In the presence of a "large audience of members" and "Mr. Parkman's relatives," Ellis, the Society's President, broke the seal on the package, which he had had in his possession since 1868. He then, in what must have been truly a moment of anticipation for all those present, read a "private note" in which Parkman had mentioned his "egoism" in composing the letter. After Ellis decided that he found no "egoism" in "the autobiographical paper in his hands," he told his audience, "he would read it." The letter, later printed in full in the society's *Proceedings,* included excerpts from the second, shorter letter, which had been sent to Martin Brimmer, fellow member of the society. It was announced that both letters were to be given to the society.[41]

Following the reading of the autobiographical letter, Oliver W. Holmes read his poem setting forth the theme of Parkman as "a silent hero." Then followed eulogies by other prominent Bostonians and members of the society: Robert C. Winthrop, George S. Hale, John Lowell, and Martin Brimmer, each adding to the "noble tributes" already made.[42]

Both letters and other Parkman papers were soon made available to Farnham, hard at work on his biography. The first letter became the heart of Farnham's book. He quoted it from time to time and then, in a long chapter on Parkman's "spiritual growth," burdened readers with repetition of the entire manuscript. To bolster their interest, Farnham perceptively tells his readers that the "story" they are about to read is about a man whose "most insidious enemy was his brain trouble."[43] We see here a ready adaptation of Parkman's language about himself by use of the word *enemy.* Then follows the theme of personal valor heralding the intimate story of Parkman's "personality and inner experiences."[44]

Farnham knew his subject from years of friendship and gave his readers insights. But he never strayed from the path of Parkman veneration. Writing soon after Parkman's death, he was under pressure from the establishment to render a proper image, and he knew he had Parkman's sister Eliza at his elbow, who would tolerate little criticism of her brother. Moreover, Farnham, a writer and journalist, was not from the inner circle of Boston's patrician society. He had been given an opportunity to make his way into the literary world, and he had no desire to deviate from the now accepted posture of Parkman hero worship.[45]

Farnham, of course, knew that he was not the first to fashion a halo around Parkman's life and work. The hallowed image of Parkman made its appearance before Parkman died and crystallized into a legend in print emerging from a flurry of memoirs composed by admirers. Following the memorial meeting and the subsequent printing of the letter of 1864 and all other encomiums in the society's *Proceedings,* newspapers and magazines throughout America came forth with accounts of his life that made him appear a national hero. Along with these, a new spate of memoirs set forth a particularly reverential image of Parkman, many with quotations from the letter of 1864. The Reverend O. B. Frothingham, in a lengthy tribute, concluded that Parkman was "like a granite mountain in the sea, noble," but a man with "a self-estimate too proud and firm."[46]

Frothingham's hint that there were cracks in the "granite mountain" was not developed by Farnham, although, as a biographer chosen by Parkman's family, he did have access to all memoirs together with Parkman's autobiographical letters. Farnham surrendered completely to the tragic hero image of Parkman by comparing the historian to an Indian warrior courageously singing his death song and to Father Isaac Jogues's patient endurance facing Iroquois torment.[47]

Reinforcement for Farnham's eulogistic portrait of Parkman soon came from another source. Parkman's second letter, repetitious of the first except in a brief account of his childhood experiences with his grandparents, was printed in full in one more early biography by Henry Dwight Sedgwick in 1906.[48] Both letters, now widely known, along with the biographies, marked the appearance of a widespread Parkman cult of admirers, encompassing North America, France, and England. Parkman's correspondence, flooded with letters from distinguished figures (including Theodore Roosevelt, who dedicated books to Parkman) showed that this audience had been completely captivated by his storylike histories.

There are other interesting facets about Parkman's plans for preserving and enhancing his place in the sun. We have noted that the first letter is written entirely in the third person, giving Parkman a chance to depersonalize his situation. Although he used a literary device to tell his story, one has the impression that standing back and assessing his illness gave him a measure of relief. He could tell the world about "exhaustion and total derangement of the nervous system . . . the irritability of the nervous system centered in the head . . . the tension of an iron band, secured around the head and contracting with extreme force."[49]

Then, too, he put his life story in the context of a career revolving around two romantic ideals: "One was to paint the forest and its tenants in true and vivid colors; the other was to realize a certain ideal of manhood, a little medieval, but nevertheless good." He held "the pen with a hand that should have grasped the sword."[50] What a line for remembrance of a courageous literary figure! It is so quotable that it reappeared in articles and books about Parkman and his work.

JOHN FISKE'S PANEGYRICS

One of those who enthusiastically promoted Parkman's noble imagery was the historian and international public lecturer, John Fiske. For Fiske, Parkman had no equal as a "great" American historian. During Parkman's lifetime, Fiske, on a lecture circuit, spoke glowingly of "Pontiac and his conspiracy" at Hawthorne Hall in Boston in 1879. As Fiske later told us in a biographical essay on Parkman, "I said, among other things, that it [Parkman's conspiracy thesis] was memorable as 'the theme of one of the most brilliant and fascinating books written by any historian since the days of Herodotus.'" As Fiske recalled his lecture, he was startled to see Parkman's face appearing suddenly before him in the audience: "I had not observed him before, though he was seated quite near me. I shall never forget the sudden start which he gave, and the heightened color of his noble face with its curious look of surprise and pleasure as honest and simple as one might witness in a rather shy schoolboy suddenly singled out for praise."[51]

One can be reasonably sure that the "shy schoolboy" with the "noble face" was expecting to hear some kind of compliment, for Fiske was on an American tour repeating lectures he had already given in London. The fact that he had extravagant praise for *Pontiac* was undoubtedly known to Parkman. What is intriguing about this encounter is that by the late 1870s Parkman was already singled out in international public lectures by Fiske as a "great historian."

Following Parkman's death, and after the Massachusetts Historical Society memorial meeting, Fiske had another opportunity to expound on Parkman's work at a second "meeting," sponsored by Harvard College at Sander's Theater on 6 December 1893. No less than Harvard's president, Charles W. Eliot, presided (he had been unable to attend the previous meeting because of "a previous engagement on college business"). Justin Winsor and Fiske, "eminent authorities on historical subjects," were speakers, and Winsor, who had disagreed with Parkman on data concerning discoveries in North America, gave restrained praise, citing Parkman for "honesty of citation" and "for the integrity of his art."[52]

Fiske, however, rose once more to give Parkman unstinting acclaim with a colorful panegyric. "Parkman," he intoned in the sonorous voice of a powerful orator (Fiske was a huge, bearlike man with a commanding presence on the podium), "is the most American of all our historians, because he deals with purely American history; but at the same time he is a historian for all mankind, and all time, one of the greatest who ever lived."[53]

One might believe that Fiske, orator and historian, might consider more restrained language when he later wrote two lengthy essay-biographies for the introduction to the beautifully bound Frontenac edition of Parkman's works, published in 1899. Fiske, time and again in these essays, gives Parkman accolade after accolade. There was seemingly not a line written by Parkman that Fiske did not praise. Even Parkman's articles opposing universal and woman's suffrage Fiske declared to be of "the highest value," having been based upon "impartial survey of essential facts." But the crown jewel of evidence for Fiske's argument was Parkman's autobiographical letter of 1864. Here, Fiske maintained, was the hidden story of Parkman's "marvelous heroism." In a final, somewhat repetitious encomium, Fiske wrote that Parkman's books belonged "among the world's masterpieces of highest rank, along with the works of Herodotus, Thucydides, and Gibbon."[54]

THE PARKMAN LEGEND

Fiske's portrait of Parkman, published in two eloquent essays in *Pioneers* (dealing with the historian's life and work) were prime movers in trumpeting heroic images. What is particularly interesting is that both are built around the autobiography of 1864. The full impact of both the letter and Fiske's eulogies is readily visible in Mason Wade's popular biography of 1942, *Francis Parkman: Heroic Historian*. Wade concludes that Parkman "is perhaps the greatest American historian," after relying on the letter of 1864 to chronicle the high noon of Parkman's sickness as he emerged from the "dungeon of the spirit."[55] What impressed Wade about Parkman's lifetime writings was the heroic ardor of the letter of 1864, which by now had attained its own immortality. Like Fiske and others before him, Wade was completely captured by the letter's portrayal of Parkman's valorous behavior and his quality of mind in the face of afflictions and a sea of troubles. As Wade argued: "This letter, written in the third person, was the first revelation of the odds that Parkman faced and overcame, and its simple statement of facts is more eloquent than any of the panegyrics on that or later occasions."[56] It was Wade, then, biographer and editor of a handsome edition of Parkman's journals, who encouraged the growth of a Parkman cult and set the stage for new reverberations of the Parkman legend.

Parkman, it would seem, reached out from his grave to pick Mason Wade as a twentieth-century biographer to preserve his legend. Wade, a former student of a fervent Parkman admirer, Bernard DeVoto, in a masterstroke of diligent research, discovered Parkman's journals, filled with accounts of White Mountain and Oregon Trail expeditions. The journals, left by Parkman in his study at his 50 Chestnut Street, Beacon Hill home, gave new impetus to the heroic image because of their detailed record of exhausting, sometimes dangerous expeditions and field trips. The journals, plus Parkman's autobiographical letter of 1864, were prime sources for Wade's portrait of Parkman in an epic-hero format.

Could Parkman have anticipated Wade's foraging through his study to find the journals? Probably not, but the journals were there, and he knew someone would find them. The small journal books were easily identified, as I found in going to the same room some years later to discover Parkman's original Oregon Trail letters written to his parents. What we can be reasonably certain about is that the neurotic Parkman did unconsciously create a heroic struggle to cope with his "enemy." At the same time, he was calculating in trying to preserve his heroic legacy for posterity. In all this, Parkman could be said to be crazy like a fox. He was so successful that he is at least partly responsible for generating a strong backlash by modern critics who seek his decanonization. As his critics insist, he did and still does represent a canon of white-male superiority over people of color and women,[57] and although he admired French aristocrats in pioneer roles, for him the French were inferior to the Anglo-Saxons.

If we look at Parkman and his work from the posture of nineteenth-century Anglo-Saxonism, it is evident that he was not alone in picturing the French Celt as compulsive and irrational and unable to cope with Anglo-Saxon ideals of freedom. Parkman viewed himself as an intellectual leader of his time and a liberal who supported Civil Service reform and Mugwump politics. He also saw himself as a narrative historian who gave American readers a pattern of understanding and guidelines for interpreting the roles of Anglo-Saxons in the formative years of their nation.

But even as Parkman was writing, in the second half of the nineteenth century, liberal Anglo-Saxonism showed transfusions of racism, sutured by "scientific" advances in phrenology and craniology, which resulted in beliefs in race types and racial inequality. Traditional Anglo-Saxonism be-

FRANCIS PARKMAN

came tainted with elitist blood and ethnocentrism. A natural conclusion for Parkman was that Anglo-Saxons, particularly those of the "Germanic race," were especially fitted for the masculine task of self-government.[58] Other historians following Parkman, such as Frederick Jackson Turner and his mentor, Herbert Baxter Adams, held similar views.[59]

We must recognize that Parkman was an early and powerful advocate of this skewed version of history. With patriotic overtones and vibrant narratives of heroism, he courted his readers. It gave him great pleasure to know that his volumes had wide appeal in his generation. Millions of twentieth-century readers also found enjoyment and pride in the Parkmanesque version of history, beginning with *The Oregon Trail* and *Pontiac*.[60]

These readers, including many in a new generation of professional historians and critics, were unconcerned about an obverse weakness of Parkman's storylike narratives, that he treated selective evidence for incidental events as reality. The fact that his novelistic style of history was therefore inherently facile and superficial did not impinge on his popularity.

We can be sure that Parkman's skillfully crafted description of intrinsically valuable aspects of our Anglo-Saxon legacy gave his work precise signification in American historiography. Despite his invigorating style, the shadows of his astigmatism and his social bias and elitism are visible in *The Oregon Trail*, in *Pontiac*, and in his later volumes. Parkman was able to camouflage some of these shaded passages by an impressive array of references that were blended into a data base enabling him to document his narrative, month by month and year by year. His heavily annotated narrative won admiration and respect from generations of scholars. So great was the impact of Parkman's bibliographic annotation in *Pontiac* that henceforth he could ask to be accepted with trust, citing fewer sources of information.

With his powers of memory he made his infirmity into an asset by quietly sitting in his study digesting sources and organizing chapters. He did all this without note cards or outlines to organize and fashion a narrative, fresh and original in its own time and still inspiring today. What is even more amazing is that Parkman made no drafts. In his boyish handwriting he wrote or dictated to an assistant. There were revisions but no rewritings. The penciled original went to the printer. His chapters glided smoothly over the surface of thousands of pages of journals, letters, and reports. How did he do it? One answer is that when in his study, it became his room of dreams. In a half-joking letter to his friend Pierre Margry in 1885 he wrote: "I have chatted several times with Champlain, Frontenac, Montcalm, Brébeuf, and many more. Brébeuf calls me a heretic and says it is wrong for me not to be down in the flames. I am just fine here, considering the disorders of my past life."[61]

Although Parkman made light about chatting with historic characters, one suspects that on other occasions he might indeed have had imaginary chats with Brébeuf and Frontenac. In this self-revealing letter, written at the age of 62, Parkman went on to tell his friend that although he had been sick he was "still busy on history. I ride horseback, dine at my neighbor's or else pay my respects to some beautiful lady of the neighborhood." Parkman did all this, he said, while living in his country home "on a pretty little lake called Jamaica Pond—*Étang de Jamaique.*"

An attractive woman whom Parkman especially liked to visit was the wife of his historian friend, Henry Adams—Marian, or Clover, as she was known. Throughout the 1870s, before Clover's death in 1879, Parkman was a guest of the Adamses at their homes in Beverly Farms, Massachusetts, or in London, England. It is clear from Clover's letters that Parkman was not always her favorite dinner guest. She respected him as a historian but regarded his unchanging views as wearisome. A photographer with professional skills, she found him an intriguing subject and took his picture sitting jauntily on a wicker chair, wearing a saucy derby hat. Frank Parkman does not appear to be an unhealthy man (she ignored his illness). What impressed her was that he was such a vigorous proponent of antifeminist views. Clover and her close friend, Mary Dwight Parkman, avoided talk with him about politics. He had not changed, she wrote, in "three years" on a variety of "topics or opinions." Frank Parkman was "no less conservative" and as "immutable as Faneuil Hall."[62]

Clover had uncovered Parkman's unchanging "historic constancy." He appears to have found personal strength in a stubborn refusal to alter his outlook on life and history. He achieved what a man like LaSalle attained, constancy in thought and action in the tradition of the epic hero,[63] and he waged a lifelong battle for self-validation. Parkman could appear outwardly affable and courteous while he disguised his rage against the Catholic church and the suffragists. He would not compromise in his views. To yield would be a visible sign of weakness. He never waned in his passion to further his career without compromising his principles.

We should also remember that throughout his life Parkman demonstrated a love for the virgin woods and the naked primeval beauty of our lakes and riverlands. Lifelike panoramas of these are forever embodied in the splendid cadences of his *History.* As a gifted writer who overcame adversity to fashion legends of heroic nobility about himself and his nation's colonial past, Parkman became a significant part of our literary heritage.

Three portraits of Parkman after putting on weight and losing it by following Dr. S Weir Mitchell's dietary advice: *a*. Parkman in his late fifties, *b*. Parkman in his middle sixties, *c*. Parkman in his late sixties. (All W. R. Jacobs Photography Collection.)

PARKMAN'S COMMENCEMENT ORATION, "ROMANCE IN AMERICA"

ON 28 AUGUST 1844, TWENTY-ONE-YEAR-OLD Francis Parkman delivered a commencement oration on the occasion of his graduation from Harvard. The original manuscript, among his papers in the Harvard College Library, is in Parkman's handwriting, signed "F. Parkman, August '44."[1]

In early summer of 1844, after returning from Europe, before writing his oration and before his graduation (a graduation that seems to have been delayed from early summer because of his temporary absence from college), he gave evidence of his state of mind with these random jottings in his journal:

> The traveller in Europe
> Art, nature history combine
> In America Art has done her best to destroy nature,
> association nothing.[2]

The quiet beauty of the English countryside had impressed the youthful tourist; in Scotland he was captivated by the "heathery" hills closely associated with the life and writings of Sir Walter Scott. Here were art, legend, nature, and history. America, by contrast, had failed to appreciate the romance of its wilderness heritage, and it was this failure that Parkman hoped to rectify by writing a good—perhaps a great—book on a North American theme, a book that would be recognized as a product of the New World. His feeling for his theme is exhibited by the comments of Vassal Morton, the hero of his novel. "Here in America," declares Vassal, "we ought to make the most of this feeling for nature; for we have very little else . . . savageness and solitude have a character of their own; and so has the polished landscape with associations of art, poetry, legend and history."[3] The polished landscape of Europe had little enchantment for Parkman. Rather, he turned to the mountains and the virgin forests for his New World symphony.

"Romance in America," as Parkman called his oration, reveals for us the springs from which his later work flowed, providing new insight into his romantic concept of history. Yet Parkman's treatment of Indians, as seen in the preceding chapters of this book, was far from romantic. He rejected completely the idea of the noble savage, depicting the warrior instead as a barbarian of the wilderness. Despite his unromantic attitude toward Indians, his enthusiasm for Indians became a lifelong affair. His early fascination with Indian history blended with an interest he developed in studying the heroic figures of early Canadian history. Parkman partook of a virtual wilderness psychodrama with dangerous Indians, beautiful but hostile environments, and courageous leaders such as the chivalrous Marshall Louis de Montcalm, who captured Fort William Henry.

That Parkman as a graduating senior had learned his art is clear from his oration. The language reflects Parkman's youthful affection for poetry, particularly his admiration for the Byronic hero and the forest hymns of William Cullen Bryant. The excellent vocabulary, the graceful sentences merging into smoothly molded paragraphs and transitions, the skillful characterization of the slatternly log-hut pioneer—occupied with reading newspapers and cultivating potatoes—suggest literary sophistication. His prose is made vivid by its appeal to the senses of sight, hearing, and smell. At Lake George "a gentle girl . . . gazes . . . down the Lake"; the sound of a "gun reverberates down the long vista of mountains, and the sullen murmurings dwell for many moments on the ear"; and a raven appears that "once gorged on the dead."

For Lake George, Parkman uses the image of the "holy lake," christened Lac St. Sacrament by Father Isaac Jogues, before he was tormented by the Mohawks. The lake was also the scene of Sir William Johnson's bloody victory over the French, and afterward it was a silent witness of escapades of Robert Rogers, the colonial ranger, whose "slide," on the edge of an escarpment on the lake, even today awakens memories of the "Old French War." Lake George was a kind of historical focus for Parkman, a geographical center for his narratives. The description of the lake in *Montcalm and Wolfe*, written forty years after his graduation, is a clear echo of his graduation oration.[4]

In later years Parkman deeply resented the changes on the shores of the lake brought about by real-estate promoters. As he wrote a friend about the encroachment of the nouveau riche around the lake in 1892, a year before his death, "For my part, I would gladly destroy all his works and restore Lake George to its native savagery."[5]

"ROMANCE IN AMERICA"

The tourist in Europe finds the scenes of Nature polished by the hand of art, and invested with a thousand associations by the fancies and the deeds of ages. The American traveller is less fortunate. Art has not been idle here for the last two centuries, but she has done her best to ruin, not to adorn, the face of Nature. She has torn down the forests, and blasted the mountains into fragments; dammed up the streams, and drained the lakes, and threatens to leave the whole continent bare and raw. Perhaps the time will come when she will plant gardens and rear palaces, but the tendency of her present efforts forbids us to be too sanguine.

When Columbus first saw land, America was the sublimest object in the world. Here was the domain of Nature. For ages her forest-trees had risen, flourished, and fallen. In the autumn, the vast continent glowed at once with red, and yellow, and green; and when winter came, the ice of her waters creaked and groaned to the solitude; and in the spring her savage streams burst their fetters, and swept down the refuse of the wilderness. It was half the world a theatre for the operations of Nature! But the charm is broken now. The stern and solemn poetry that breathed from her endless wilderness is gone; and the dullest plainest prose has fixed its home in America.

Once Spain, Italy, England was also a wilderness. The haunts of Nature were *there* in like manner invaded, and her charm broken; but since that remote day, the deeds of many a generation of wise and gallant men have flung around that land the halo of romance and poetry. Its streams and mountains are hallowed by associations that ours have not, and may never have; and the hand of art has polished the rough features of Nature. The warfare of fierce and brave men, seen through the obscure veil of centuries, has given a charm to the Cheviot Hills that will never belong to ours, though our forests have seen struggles more savage and bloody.

The fanciful child, as he journeys through the passes of our northern mountains, looks with awe into the black depths of the woods, and listening to the plunge of the hidden torrent, he recalls the stories of his nursery of Indian wars and massacres. A fearful romance invests all around him, for he associates it with those scenes of horror. And surely the early days of no nation could afford truer elements of romance. They need but to be magnified by superstition and obscured by time. But we live in an enlightened age. History has recorded the minutest circumstance of our fathers' wars; and when we look at the actors, we find the same cool-blooded, reasoning, unyielding men who dwell among us this day—the very antipodes of the hero of romance.

The traveller may pause over the battle-fields of Saratoga or Bennington, and moralize, if he pleases, or give vent to his patriotic ardor. But they have none of the romantic charm, so hateful to the Peace-society. He will not feel the inspiration of Flodden or Otterburn. Here, on these American fields, was no display of chivalry or of headlong passion, but a deliberate effort in favor of an abstract principle. Cool reason, not passion, or the love of war, sent the American to the battlefield. When Napoleon placed his brother on the throne of Spain, the Spanish peasant sprang to the gun and the dagger and leaped on the invader with the blind fury of a tiger. The men of New England heard that they were taxed, called a meeting, and voted resistance. Philanthropists may rejoice over the calm deliberation of such proceeedings, but the poet has deep reason to lament.

The soldier of the Revolution has handed down to his grandchildren his own cool reasoning temper, so that the traveller finds even fewer elements of the picturesque in the character of the men, than in the aspect of the country. But, perhaps, being young and inexperienced, and having heard that wild men still linger in the recesses of the Scottish Highlands and the mountains of Wales, he imagines that the depths of the yet unwasted forest may contain some form of human nature more strange and wonderful to his American eye. So, with infinite toil, he penetrates to a narrow gap in the woods on the outskirts of civilization;—a small square space hewn out of the forest, and full of the black and smoking carcases of the murdered trees, while the still living forest palisades the place around. Here dwells the pioneer, in his log-hut. The disappointed traveller finds him like other people, with no trace of primitive ignorance or romantic barbarism. He reads the newspapers; supports Polk and Dallas with fiery zeal; knows the latest improvements in agriculture, and keeps a watchful eye on all that is going on in the great world. Though quite confident in his power to match the whole earth in combat, he has no warlike ardor, preferring to watch his saw-mill and hoe his potatoes, since these seem to him the more rational and profitable occupations. In short, the enthusiast can make nothing of him, and abandoning the thought of finding anything romantic on his native continent, he sighs for Italy, where there are castles and convents, stupid priests, and lazy monks, and dresses of red and

APPENDIX

green; where people are stabbed with stilettos, instead of being slashed with bowie-knives, and all is picturesquely languid, and romantically useless.

Yet beauties enough be on the northern traveller's path; beauties scarce surpassed on earth, and one spot, at least, whose wild scenery has gained a deeper interest from the early history of his country. A lake which Romish priests, charmed by its matchless beauty, consecrated to the Prince of Peace when that country was an untrodden wilderness, yet which has seen a thousand death-struggles, and been dyed with the blood of legions. To the eye, Lake George seems the home of tranquillity and mild repose. The gentle girl sits on the green mound of the ruined fort, and gazes in quiet happiness down the Lake. All is calm and peaceful, yet lovely and wild, by the red light of evening; waters as deep and pure as the eyes of the gazer; mountains whose sternness is softened into a wild beauty. The evening gun reverberates down the long vista of mountains, and the sullen murmurings dwell for many moments on the ear.—There was a time when other sounds awoke those echoes,—the batteries of Montcalm; the yells of a savage multitude, and the screams of a butchered army. Blood has been poured out like water over that soil! By day and by night, in summer and in winter, hosts of men have struggled and died upon it. It is sown thick with bullets and human bones, the relics of many a battle and slaughter. The raven that plucks the farmer's corn once gorged on the dead of France, of England, and a score of forgotten savage tribes.

But the Holy Lake is alone. There are other scenes of grandeur and beauty, yet none where associations throng so thick and fast; and as they seem doomed to rest undistinguished in song, we must hope for them the colder honors of prose, and look forward [to] the day when the arts of peace shall have made them illustrious.

F. Parkman, August '44

The hero in the garden ca. 1870. Photographed by Clover Adams (Mrs. Henry Adams), who had professional skills in portrait photography. (From *The Education of Mrs. Henry Adams*, by Eugenia Kaledin; © 1981 by Temple University, reprinted by permission of Temple University Press.)

NOTES

I. THE HERO-HISTORIAN AND HIS ILLNESS

1. For heroic Parkman imagery, see Charles H. Farnham, *A Life of Francis Parkman,* Frontenac ed. of Parkman's works (Boston: Little, Brown & Co., 1901). All citations are to this edition, which includes Parkman's last revisions and has a factual summary of Parkman's youth and family background, pp. 11–24. See also Edward Wheelwright, "Memoir of Francis Parkman," *Publications of the Colonial Society of Massachusetts* 1 (1895): 304–350, and three biographical studies: Mason Wade, *Francis Parkman: Heroic Historian* (New York: Viking Press, 1942); Howard Doughty, *Francis Parkman* (New York: Macmillan, 1962; reprint, Cambridge, Mass.: Harvard University Press, 1983); and Robert L. Gale, *Francis Parkman* (New York: Twayne Publishers, 1973).

2. See the epilogue for a discussion of Parkman's self-fashioning of a hero image. For a commentary on the artist in society from a viewpoint of modern psychoanalysis, see Lawrence J. Hatterer, *The Artist in Society: Problems and Treatment of the Creative Personality* (New York: Grove Press, 1965), p. 27, which argues that the artist who fails competitive activities may invoke his talent to provide a feeling of superiority. Through his artistic activity, he can thereby release fantasies and permit them to become acceptable. In building an image for himself, the writer creates what is called a "reader-author alliance" to persuade the reader to accept his version of the truth. There are ethical problems here, but Parkman went to extraordinary lengths to convince his readers that his romantic vision of the past was truthful and authentic and not exaggerated. For a discussion of the complexities of the reader-author relationship, see Maurice Levine, *Psychiatry and Ethics* (New York: G. Braziller, 1972), pp. 38–42. For an appraisal of Parkman's research techniques, see my analysis in chapter 6 dealing with Pontiac's "conspiracy."

3. Farnham, *Life of Francis Parkman,* pp. 11–13, details Parkman's Huguenot and Puritan background. The Parkman Papers (hereafter cited as PP), Massachusetts Historical Society (hereafter cited as MHS), include data on the generations

of Parkmans. For instance, the diary MS of grandfather Ebenezer Parkman is preserved at the MHS and was published by the Westborough Historical Society in 1904. Dr. Francis Parkman's diaries are also at the MHS, as well as a listing of books in his library ("Library Catalogue of [the Reverend Dr.] Francis Parkman").

4. For Parkman's academic record, see "Record of the College Faculty," XII, 4, 23, Harvard Archives.

5. Parkman's extensive reading lists are found in Term Books, Library Charge Lists, Harvard Archives and "Entry of Books Borrowed," Boston Athenaeum.

6. See chapter 6 for a critique of Parkman's problems in documenting the "conspiracy" of Pontiac. His legal training may or may not have helped him. The argument can be made that rules of evidence used by a lawyer are quite different than those used by a historian. John Reid, legal historian at New York University, has argued that lawyers may stress the importance of an individual fact in examining controversial material according to rules of evidence. A single fact may overturn a case. Conversations with John Reid, Huntington Library, 2 November 1989. R. G. Collingwood in the *Idea of History* (Oxford, England: Clarendon Press, 1946), p. 268, states that the lawyer is bound by rules of evidence in court cases that involve a verdict that must be given. Moreover, "it is that you give a verdict now."

7. Parkman was an excellent "observer." For instance, he took detailed notes from sites such as Fort William Henry and then entirely reconstructed the fort and its environs on a map with drawings of lines of defense, cannon positions, elevations, and positions of attacking forces. From this visual representation he reconstructed a narrative of the siege. This Fort William map as well as many others is in his collection of maps, Harvard Archives.

8. Wilbur R. Jacobs, ed., *Letters of Francis Parkman*, 2 vols. (Norman, Okla.: University of Oklahoma Press, 1960), I, 16–17. In addition, Parkman describes this episode in his journals. Herein are also handwritten notebooks on Parkman's various expeditions preserved at the MHS. With minor variations these have been edited by Mason Wade, *The Journals of Francis Parkman*, 2 vols. (New York: Harper, 1947). My citations are to the original manuscript journal notebooks in the PP, MHS.

9. The original MS is in the Harvard Archives, Class of 1841. See Appendix.

10. Ibid.

11. *Letters of Francis Parkman,* I, 48–49.

12. Ibid.

13. Ibid.

14. Ibid., II, 53 and n.

15. Ibid., 176. There is a mass of data on the young Parkman in the Parkman family papers, MHS, in PP, MHS, and in Farnham's *Life of Francis Parkman,* pp. 5 ff.; and in Henry Dwight Sedgwick, *Francis Parkman* (Boston: Houghton Mifflin Co., 1904), pp. 3 ff. These two biographies are especially useful because the authors were contemporaries of Parkman and knew him personally.

16. *Letters of Francis Parkman,* I, 176.

17. Parkman's autobiographical letter of 1864, ibid., I, 175–184.

18. See Sigmund Freud, "The Psychology of Dream Processes, Wish-Fulfillment," in *The Standard Edition of the Complete Works,* ed. James Strachey, 24 vols.

(London: Hogarth Press, 1973), IV, 129 ff. Freud's observations on dreams led him to state that dreams have at their command memories that are inaccessible when awake. Parkman's apparitions in dreams mystified him and led him to conclude that because of stress he had "exhausted" his brain.

19. See, for example, Parkman to his father, 22 June [1841], *Letters of Francis Parkman*, I, 5–7.

20. Erik Erikson's comments on identification throw light on Parkman's relationship with his father. See Erikson's *Identity and the Life Cycle* (New York: Norton Co., 1959) for his view that the son may identify with the father's "hurt" or illness. See especially Erikson's discussion of Bernard Shaw's father's alcoholism, pp. 103 ff. Erikson goes on to argue that increased identification, and confidence in knowing where one is going with the development of self, gives one a sense of well being. See p. 118. This observation gives insight into the improvement of Parkman's health as he matured and had self-confidence in his literary objectives.

Sexual origins of father identification are described by Sigmund Freud in *Standard Edition*, XIX, 28 ff., 176 ff. Freud argues that the relationship of a youth to his father is often ambivalent, ranging from hate to admiration. See ibid., XXI, 183.

21. *Letters of Francis Parkman*, I, 17.

22. See reproductions of Remington's drawings in the Remington edition of *The Oregon Trail* (Boston: Little, Brown & Co., 1892).

23. Caroline Hall Parkman to Caroline Parkman, 29 March 1849, PP, MHS.

24. *Letters of Francis Parkman*, I, 60.

25. Ibid., I, 71.

26. Ibid., I, 77.

27. Ibid., I, 88, 90.

28. Ibid., I, 103.

29. Ibid., I, 97, 127.

30. Ibid., I, 175–184, 184n.

31. Ibid., II, 58, 64.

32. Ibid., II, 196 and n., 210, 211n, 236.

33. Benjamin Perley Poore, journalist, editor, and author, sold Parkman duplicates of documents already available to him and tried to sell him "an elaborate and artistic collection" on linen paper. Parkman accused Poore of fraud and turned over his records of Poore's duplicity (along with accounts of funds loaned to Poore) to his attorney, Francis E. Parker, in 1856. Parkman demanded a note from Poore for $128, "payable in three years, with full security for principal and interest." See ibid., I, 109–112 and n.

34. Ibid., I, 69, 70 and n., and Cleveland Amory's "Dr. Parkman Takes a Walk," in William Bentinck-Smith's *The Harvard Book* (Cambridge: Harvard University Press, 1953), 119–134; Simon Schama, *Dead Certainties: Unwarranted Speculations* (New York: Alfred Knopf, 1991), pp. 171–318.

35. *Letters of Francis Parkman*, I, 175–184, 184n ff.

2. THE CONQUEST OF THE "ENEMY"

1. *Letters of Francis Parkman,* I, 134n., 137; Nathan G. Hale, Jr., *Freud and the Americans: The Beginnings of Psychoanalysis in the United States* (New York: Oxford University Press, 1971), p. 36.

2. *Letters of Francis Parkman,* I, 137.

3. Parkman's correspondence reveals that his complaints about illness showed a sharp decline after he came under Mitchell's care, 1869−1870.

4. I am indebted to Edward Harnegel, M.D., San Marino, California, internist and historian of medicine and an authority on Dr. S. Weir Mitchell, for advice on Mitchell's prescriptive techniques and uses of arsenic. See also Mitchell's volume, *Clinical Lessons on Nervous Diseases* (Philadelphia, 1897), Huntington Library, Rare Book No. 3921FEAZ, pp. 3, 14, 28, 29, 58, 89, 220, 233; Hale, *Freud and the Americans,* pp. 34, 41, 46.

5. See note 4 above.

6. See Ernest Earnest, *S. Weir Mitchell: Novelist and Physician* (Philadelphia: University of Pennsylvania Press, 1950), p. 83. Many of Mitchell's publications are cited and quoted in this older, factual biography. See pp. 80−86, 227−228, 253.

7. Hale, *Freud and the Americans,* pp. 40 ff. has a discussion on American "civilized" morality and dangers of exhaustion because of too much "brain work."

8. Hale makes a perceptive analysis of Howells's view of proper behavior. See *Freud and the Americans,* pp. 43. Parkman's correspondence indicates that he read Howells's novels and was critical when Howells allowed characters, such as the businessman Silas Lapham, to take on manners of a gentleman. See *Letters of Francis Parkman,* II, 70, 70n; William Dean Howells, *Literary Friends and Acquaintance* (New York: Harper, 1900), pp. 140−142.

9. Hale, *Freud and the Americans,* pp. 40 ff. Karen Lystra, in her penetrating book on Victorian romantic love, *Searching the Heart: Women, Men, and Romantic Love in Nineteenth-Century America* (New York: Oxford University Press, 1989), points out that Victorian advice books (see list of titles, pp. 325−328) were written by "restrictionists," some of them suggesting continence for long periods. See pp. 108 ff.

John Cowan, M.D., an "extreme restrictionist," in his *The Science of Life* (New York: Cowan & Co., 1873), Huntington Library, Rare Book No. 145321, in his chapter on the "Law of Continence," pp. 114−130, cautions that the male "sexual organism" should not be exercised "unless for reproduction." He advocates male continence for twenty-one months and daily walks of five to ten miles. See pp. 117, 130. The first nine pages of Cowan's book contain excerpts from enthusiastic reviewers, including Parkman's friend and future biographer, Unitarian minister Octavious B. Frothingham, who reported that the book's "purpose was high, its counsel noble, its spirit earnest, humane and pure" (p. 3).

Parkman was undoubtedly familiar with this book, considering the wide publicity it had. Moreover, Cowan's advocacy of five- to ten-mile walks for the "gentleman" may have influenced Parkman, who did take such walks, aided by his cane. See Howells, *Literary Friends and Acquaintance,* p. 141.

Despite the impact of many Victorian advice books, Lystra argues convincingly that the restrictive advice was ignored by the many lovers she studied. (See Lystra, *Searching the Heart*, p. 101.) Nevertheless, it is my opinion that Parkman was one of those exceptions who, under the guiding eye of members of his extended family and later, Dr. Mitchell, treaded the Puritan path of continence no matter what the price in anxiety.

10. The vivacious Sybil would have nothing to do with female physicians, but she regarded her male doctor as "a priceless friend." Silas Mitchell, *Dr. North and His Friends* (Bloomington, Ind.: Indiana University Press, 1950), p. 241.

11. Insight on Parkman's illness is offered by Karen Horney in the *Collected Works of Karen Horney*, 2 vols. (New York: W. W. Norton & Co., 1945). She argues that a person under inner stress may become alienated from his real self and then shift his energies to a task of remodeling himself. In a search for self-realization and self-idealization the person with neurotic ambition may embark upon a "search for glory" and attempt to excel in all things. See I, 186 ff.; II, 13, 23, 65–88. Heinz Kohut offers further insight on Parkman's illness in his *Restoration of the Self* (New York: International Universities Press, 1977), where he discusses Parkmanlike narcissistic personality disorders and the problems such a person has in maintaining a sense of equilibrium. See pp. 13 ff., 122 ff., and 192 ff.

12. *Letters of Francis Parkman*, II, 181.

13. Ibid., I, 80.

14. See Parkman's autobiographical letter of 1864, ibid., I, 175–184.

15. Ibid., II, 141.

16. Conversations with medical historian Edward Harnegel, M.D., Huntington Library, 20–27 November 1989.

17. Found by Mabel Billington, wife of the late historian, Ray A. Billington, in a secret drawer of Parkman's desk. The desk is a large one with multiple drawers on two sides and several small compartments deep inside larger storage areas. It had been moved from his former home at 50 Chestnut St., Boston, to a room restored as his study at the Colonial Society of Massachusetts building on Beacon Hill at 87 Mount Vernon Street.

18. For an account of Lord Randolph Churchill's long battle with syphilis, see R. F. Foster, *Lord Randolph Churchill: A Political Life* (Oxford: Oxford University Press, 1981), pp. 58, 59, 218–219, 377, 389.

19. Consulting physicians of the Santa Barbara Mental Hygiene Clinic and members of the Psychology Department of the University of California, Santa Barbara. I am also grateful to the late Henry Murray of Harvard University, Peter Loewenburg of the University of California, Los Angeles, and Andrew Rolle of Occidental College for assistance in describing Parkman's illness.

Further information on a possible Parkman diagnosis can be found in the *Diagnostic Statistical Manual for Mental Disorder*, 3d ed., rev. (Washington, D.C.: American Psychiatric Association, 1987), p. 459. Here, coded, 300.5, is the neurotic disorder, neurasthenia, characterized by "fatigue, irritability, headache, depression, insomnia, difficulty in concentration, lack of capacity for enjoyment . . ." Neurasthenia can be associated with physical disorders. I am especially grateful to Peter

Loewenburg for calling my attention to this disorder that appears to fit Parkman's mental illness.

20. Parkman's autobiographical letter in *Letters of Francis Parkman*, I, 175–184.

21. See note 20, chapter 1.

22. *Letters of Francis Parkman*, I, 169.

23. Louis Casamajor, "The Illness of Francis Parkman," *American Journal of Psychiatry* 107 (April 1951): 749–752. Casamajor further argues that Parkman's eye trouble could not be traced to compound astigmatism or to anisikonia, as suggested by George M. Gould, *Biographic Clinics* (Philadelphia: P. Blackiston's Son & Co., 1904), pp. 131–193, and Bernard DeVoto, *Year of Decision* (Boston: Little, Brown & Co., 1943), p. 496.

24. E. C. Atwater, "The Lifelong Sickness of Francis Parkman (1823–1893)," *Bulletin of the History of Medicine* 41 (September–October 1977): 413–439. Dr. Atwater has also written about William H. Prescott's illness, stressing iritis and arthritis: "William H. Prescott, 1796–1859, An Early Report of Iritis with Arthritis," *New England Journal of Medicine* 225 (1 December 1966): 1228–1232.

25. See Parkman's letters to Charles Eliot Norton, 13 July 1848, and 22 September 1850, *Letters of Francis Parkman*, I, 54–55, 76–77.

26. Ibid., I, 98–99.

27. Parkman was preparing his new edition as early as 1866. See *Letters of Francis Parkman*, II, 7. Parkman later told Edward Eggleston in a letter of 27 April 1879 that *Pontiac* was based upon "Time and labor employed in gathering obscure and widely scattered material visiting and studying localities, and becoming personally familiar with Indians under their primitive conditions." Ibid., II, 128.

28. Parkman's first edition of LaSalle was written without use of a corpus of documents owned by the Parisian archivist, Pierre Margry. Parkman's perseverance in assisting Margry to publish his documents (through a U.S. Congressional appropriation) is described in *Letters of Francis Parkman*, II, 4. Parkman's only reward was the chance of changing certain parts of his earlier biography of LaSalle for a new edition. E. N. Feltzkog, in his edition of *The Oregon Trail* (Madison: University of Wisconsin Press, 1969), pp. 11a–75a, states that Parkman made some seven thousand changes in the three main editions of the book, those of 1849, 1872, and 1892, the first version being printed in the *Knickerbocker Magazine*. A full collation of all nine so-called "editions" is in Feltzkog's unpublished doctoral dissertation, "Francis Parkman's Oregon Trail . . ." (University of Illinois, 1966).

29. "Records of the St. Botolph Club," St. Botolph Club, Boston.

30. "The Tale of the Ripe Scholar," *Nation* 9 (23 December 1869): 558–560.

31. Underwood to Parkman, 7 September 1887, PP, MHS.

32. Henry Cabot Lodge, *Early Memories* (New York: C. Scribners, 1913), p. 323. For Lodge, Parkman, despite his disabilities, had the image of a man with heroic qualities. "I have never seen a finer face," he wrote. "Whatever the details, the effect was beauty; intellect, force, character, breeding, distinction . . . and, despite all that he had passed through, so powerful had been his will that he had no expression of suffering nor in the least the look of an invalid" (p. 324).

33. Special Meeting, 21 November 1893, Dr. George Ellis in the Chair, *Proceedings of the Massachusetts Historical Society, 1892–1894*, 2d ser., 8 (1894): 360–361.

This heroic portrait of Parkman appears again in an essay on Parkman after an interview conducted shortly before his death. See Julius H. Ward, "Francis Parkman," *McClure's Magazine* 2, no. 2 (January 1894): 185–198. Although "to realize his personality is difficult," the author concluded, Parkman "remade himself." "He brought his will into subjection to an enfeebled body, and determined to put every bit of strength that was left to him into the work he wished to do. I have never met a man with the same superb gifts of mind and soul" (p. 191).

3. THE HERO ON THE OREGON TRAIL

1. Stimulated by Parkman's experience and the fieldwork of modern anthropologist friends, I have visited numerous Indian reservations and spent a short time with Australian aborigines and native people of the Sepic River area of New Guinea. The results of my research are in a chapter, "The Price of Progress," in *Dispossessing the American Indian*, 2d ed. (Norman, Okla.: University of Oklahoma Press, 1985), pp. 126–149.

2. I am indebted to anthropologist Henry Dobyns for these comments on Parkman's "fieldwork."

3. Samuel E. Morison, ed., *The Parkman Reader: From the Works of Francis Parkman* (Boston: Little, Brown & Co., 1955), p. 16. Morison's interpretation is documented by Parkman's views as expressed in his letters. For instance, in writing to Henry Stevens from Boston on 29 October 1846, he reported: "I have just returned from a rather long trip—to the Rocky Mountains, where I saw plenty of Indians, and had fine opportunities of observing them in all circumstances. They were the true Simon pure—no beggarly reprobates such as you see on the frontier. I was about fourteen hundred miles west of the Mississippi—travelled twenty three hundred miles on horseback—and hunted buffalo to my heart's content." John Buechler, ed., *The Correspondence of Francis Parkman and Henry Stevens, 1844–1885*, Transactions of the American Philosophical Society, New Series, vol. 57, part 6 (Philadelphia, Pa.: American Philosophical Society, August 1967), p. 16.

4. See chapter 6 for an analysis of Parkman's conception of the forces of nature and their role in reconstructing key episodes in history, and chapter 7 for discussion of Parkman's literary skills as a historian storyteller.

5. *The Oregon Trail*, pp. 4–5. (Unless otherwise indicated, references to *The Oregon Trail* are to the volume in the 1899 Frontenac edition of Parkman's works.) Jack Scherting in a provocative article suggests that wide, rolling, watery plains in *The Oregon Trail* narrative influenced Herman Melville's imagery in *Moby Dick*. See Scherting, "Tracking the *Pequod* along the Oregon Trail: The Influence of Parkman's Narrative on Imagery and Characters in *Moby Dick*," *Western American Literature* 22, no. 1 (May 1987): 3–15.

6. Oregon Trail Journals, original MS, vol. 2, pp. 103–104, PP, MHS.

7. *The Oregon Trail*, pp. 331–335.

8. This passage, especially the words, "surely there could be no harm in shooting such a hideous old villain," reveals a streak of cruelty in Parkman's character. In one of his early letters to his friend, Henry O. White, 5 February 1843, (*Letters of Francis Parkman*, I, 12), Parkman tells of his pleasure in killing chickadees, one of the tamest of all North American wild birds: "One great amusement of mine has been to sit in a grove of pine or hemlock, a cigar in my mouth, and rifle across my knee, and take off the heads of the chick-a-dees with a bullet. But I have come to the conclusion that the sport is too barbarous." In concluding that the indiscriminate slaughter of the chickadee was barbarous and by eliminating the passage about shooting the old Indian, Parkman showed that he was aware of possible criticism for cruelty in contemplating the murder of another human being. In the paragraph inserted in the 1849 edition of *The Oregon Trail* and later deleted, Parkman compared the killing of a buffalo with the thrill and "fierce delight of the battlefield." Although Parkman never participated as a soldier in the Civil War battles, he seems to have found his substitute in hunting.

The chapter on "The Buffalo Camp," detailing hunting in September 1846, is filled with descriptions of wanton slaughter of buffalo. Quincy Shaw delighted in cutting off tails for trophies. Henry Chatillon killed for meat needed for food, but Parkman and Shaw seem to have had enormous pleasure in killing for sport. Parkman justifies the killings, arguing that no one could have sympathy for huge ugly bulls: "The buffalo came issuing from the hills . . . to drink at the river. All our amusements were to be at their expense. An old buffalo is a brute of unparalleled ugliness. At first sight of him every feeling of pity vanishes . . . against the bulls we waged unrelenting war. . . . Waylaying the buffalo . . . and shooting them as they come to the water is the easiest method of hunting them." See *The Oregon Trail*, pp. 418–421.

9. There is uncertainty about Norton's role in assisting Parkman with the publication of the 1849 edition. Parkman's correspondence of 1848 with Norton indicates that Norton probably made few changes beyond correcting proofs of the book. Parkman to Norton, 12 September 1848 contains this acknowledgement to Norton: "With regard to your very friendly offers to read proofs on *The Oregon Trail*, I think I may very thankfully accept them." In an autobiographical letter, Norton later described the assistance he gave Parkman: "During my years in the countinghouse [of the East India Merchants Bullard and Lee] a casual acquaintance with Frank Parkman developed into a friendship which lasted through life. He was then printing in the 'Knickerbocker Magazine,' if I remember rightly, his first book, 'The Oregon Trail,' and when it was to be published as a volume he asked me to revise the numbers, and many an evening, when there was not other work to be done, was spent by me and him in the solitary counting-room in going over his work." See *Letters of Francis Parkman*, I, 55n, 56. E. N. Feltskog, in his introduction to *The Oregon Trail*, argues that Norton did little more than correct Parkman's proofs, an interpretation that varies with Mason Wade's view that Norton took a large part of the spontaneity out of Parkman's narrative. See Feltskog, ed., *The Oregon Trail*, pp. 60a–63a, and Wade, *Francis Parkman*, pp. 286–287.

10. "The Oregon Trail: Or a Summer's Journey Out of Bounds," by a Bostonian, appeared in successive issues of the *Knickerbocker Magazine,* vol. 29 – 30, February 1847 to February 1849. Chapters 10, "The War Parties," 12, "Ill-Luck," and 17, "The Black Hills," were not published in the *Knickerbocker,* appearing for the first time in the 1849 edition.

This first edition was published in both paper and cloth covers with a lithographed frontispiece (portraying Indians on horseback) by Felix O. C. Darley, who was later commissioned to illustrate Washington Irving's works. G. P. Putnam, writing to Parkman 30 March 1849, complained that paper-covered volumes were going out of style: "The last ed. n. (1000) of the Trail is now all sold—including paper covers—The second ed. n (500) will be ready tomorrow . . . The paper books are fast going out of favor—& I dislike them particularly." This letter is quoted in James E. Walsh, "The California and Oregon Trail: A Bibliographical Study," in *The New Colophon: A Book-Collector's Miscellany,* 3 vols. (New York: Duschnes, Crawford, 1948 – 1950), III, 279 – 285.

Putnam's reference to a second edition is, of course, reference to a second printing. The article cited above by James E. Walsh has a detailed description of minute differences (differences in type, advertising, and pagination) between the first, second, and third printings of *The Oregon Trail* in 1849. Copies of 1849 printings are located in the Massachusetts Historical Society, the Huntington Library, San Marino, and in the Bancroft Library (Berkeley, California), and in the Brown, Harvard, Yale, University of California, Santa Barbara, and New York Public Libraries. The Huntington Library owns a copy of the 1872 edition (Rare Book No. 337235) that formerly belonged to Jack London with marginal notations on such varied topics as Daniel Boone's grandson (p. 127), Catlin the artist (p. 103), and the American fur company (p. 99).

Under the imprint of J. C. Riker in 1854, an additional reprint was published that retained the word *California* in the title. Orville A. Roorbock, *Supplement to the Bibliotheca Americana, A Catalogue of American Publications* . . . (New York, 1855), p. 149.

11. *The Oregon Trail* continued to be published as a volume in Parkman's collected works in successive editions by Little, Brown & Co.: 1894 (Author's ed.); 1898 (Chaplain ed., limited to 1,200 copies); 1899 (New Library ed.); 1899 and 1907 (Frontenac eds.). In 1925 it appeared once more (color illustrations by N. C. Wyeth) under the Little, Brown imprint.

In addition, the book has been continually reprinted in the last fifty years with introductions by a number of writers: David Levin (New York: Penguin Library, 1954); Henry Steele Commager (New York: Modern Library [1949]); A. B. Guthrie, Jr. (New York: New American Library [1950]). An attractive edition was edited by Mason Wade and illustrated by Maynard Dixon under the imprint of the Heritage Press (New York, 1943). A 1911 edition with an introduction by William Macdonald (Chicago: Scott, Foresman) was designed for use in secondary schools.

According to figures supplied by Little, Brown & Co., sales for *The Oregon Trail* were 13,541 copies in the period 1873 – 1893, and in the years since 1893, 103,279.

In addition, 7,549 copies were sold in sets of Parkman's works. Morison, ed., *The Parkman Reader*, p. 523.

12. Parkman's fascination with exploration, both as an explorer-hero, as a young man, and as a writer about North American explorers in his mature years, may also be related to what has been called the Ulysses factor. The English writer, J. R. L. Anderson, in his volume *The Ulysses Factor: The Exploring Instinct in Man* (New York: Harcourt Brace Jovanovich, 1970) states that this factor involves, on the part of explorers, "deliberate risk-taking in pursuit of a goal of no apparent value" (pp. 20–21). These explorers are, he states, type figures in a real world of "heroes, or their prototypes" (p. 23). Andrew Rolle, psychoanalyst as well as professional historian, sees the Ulysses factor as a possible explanation for the behavior of the young John Charles Frémont in a convincing essay, "Exploring an Explorer: Psychohistory and John Charles Frémont," *Pacific Historical Review* 51, no. 2 (May 1982): 135–163. There appear to be some parallels in the behavior of the youthful Frémont and Parkman. See especially Rolle's discussion of Frémont's narcissism and bravura, pp. 152–157.

4. *PONTIAC*: THE STRUGGLE TO RE-CREATE FRONTIER HISTORY

1. Parkman's autobiographical letter to Martin Brimmer [1885], PP, MHS. Printed in Sedgwick, *Francis Parkman*.

2. Ibid. See also *Letters of Francis Parkman*, I, 175–185; II, 198n.

3. Farnham, *Life of Francis Parkman*, pp. 52, 68, 78.

4. Doughty, *Francis Parkman*, p. 162.

5. Mason Wade makes a convincing argument on this point. *Francis Parkman*, p. 327.

6. *Vassal Morton: A Novel* (Boston: Philips, Sampson & Co., 1856), p. 37. An English edition of Thierry's *History of the Conquest of England by the Normans* was printed in London as early as 1841, but Parkman may have used French editions, published in Paris throughout the 1830s.

7. Farnham, *Life of Francis Parkman*, pp. 143–144; *A Half-Century of Conflict*, Frontenac ed. (Boston: Little, Brown & Co., 1899), I, 345, has an account of Parkman's first observation of Indians at the age of thirteen while they were dancing on the Boston Common.

8. Translation of Loudoun Papers, No. 4134, Huntington Library, an original manuscript signed in Montcalm's childlike handwriting.

9. Loudoun Papers, No. 4050. See also E. B. O'Callaghan et al., eds. *Documents relative to the colonial history of the state of New York*, 15 vols. (Albany, N.Y.: Weed Parson and Co., 1853–1887), X, 602, 612, 628.

10. "Opinion of the Several Officers Regarding the Defense of Fort William Henry," 9 August 1757, Loudoun Papers, No. 4158 A.

11. Loudoun Papers, No. 4050.

12. James Fenimore Cooper, *The Last of the Mohicans* (New York, 1826), p. 207.

13. *The Works of James Fenimore Cooper*, Author's rev. ed. (New York: G. P.

Putnam, 1851). *North American Review* 74 (January 1852): 147–161. This is an unsigned review, but internal evidence and citations by Farnham indicate that Parkman was the author.

14. *North American Review* 74 (January 1852): 155. Robert F. Sayre, in a discussion of Cooper's Indians in his volume on *Thoreau and the American Indians* (Princeton: Princeton University Press, 1977), argues that Cooper put words of criticism about whites in the mouths of "bad" Indians such as Magua. More philosophic utterances are in the words of doomed but "good" Indians. And the thoughtful comments are by the white man, Leatherstocking, possessor of Indian skills and the better traits of Indians, p. 13.

15. *North American Review* 74 (January 1852): 155.

16. Ibid., pp. 156–167. There are passages in this review that show that Parkman saw Leatherstocking as a blend of Puritan and Indian virtues. See ibid., and Richard Slotkin, *Regeneration Through Violence: The Mythology of the American Frontier, 1600–1860* (Middletown, Conn.: Wesleyan University Press, 1973), p. 512.

17. *The Old Régime*, Frontenac ed. (Boston: Little, Brown & Co., 1899), I, 118 ff. This battle, the most celebrated of Canada's "Heroic Age," still has Parkman's coloration in later Canadian histories. See also Bruce Trigger's comments on the episode in *Natives and Newcomers: Canada's "Heroic Age" Reconsidered* (Kingston, Canada: McGill-Queens University Press, 1986), p. 281.

18. Mark Twain, "Fenimore Cooper's Literary Offenses," in *How to Tell a Story and Other Essays* (New York: Harper & Brothers, 1897), p. 82.

19. *North American Review* 74 (January 1852): 149.

20. Ibid., 155.

21. Ibid., 155–156. Lee Clark Mitchell, in his well-documented study, *Witnesses to a Vanishing America: The Nineteenth Century Response* (Princeton: Princeton University Press, 1981), pp. 43–44, 173, argues that Cooper in *The Deerslayer* gave us one of "the first [writings] devoted to faithful fictional portraits of native tribes" because he read extensively in missionary accounts, government reports, and histories. Mitchell cites articles by Paul A. W. Wallace, "Cooper's Indians," *New York History* 35 (October 1954): 424–427; Gregory L. Paine, "The Indians in the Leatherstocking Tales," *Studies in Philology* 23 (1926): 20–21, 30, 39; and William Goetzmann, "James Fenimore Cooper," in *Landmarks of American Writing,* ed. Hennig Cohen (New York: Basic Books, 1969), p. 71 (in Cooper "time *and* progress stand still"). See also Doughty, *Francis Parkman*, pp. 89 ff.; Louis O. Saum, "'Nature's Nation,' Enlarged and Penitent," *New Mexico Historical Review* 57, no. 2 (April 1982): 183–189. In H. Daniel Peck, *A World By Itself: The Pastoral Moment in Cooper's Fiction* (New Haven: Yale University Press, 1977), a chapter on "The Primacy of the Image," pp. 3–17, stresses Cooper's penchant for visual accuracy. He wrote *The Pilot* to correct inaccurate images of nautical life found in Sir Walter Scott's sea novel, *The Pirate*. His images of Lake George, "the Holy Lake," and the distant view of nature tending to mitigate the harsh realism of "extensive earthen ramparts" (p. 112), were copied by Parkman and incorporated into a college oration, "Romance in America."

22. Jared Sparks in a letter to Parkman on 30 April 1842, PP, MHS, in a "list of

books relating to the Old French War," recommended Mante's *History* along with the *Annual Register*, with its "chapters relating to America," *Washington's Writings*, "Major [Robert] Rogers' *Journal*," and a set of plans of forts and maps.

23. Parkman to Lyman C. Draper, 23 December 1845, *Letters of Francis Parkman*, I 32.

24. Edited and translated by William N. Fenton and Elizabeth L. Moore under the title of *Customs of the American Indians Compared With the Customs of Primitive Times*, 2 vols. (Toronto: The Champlain Society, 1974). Parkman regarded Lafitau as a pioneer in scientific anthropology, and Fenton states that the Jesuit missionary was one of the first of the Iroquoianists. See I, xxix, 60n, 291, 292n, 294n, 296n, 297n. Editor Fenton, principal Iroquois scholar today, uses Parkman's *History* for identification and expansion of details in Lafitau. Parkman's *Jesuits'* introduction on the woodland Indians was drawn partly from Lafitau. And although Parkman had used Schoolcraft's *Notes on the Iroquois* and Lewis H. Morgan's *League of the Iroquois* (1851), he still returned to consult Lafitau because "none of the old writings are so satisfactory as Lafitau." Fenton, ed., "Lafitau," in *Customs of the American Indians*, I, 291n. Parkman, *The Jesuits of North America in the Seventeenth Century*, Frontenac ed. (Boston: Little, Brown & Co., 1899), I, 44.

25. Parker to Parkman, 22 December 1851, PP, MHS, printed in Farnham, *Life of Francis Parkman*, Appendix C, pp. 374–378.

26. Ibid.

27. Ibid.

28. Wade, *Francis Parkman*, pp. 314–315, comments on this part of Parkman's plan of writing.

29. Mitchell, *Witnesses to a Vanishing America*, pp. 18–19, stresses this point.

30. Lewis H. Morgan, *Ancient Society, or Researches in the Lines of Human Progress from Savagery Through Barbarism to Civilization* (New York: Henry Holt & Co., 1877), pp. 458–508. Morgan illustrated his theme by citing the invention of the arrow by the savage, followed by the discovery of iron smelting by barbarians and the construction of railroads as an achievement of civilization. Parallel evidence of cultural evolution could be found in similarity of kinship terminology among some seventy Indian tribes and in the transition of the family from savage promiscuity to the patriarchal family of early civilization. These theories are questioned today by many anthropologists. Henry Dobyns, leading anthropologist, has affirmed this point in correspondence, August 1984.

31. William N. Fenton, "The Iroquois Confederacy in the Twentieth Century: A Case Study of the Theory of Lewis H. Morgan in 'Ancient Society,'" *Ethnology* 4 (July 1965): 263. See also Morgan, *Ancient Society*, p. 146, for the statement that the "germ" of the chief executive concept among the Five Nations was "the Great War Soldier of the Iroquois."

32. Morgan, for example, did use the phrase, "our Indian people." See *League of the Ho-de-Ne-Sau-Nee, or Iroquois* (New York, 1851), p. 456. Francis Jennings stresses this issue in a critique of Morgan in *The Ambiguous Iroquois Empire: The Covenant Chain Confederation of Indian Tribes with English Colonies from its Beginnings to the Lancaster Treaty of 1744* (New York: W. W. Norton, 1984), pp. 18–19.

33. Margaret T. Hodgen, *Early Anthropology in the Sixteenth and Seventeenth Centuries* (Philadelphia: University of Pennsylvania Press, 1964), p. 369. Hodgen maintains that often missionaries were inclined to treat the failings of their charges with indulgence. Sometimes, too, praise of aborigines was linked to economic motives, including propaganda to encourage colonial emigration. Ibid. At the same time there were instances of cultural relativism because of the countless types of Indian behavior. It was not sufficient to give an image of a tribe as good or bad. Cultural diversity however was an escape as a statement of fact, because it enabled the writer or observer to avoid accepting a new moral criterion or an older one. Ibid., p. 373.

34. Ibid., p. 369. For an example of Las Casas' imagery of maltreated Indian people, see his *The Tears of the Indians: Being An Historical and True Account of the Cruel Massacres and Slaughters of Above Twenty Millions of Innocent People Committed by Spaniards* . . . (London, 1656), pp. 1–3, 20, 44–45, 109. Lafitau gives us the image of an Onondaga council as a greasy assemblage of Indians sitting with their knees high in front of them, debating affairs of state. His *Moeurs des sauvages ameriquains* . . . (Paris, 1724), 2 vols., was edited and translated by William F. Fenton and Elizabeth L. Moore. See Hodgen, *Early Anthropology,* p. 94. For an excellent description of stereotyped images of Indian treachery, savagery in treatment of captives, and barbaric behavior, see descriptions from seventeeth-century sources in Maurice Marc Wasserman, "The American Indian as Seen by the Seventeenth Century Chroniclers," (Ph.D. diss., University of Pennsylvania, 1954, University Microfilms, Xerox copy No. 7818), pp. 310, 324, 336 ff. A number of these chroniclers, some of them eyewitnesses, are cited by Parkman. Most Europeans, including explorers and conquistadors from Columbus to Cortez, considered Indians far from being enlightened children of nature; they were, instead, as Anthony Pagden argues in a well-documented essay, "debased" creatures who had demonstrated that they were "incapable of understanding God's design for the world . . . more like tame animals than real men because they 'had no knowledge . . . and no experience whatsoever of things.'" "The Savage Critic: Some European Images of the Primitive," in *The Yearbook of English Studies: Colonial and Imperial Themes,* ed. G. K. Hunter and C. J. Rawson, 20 vols. (Leeds, England: Modern Humanities Research Association, 1983), XIII, 32–45. Karen Kupperman, in her perceptive work *Settling with the Indians: The Meeting of English and Indian Cultures* (Totowa, N.J.: Rowman and Littlefield, 1980), concludes that Indians were seen as "treacherous" and inferior, pp. 170–176. Robert F. Berkhofer argues that early images of Indian "deficiency" justified secular and religious policies of exploitation. *The White Man's Indian* (New York: Alfred Knopf, 1978), pp. 132–134.

5. NOBLE-IGNOBLE INDIAN PORTRAITS

1. *The Oregon Trail,* p. 356, quoted in Louise K. Barnett, *The Ignoble Savage: American Literary Racism, 1790–1890* (Westport, Conn.: Greenwood Press, 1975), p. 127. Elsewhere in *The Oregon Trail,* Parkman refers to "half-breeds" as part of "a mongrel race," p. 87. The Indian "half-breed" had a "black and snakey eye," but the

French "half-breed" such as Le Rouge had "small eyes that twinkled . . . with a mischievous luster." For Parkman, the greater the Indian blood, the greater the "half-devil" image. See *The Oregon Trail,* pp. 356 ff.

2. E. N. Feltzog, in his edition of *The Oregon Trail,* p. 646, makes this argument, quoting Alexander Ross's *Fur Hunters of the Far West,* ed. Kenneth A. Spaulding (Norman, Okla.: University of Oklahoma Press, 1956), p. 196: "Half-breeds, . . . from the peculiar color of their skins, being of swarthy hue, as if sunburnt, as they grow up resemble, almost in every respect, the pure Indian. They are indolent, thoughtless, and improvident. Licentious in their habits, unbounded in their desires, sullen in their disposition. Proud, restless, and clannish, fond of flattery. They alternately associate with the white and the Indians. . . . They form the composition of all the bad qualities of both."

3. A. Irving Hallowell, "The Backwash of the Frontier: The Impact of the Indian on American Culture," in *The Frontier Perspective,* ed. W. D. Wyman and C. B. Kroeber (Madison: University of Wisconsin Press, 1957), pp. 246 ff. There is a corpus of literature on the noble- versus ignoble-savage concept in American literature and history in which Parkman is consistently mentioned. Roy Harvey Pearce, *The Savages of America: A Study of the Indian Idea of Civilization* (Baltimore: Johns Hopkins University Press, 1953), pp. 163 ff. sees the "Indian problem" in terms of "the victory of civilization over savagism." Not unexpectedly, Pearce concludes that Parkman's *Pontiac* was "the greatest record of that victory" and that Parkman himself was "the prime historian of the victory of civilization over savagism." Bernhard W. Sheehan in a doctoral dissertation argued in the same vein: "The Indian's penchant for the most exotic brands of violence . . . commanded a realistic appraisal of his savage character." "Civilization and the American Indian in the Thought of the Jefferson Era," (Ph.D. diss., University of Virginia, 1965), pp. 251, 325; later published in substantially the same form by the Institute of Early American History and Culture, Williamsburg, Va. In a later book Sheehan separates statements of fact from attitudes of colonial Virginians toward Indians ("the ignoble savage's character"), p. 64, in *Savagism and Civility: Indians and Englishmen in Colonial Virginia* (Cambridge, England: Cambridge University Press, 1980). Mitchell in *Witnesses to a Vanishing America,* in discussing frontier concepts of Indian barbarity has commentaries on cultural absolutism, cultural relativism, and ethnocentrism, pp. 18−20 ff., 157−159, 246n−248, 274−275. Calvin Martin in *Keepers of the Game: Indian Animal Relationships in the Fur Trade* (Berkeley: University of California Press, 1978), pp. 166 ff., and in "The War Between Indians and Animals," in *Indians, Animals and the Fur Trade: A Critique of Keepers of the Game,* ed. Shepard Krech (Athens, Ga.: University of Georgia Press, 1981), asserts that certain tribes killed off beaver because their wildlife spirits had infected Indians with disease. See Krech, *Indians, Animals,* pp. 13−18, 174−188.

4. Clifford Geertz, *The Interpretation of Culture: Selected Essays* (New York: Basic Books, 1973), p. 346.

5. *A Half-Century of Conflict,* I, 223. Parkman goes on to ridicule contemporary "apologists" for the Indians, such as "that relic of antique Puritanism, old Samuel Sewell . . . sometimes absurd . . . whose benevolence towards the former

owners of the soil was trebly reinforced by his notion that they were the descendants of the ten lost tribes of Israel."

6. See *North American Review* 103 (July 1866):1−18, "Indian Superstitions," an essay dealing with Schoolcraft's works. Parkman did conclude from his investigations that "the primitive Indian did believe in the immortality of the soul." See p. 11.

7. Parkman did, however, consult Morgan's "letters" on the Iroquois printed in the *North American Review* as early as 1847. These were later incorporated into the *League*. He also corresponded with O. H. Marshall and E. G. Squier, archeologists, and consulted their publications on the Iroquois for *Pontiac*. *Pontiac*, Frontenac ed. (Boston: Little, Brown & Co., 1899), I, 19−20.

8. *Jesuits*, I, 3−87.

9. Parkman was particularly influenced by Lalemant's grisly reports. See R. G. Thwaites, ed., *Jesuit Relations* . . . , 72 vols. (Cleveland, 1898), XVII, 76−77 on feasts and human hands, and *Jesuits*, I, 229, and a variation repeated by Willa Cather, *Shadows on the Rock* (New York: A. A. Knopf, 1931), p. 152 ff.

10. See footnotes in *Pontiac*, I, 4 ff. and *Jesuits*, I, 3 ff. and 22−34. See also index in vols. I and II in *Letters of Francis Parkman* for correspondence relating to Indian history and culture. Herein are references to Parkman's contacts with George Copway, the Ojibwa historian whose work Parkman believed to be unreliable. *Letters of Francis Parkman*, I, 78−79.

11. There is a degree of exaggeration here. Individuals were under the social pressure of well-organized societies. Iroquois clans were very powerful social structures with ritual functions. Chieftainship was formal, well-defined, responsible. Much of this is described in Morgan, *League of the Ho-de-Ne-Sau-Nee, or Iroquois*, and in Bruce G. Trigger, ed., *Handbook of the North American Indians* (Washington, D.C.: Smithsonian Institute, 1978), vol. 15, *The Northeast*, 85−86, 156−167 ff., 308−316, 530−540. As Oren Lyons, Onondaga spiritual leader, recently defined the Iroquois concept of liberty: "The basis of our nation is that the sovereignty of the individual is supreme." Lyons, "An Iroquois Perspective," in *American Indian Environments: Ecological Issues in Native American History*, ed. Christopher Vecsey and Robert Venables (Syracuse, N.Y.: Syracuse University Press, 1980), p. 171. In discussions of Iroquois concepts of liberty, Lyons has stressed the point that his people believe that "an Indian may not be driven from his own land." Hence the Iroquois offered sanctuary to the American Indian Movement leader, Dennis Banks. Because the Iroquois believe in freedom of movement (and have made a determined defense of their treaty rights in the Jay Treaty and later ones, giving the Iroquois free movement across the Canadian-U.S. border), they have their own international passports, now accepted in nineteen nations. Lyons' comments were made in sessions of the conference on "Indian Self-Rule," 17−20 August 1983, Institute of the American West, Sun Valley, Idaho. I have been a speaker on Indian treaties at the Six Nations Longhouse at Onondaga and have heard, with minor variations, Iroquois speakers express concepts of Iroquois freedom and free move-

ment that are similar to those of Oren Lyons. Some of these Iroquois leaders have been visiting speakers in my graduate seminars at the University of California, Santa Barbara.

12. *Pontiac*, I, 4 ff.

13. Ibid.

14. Ibid.

15. *Pontiac*, I, 19–20. Parkman's ability to reconstruct elements of Iroquois life and history is now recognized by some Iroquois scholars. Conversations with Elisabeth Tooker, American Society for Ethnohistory, Annual Meeting, Nashville, Tenn., 13–16 October 1982, and with William Fenton, American Society for Ethnohistory, Annual Meeting, Williamsburg, Va., 10–13 November 1988.

16. *Pontiac*, I, 20–21, 26. See also Trigger, *Handbook of the North American Indians*, vol. 15, *The Northeast*, 303–306, 315–316, 344–356, 544 ff., for an excellent modern description of the history and culture of the Iroquois.

17. *Pontiac*, I, 25.

18. Ibid., I, 31.

19. Ibid., I, 31–32. The word, "perfect," deleted in later editions, appeared in the first edition of *Pontiac* (Boston: Little and Brown, 1851), p. 25.

20. Early anthropologists who wrote on the culture-area concept did not stress archetypes. They discussed diffusion from innovative centers. The theory was clearly proposed as early as 1895 by Otis T. Mason, who suggested twelve "ethnic environments" for the study of Indians in an article, "Influence of Environment upon Human Industries or Arts," in the *Annual Report of the Board of Regents of the Smithsonian Institution, 1895* (Washington, D.C., 1896), pp. 639–665. A. L. Kroeber, Clark Wissler, and later A. Irving Hallowell, Jesse D. Jennings, Harold Driver, and Wendell H. Oswalt have expanded on the theory. Oswalt, for instance, in his *This Land Was Theirs: A Study of the North American Indians*, 3d ed. (New York: Wiley, 1978), pp. 420–453, in a section called "The Iroquois: Warriors and Farmers of the Eastern Woodlands," gives his readers a portrait of the Iroquois as a cultural archetype of the eastern woodlands. He relies in part on Parkman as well as sources Parkman used, including Father Lafitau, Henry Schoolcraft, and Lewis H. Morgan. Much of the same kind of culture-area discussion on the Iroquois and other woodland Indians is in Oswalt's mentor's book, Harold Driver, *Indians of North America*, 2d ed. (Chicago: University of Chicago Press, 1969), pp. 48, 279, 302 ff.

21. *Pontiac*, I, 35. It was the Iroquois who asserted in the 1740s (as early as 1742) that the Delaware were "women" after the Delaware were obliged to move to Iroquois-conquered lands because of land cessions. The metaphor was used by Iroquois chiefs, and attempts were made to read into it deeper connotations. The Delaware later asserted their independence (especially in a speech by Chief White Eyes in 1775). Gregory Schaaf, "George Morgan and George Washington: Beginnings of American Indian Policy in 1775–76," (Ph.D. diss., University of California, Santa Barbara, 1984); Trigger, *Handbook of the North American Indians*, vol. 15, *The Northeast*, 223.

22. *The Oregon Trail*, p. 26.

23. See Parkman's introductory comments on the manuscript in Appendix C, *Pontiac*, II, 352–353; Howard H. Peckham, *Pontiac and the Indian Uprising* (Princeton: Princeton University Press, 1947), pp. III ff., and Wilbur R. Jacobs, *Dispossessing the American Indian*, 2d ed. (Norman, Okla.: University of Oklahoma Press, 1985), pp. 83–93, 201–204. The "Pontiac Manuscript" has been translated as Robert Navarre's *Journal of the Conspiracy of Pontiac* (Detroit: Speaker Hines Printing Co., 1910), by R. Clyde Ford.

24. *Pontiac*, I, 279 and n.

25. Ibid.

26. *Jesuits*, I, 28 and n.

27. Parkman cites Father Vimont's *Relation* of 1642.

28. Thomas S. Abler, "Iroquois Cannibalism: Fact Not Fiction," *Ethnohistory* 27:4 (Fall 1980):309–315. Abler's essay, a refutation of W. Arens, *The Man-Eating Myth: Anthropology & Anthropophagy* (New York: Oxford University Press, 1979), a work that questions Iroquois anthropophagy because, Arens says, there are no eyewitness accounts. Certainly Jesuit accounts must be treated with caution, but as Abler points out, there are indeed eyewitness episodes from the *Jesuit Relations*, and these are similar to nonmissionary accounts, even in details. Abler goes on to state that the writings of Iroquois anthropologists Elisabeth Tooker and Bruce Trigger confirm the reality of torture and cannibalism that he first encountered in reading Parkman.

In a long, heavily documented article on the Huron-Iroquois, the Canadian geographer Conrad E. Heidenreich (see Trigger, *Handbook of the North American Indians*, vol. 15, *The Northeast*, 368–392), describes Huron-Iroquois torture very much as it is found in Parkman (p. 386):

> The torture and death of a prisoner was a highly ritualized affair in which all members of a village participated. Torture was often preceded by adoption into a family who would then address the prisoners as "brother" and "nephew" throughout the ceremony. During the ceremony, which could last several days, the prisoner sang songs and generally tried to project an image of bravery that would reflect favorably on himself and his tribe. At the same time the torturers would increase the ferocity of their activities, culminating in the eating of the heart and other parts of the body. Archeological proof of this activity is sometimes found in middens in the form of bits of human bone.
>
> Descriptions of torture and cannibalism among the Huron indicate that this ritual involved the transformation of normal group behavior into a universal outpouring of pent up emotions. The person who was tortured became in fact a symbol of the tribe he represented, a hate object on whom the frustrations of life and past wrongs could be expended.

29. *Jesuits*, I, 27–28.

30. Ibid., 1–87.

31. Ibid., 87.

32. *Pontiac*, I, 42–43.

33. Although Parkman oversimplified Indian cultural traits with his persistent comments on Indian savagery, there is evidence that he was not in error in attributing certain tribal personality traits to individual tribes. When he pinpointed Iroquois "pride," for instance, he was probably correct. In conversations with me, Elisabeth Tooker, Iroquois specialist, has argued that Parkman was accurate in pointing out that other tribes disliked trading with the Iroquois because of their fickle and sometimes arrogant manner.

D'Arcy McNickle in his influential volume *Indian Tribalism, Indian Survivals and Renewals* (New York: Oxford University Press, 1973), pp. 8 ff., argued persuasively that there are basic Indian personality traits that persist among Indians. The cultural persistence of these personality traits can be observed among Indians tribe by tribe, although there are some traits that can be identified with all Indian peoples. McNickle relies in part on the work of A. Irving Hallowell, who with some of his advanced students, studied two groups of Ojibwa Indians, one with a fishing, trapping, moccasin-wearing lifestyle, a Western Ontario people who lived much as their aboriginal ancestors lived; and another people, a Wisconsin Chippewa (or Ojibwa) who spoke English and lived much as their white neighbors. Hallowell found that his data showed that there was "a body of evidence that all points in the same direction—a persistent core of psychological characteristics sufficient to identify an Ojibwa personality constellation, aboriginal in origin, that is clearly discernible through all levels of acculteration." Hallowell, *Culture and Experience* (Philadelphia: University of Pennsylvania Press, 1955), p. 363. An important point to note here is that a part of Hallowell's research on identification of the Ojibwa personality constellation was his careful investigation into historical sources—the journals of trappers, traders, and missionaries—to reconstruct the basic outlines of a postcontact culture. These seventeenth- and eighteenth-century sources were the same that Parkman used in making his reconstruction of woodland Indian cultures and personality characteristics, although it must be acknowledged that Parkman and Hallowell wrote from different perspectives and frameworks of interpretation. Trigger in *Natives and Newcomers*, pp. 10–14, pinpoints Parkman's stereotypes about Indians, and concludes that "Parkman was a careful student of anthropology" besides being an admirer of James F. Cooper, p. 114.

34. Parkman's volumes are cited in the new edition on the Northeastern Indians, *Handbook of the North American Indians*, vol. 15, representing the cumulative research of leading anthropologists. For references to Parkman, see pp. 8, 47, 862–863. Echoing many of Parkman's interpretations are articles herein written by Elisabeth Tooker, William N. Fenton, and Thomas Abler on the Iroquois and individual tribes. See especially pp. 418, 466, 505, and William N. Fenton's comments on Parkman in his "The Iroquois in the Grand Tradition of American Letters," *American Indian Culture and Research Journal* 5, no. 4 (1981) : 21–39.

35. See Francis Jennings, "A Vanishing Indian: Francis Parkman and His Sources," *Pennsylvania Magazine of History and Biography* 87, no. 3 (July 1963): 306–332; *Pontiac*, I, 150 ff.; *Montcalm and Wolfe*, Frontenac ed. (Boston: Little, Brown & Co., 1899) II, 353–357.

36. There is disagreement about the view that the Iroquois had actually con-

quered an "empire." To eighteenth-century observers, such as William Johnson and Edmond Atkin, both imperial Indian superintendents, and Thomas Mitchell, cartographer, as well as to Cadwallader Colden, historian of the Iroquois, the Iroquois were indeed a redoubtable confederacy that conquered and dominated an inland empire. This concept, incorporated into the writings of Parkman and his contemporary, anthropologist Lewis H. Morgan, is disputed by Francis Jennings in his *The Ambiguous Iroquois Empire* . . . (New York: W. W. Norton, 1984), pp. 10−24, and in comments in Daniel K. Richter and James Merrell, eds., *Beyond the Covenant Chain: The Iroquois and their Neighbors in Indian North America, 1600−1800* (Syracuse, N.Y.: Syracuse University Press, 1987), pp. 75, 78. This view is contested by Calvin Martin in *Reviews in American History* 13, no. 1 (March 1934): 17−20, and by Elisabeth Tooker, *American Historical Review* 90, no. 1 (February 1985): 211−212. Tooker stresses that Parkman was influenced by memory of a formidable Indian presence that still remained in the early nineteenth century. My judgment, after reexamination of historic evidence and conflicting viewpoints in this controversy, is that Parkman, as Jennings argues, did exaggerate the concept of an Iroquois empire, but Parkman also reflected accurately the evidence in his sources and the general interpretation of the warlike Iroquois place in history as seen in the nineteenth century. Parkman's views on economic motives for Iroquois aggression (trade in beaver pelts to satisfy their increasing demands for European goods) are echoed by modern researchers. See, for example, Trigger, *Natives and Newcomers*, pp. 260−266; compare to *Pontiac*, I, 158−184.

6. PONTIAC'S "CONSPIRACY": A TARNISHED BUT ENDURING IMAGE

1. Although Parkman did not use the term *millenarian*, he clearly recognized the impact of the Prophet's prophecies ("his fame spread even to the nations of the northern lakes," *Pontiac*, I, 187) and the significance of smallpox "ravages" (*Pontiac*, I, 377, II, 14, 44−46, 77, 167) in Indian depopulation. He seems, however, not to have connected the epidemics with the Prophet's teachings and the subsequent uprising.

2. *Pontiac*, I, 167, 187; see Henry F. Dobyns, *Their Number Become Thinned: Native American Population Dynamics in Eastern North America* (Knoxville, Tenn.: University of Tennessee Press, 1984), for the impact of epidemic disease on millenarian Indian movements, especially pp. 254, 258, 260, 302−303.

3. *Pontiac*, I, 194−195. Although Parkman had reservations about the use of "conspiracy" in the title, he concluded that "Johnson's dictionary will bear me out in the use of the word." Parkman to G. E. Ellis, 16 July [1850], *Letters of Francis Parkman*, I, 73. In spite of making a number of revisions in various editions of *Pontiac*, Parkman never seems to have considered revising the title or changing his interpretation of Pontiac's role in the uprising. When in 1879 Edward Eggleston approached him on the use of the book for a juvenile-type biography of Pontiac, Parkman declined to give permission: "I would rather that another book on Pontiac should not be published. . . . You have full appreciation of the time & labor

employed in gathering obscure & widely scattered material, visiting and studying localities, & becoming personally familiar with Indians in their primitive conditions" (Ibid., II, 127–128).

4. See Kerlerec to Minister, 4 July 1963, Archives Nationales, Colonies, C13, 43:206; sketch in Reuben G. Thwaites, ed., "The French Régime in Wisconsin— III," *Collections* of the State Historical Society of Wisconsin, 30 vols. (Madison, 1908), XVIII, 221n; *Pontiac*, II, 288–289.

General Thomas Gage, who succeeded Amherst as commander-in-chief of British forces, consistently praised Pontiac's abilities, and, like Parkman, seems to have based his opinion on letters written by D'Abaddie. Writing to the Earl of Halifax, 14 April 1764, Gage said that according to "a paragraph in M. D'Abbadie's letter [no date given], there is reason to judge of Pontiac, not only as a Savage, possessed of the most refined cunning and treachery natural to Indians, but as a person of extra abilities . . . Pontiac keeps two Secretaries, one to write for him, and the other to read the letters he receives, and he manages them so, as to keep each of them ignorant of what is transacted by the other. I proposed to send advice to Major Gladwin (at Detroit) of Pontiac's designs, that he may be on his guard." E. B. O'Callaghan, ed., *Documents Relative to the Colonial History of the State of New York* (Albany, N.Y., 1856), VII, 619–620 (hereafter cited as *New York Col. Docs.*).

5. Peckham, *Pontiac and the Indian Uprising*, pp. 108–111. Peckham writes unconvincingly that "it was not the nature of the Indian mind to foresee all consequences or to prepare for all eventualities," p. 111. In his final assessment of Pontiac as a leader, he writes (p. 321): "Savage though he was, he never degenerated into a whining beggar. The advancing frontier produced many worse examples of manhood, both red and white."

With the inference that Pontiac, as an Indian, was intellectually incapable of organizing a widespread conspiracy, Peckham states, in addition, that there is no documentary evidence that Pontiac in 1762 sent "ambassadors" to other tribes. Parkman's evidence is of course questionable on this point, but Louis Chevrette in his article "Pontiac," in the *Dictionary of Canadian Biography*, vol. 3, *1741–1770*, ed. George W. Brown, David M. Hayne, and Frances L. Halpenny (Toronto: University of Toronto Press and Les Presses de l'université Laval, 1974), 525–531, states that Pontiac was "supposed" to have sent "messages" in 1763 before his attack on Detroit (p. 527). Chevrette also portrays Pontiac in much the same language as Parkman's in evaluating his ability (p. 531): "Pontiac did not lack stature and fought with exceptional discernment and tenacity . . . he also perceived with great acuteness the problems that would afflict Indians for generations to come: the threat of assimilation and the slow taking-over of their lands by a European population."

6. *Pontiac*, I, 190.

7. *Pontiac*, I, 215n.

8. Peckham, as noted above, relied primarily upon Robert Navarre's *Journal of the Conspiracy of Pontiac, 1763*, trans. R. Clyde Ford (Detroit: Speaker Hines Printing Co., 1910), for most of the material in his book relating to the immediate origin of the war. R. Clyde Ford believes that Robert Navarre, the scrivener, was probably the author. C. M. Burton, who wrote the preface to the translation, maintains

that the contents suggest that a priest was not the author of the manuscript. Peckham also relied on the General Thomas Gage Papers in the William Clements Library and the Sir Jeffery Amherst Papers, Public Record Office, War Office 34. The University of Michigan General Library has a microfilm copy of the Amherst Papers. Parkman used similar, and, in some cases, identical manuscripts or copies.

I have examined a mass of documentary material that Parkman traced down and consulted; he used manuscript and printed works relating to Robert Rogers, George Croghan, Sir William Johnson, Sir Jeffery Amherst, General Thomas Gage, General Robert Monckton, Colonel Henry Bouquet, Major Henry Gladwin, and Captain Donald Campbell. Modern guides to manuscript collections were not available to him. Much of the source material today relating to the Indian war is in the Bouquet Papers in the British Museum. The Bouquet correspondence is now published as *The Papers of Col. Henry Bouquet* by the Pennsylvania Historical Survey. Bouquet Papers are also in Series A. in the Canadian Archives. A calendar begun by Douglas Brymer, archivist, to be found in the *Reports* of the Canadian Archives, is very useful in tracing Parkman's sources. As a young man in his twenties, Parkman, of course, had to locate and identify this material, much of it available today in published form.

9. Chevrette, "Pontiac," pp. 525–531.

10. I am indebted to Michael McConnel, who gave me a critique of an earlier version of this chapter and suggested my reading Thomas J. Maxwell's "Pontiac Before 1763," published in *Ethnohistory* 4, no. 1 (Winter 1957): 41–46. McConnel's Ph.D. diss. (William and Mary College, 1983) is "The Search for Security: Indian-English Relations in the Transappalachian Region, 1758–63." See also McConnel's "Peoples 'In Between': The Iroquois and the Ohio Indians, 1720–68," in Daniel K. Richter and James H. Merrell, eds., *Beyond the Covenant Chain* (Syracuse, N.Y.: Syracuse University Press, 1987), pp. 93–112.

11. There is a body of literature on factionalism among Indian chiefs, the kind of fierce rivalry that may have been a factor in Pontiac's death. William N. Fenton points out that factionalism was often between three types of Iroquois leaders: sachems or peace chiefs; pine-tree orators, known for their sagacity and wisdom; and war chiefs, young men who often aspired to become sachems or orators. See Fenton's "Factionalism in American Indian Society," *Tirage à part: Actes du IVe Congrès International des Sciences Anthropologiques et Ethnologiques* (Vienna, 1952), II, 330–340. Modern Indians, trained as historians and anthropologists, however, point to "factionalism" as a racist term when it is confined to Indian societies and their leaders. In contrast, disagreements among white leaders are often dismissed as "politics." Panel discussions on Indian "Self-determination," "Conference on Indian Self-Rule, Fifty Years Under the Indian Reorganization Act," 17–20 August 1983, Sun Valley, Idaho.

12. See *Pontiac*, I, 179–195; Chevrette, "Pontiac," p. 531; W. R. Jacobs, *Wilderness Politics and Indian Gifts* (Lincoln, Neb.: University of Nebraska Press, 1966), pp. 184–185 and notes.

13. The major Seneca towns were located in what is now western New York. In the 1740s and 1750s there is evidence of Seneca movement into the Ohio area. See essay by Thomas S. Abler and Elisabeth Tooker, "Senecas," in Trigger, *Handbook of the North American Indians*, vol. 15, *The Northeast*, 505–507.

14. Parkman uncovered a copy of George Croghan's journal, which he cites. *Pontiac*, I, 185. The modern version is cited by Nicolas B. Wainwright, ed., "George Croghan's Journal, 1759–1763," *Pennsylvania Magazine of History and Biography* 62 (1947): 411. Seneca plans are mentioned in other sources, but Croghan gives details of the secret design of attack.

15. The ancient feud between the southern woodland tribes and the Iroquois was an almost insurmountable barrier to the formation of a large British frontier Indian alliance. As late as October 1762, the Iroquois notified the Pennsylvania government that they desired a route through the settlements so they could continue hostilities against "their old Enemies, the Cherokees." *Minutes of the Provincial Council of Pennsylvania* (Harrisburg, 1852), VII, 779–780 (hereafter cited as *Pennsylvania Colonial Records*).

16. *Pontiac*, I, 190–196. Sometimes known as Guyasuta, Guyashusta, or Kiasola. The secret Seneca plan that Pontiac himself seems to have used in his assault upon the British forts was attributed to Kaiaghshota by the archivist-historian Lyman C. Draper, who interviewed the chief's son and nephew. Draper, Parkman's correspondent, concluded that Kaiaghshota was "an arch-plotter with Pontiac" in the uprising "occasionally known as Guyashusta's War." *Collections* of the State Historical Society of Wisconsin (Madison, 1908), XVIII, 240–241n. See also the sketch of Kaghswaghtaniunt, a Seneca chief who appears to have made friendly overtures to the British at Detroit. Brown et al., *Dictionary of Canadian Biography*, vol. 3, *1741–1770*, 379–380.

17. Daniel Claus to William Johnson, 6 August 1763, in *Collections* of the State Historical Society of Wisconsin (Madison, 1908), XVIII, 256–268; Wainwright, "Croghan's Journal," p. 435. The Seneca chief Kaiaghshota (spelled Keyashuta in the document) later denied responsibility for the uprising, stating that it was the fault of the western Indians and "our foolish young men." See speeches of Seneca and Delaware chiefs, 17 October 1764, in Pennsylvania Historical Survey, *Papers of Col. Henry Bouquet*, ser. 21655 (Harrisburg, Pa., 1940–1943, Mimeographed), pp. 235–236.

18. *The Annual Register or A View of History, Politics, and Literature for the Year 1763* (London, 1796), p. 31. This time factor, mentioned in the *Annual Register*, is a key point in evaluating the Peckham and Parkman theories about the role of Pontiac. Peckham argues that widespread intervals between Indian attacks shows that Pontiac's leadership was exaggerated by Parkman. Parkman's thesis is, however, tenable. There were factors of delay, as I have pointed out, that may have prevented Pontiac from organizing his overall scheme of attack, and, as Harvard scholar Richard Sonderegger states, "We must remember that delay in military operations was a very common occurrence even in Europe in the eighteenth century. Mr. Peckham's researches have shed more light on the problem but have not super-

ceded Parkman's work." Sonderegger, *Francis Parkman,* a pamphlet in the Historiadores de America series, no. 114 (Mexico, D.F.: Instituto Panamericano de Geografia e Historia, 1951), p. 19.

19. Thomas Gage, who succeeded Jeffery Amherst as commander-in-chief, thought the only way to make peace with the Indians was to "win over Pontiac." Thomas Gage to Henry Bouquet, 10 December 1764, Bouquet Papers, A–8, pp. 491–492, Canadian Archives photostat.

20. Sir William Johnson criticized the Delaware sachem, Teedyuscung, for claiming to represent in 1756 "all the Indian Nations from the Sunrise . . . beyond the Lakes, as far as the Sun sets." James Sullivan et al., eds., *Papers of Sir William Johnson,* 14 vols. (Albany, N.Y.: University of the State of New York Press, 1921–1965), II, 826; *Pennsylvania Colonial Records,* 10 vols. (Harrisburg, Pa.: J. Severens & Co., 1851–1853), VII, 33. However, Johnson did not accuse Pontiac of misrepresenting his authority.

21. R. Clyde Ford translation of the "Pontiac Manuscript" in Milo M. Quaife, ed., *The Siege of Detroit in 1763: Journal of Pontiac's Conspiracy* (Chicago: R. R. Donnelly, 1958), pp. 14–15. An older and in some respects better translation of the "Pontiac Manuscript" is in the Pioneer Society of the State of Michigan, *Collections,* 21 vols. (Lansing, Mich.: Michigan Historical Commission, 1877–1919), VII, 266–339. The original French version together with the Ford translation is published as *Journal of Pontiac's Conspiracy,* ed. M. Agnes Burton (Detroit: Michigan Society of Colonial Wars, 1942). It was through Lewis Cass that Parkman was able to get a copy of the document (*Letters of Francis Parkman,* I, 36–37n). The entertaining story about the history of the document itself is told by Helen M. Ellis in "A Mystery of Old Detroit," Detroit Historical Society, *Bulletin* 9 (October 1952): 11–12.

22. Quaife, *Journal of Pontiac's Conspiracy,* p. 144.

23. *New York Col. Docs.,* VII, 862; Lawrence H. Gipson, *The Triumphant Empire* (New York: Alfred Knopf, 1956), p. 96n.

24. Anthony F. C. Wallace, *The Death and Rebirth of the Senecas . . .* (New York: Alfred Knopf, 1970), p. 121. See also pp. 114–121, 347. Wallace seems to have accepted the "conspiracy" theory of Parkman, however, without clearly characterizing the Indian war as a war of native self-determination.

25. Quaife, *Journal of Pontiac's Conspiracy,* pp. 14–15.

26. General Thomas Gage's term to describe Pontiac's methods.

27. Wallace, *Death and Rebirth,* p. 120.

28. Ibid., p. 117.

29. Parkman wrote extensively about Indian barbaric practices, but he also reported on white savagery. In this instance he tells of Sir William Johnson's ferocity in offering large bounties for Indian "heads." *Pontiac,* II, 122. See also note 43 below and the last section in this chapter detailing General Amherst's orders to infect Indians with smallpox blankets.

30. William Johnson to the Board of Trade, 25 September 1763, *New York Col. Docs.,* VII, 561 ff; Same to same, 13 November 1764, ibid., 572 ff.

31. William Johnson, "Enumeration of Indians within the Northern Depart-

ment," 18 November 1763, *New York Col. Docs.*, VII, 582–584. Dorothy V. Jones in her excellent study of Indian treaties, *License for Empire: Colonialism by Treaty in Early America* (Chicago: University of Chicago Press, 1982), pp. 68–69, accepts Peckham's thesis concerning Pontiac's limited role and argues that Johnson saw Pontiac as "merely" head of a "flying camp of raiders," "Detroit-based Wyandots, Potawatomis, and Ottawas." My reading of Johnson's reports and "Enumeration" gives Pontiac a more prominent role in the Indian war of 1763.

32. See synonymy under Minominee and Winnebego, Trigger, *Handbook of the North American Indians,* vol. 15, *The Northeast,* 706, 714.

33. "Enumeration," *New York Col. Docs.,* VII, 582–584.

34. See, for example, Washington's letters to the president of Congress in November and December 1776, in John C. Fitzpatrick, ed., *The Writings of George Washington . . . ,* 39 vols. (Washington: U.S. Printing Office, 1932), VI, 279, 294, 302, 303, 311, 315 ff.

35. See the above dictionaries for additional definitions of "flying camp," most of them stressing the concept of a strong, highly mobile armed force.

36. Johnson had the rank of Major General during his successful Lake George campaign of 1755 and had led more than one "flying camp" of Indians himself. See *Pontiac,* I, 96; Michael Mullin, "Sir William Johnson's Indian Policies," (Ph.D. diss., University of California, Santa Barbara, 1989).

37. See note 30 above.

38. See note 5 above.

39. As Bernard Bailyn has argued, revolutionary leaders were convinced that they faced "a deliberate conspiracy to destroy the balance of the constitution and eliminate . . . freedom." Bailyn, *Ideological Origins of the American Revolution* (Cambridge, Mass.: Harvard University Press, 1967), p. 144.

40. Parkman, however, does touch on this theme. "We may believe," he wrote, "that Pontiac was not a stranger to the high emotion of the patriot hero, a champion of not merely his nation's rights, but the very existence of his race . . . against the rock-like strength of the Anglo-Saxon." *Pontiac,* I, 225.

41. *Pontiac,* I, 238.

42. Ibid., 225.

43. Ibid., 237.

44. Ibid., 267.

45. In describing the barbaric murders of Indians by the provincial, David Owens, Parkman wrote: "His example is one of the many in which the worst acts of Indian ferocity have been thrown in the shade by the enormities of white barbarians." *Pontiac,* II, 217. Parkman also wrote about the brutal massacre of Conestoga Indians by the Paxton boys. Ibid., 125–144. See also note 29, above.

46. Father Joseph-Francois Lafitau. See *Letters of Francis Parkman,* I, xxxvl, 23, 23n.

47. In my judgment, there is good reason to believe that such distortion of the record was at least in part a projection of Parkman's mental illness.

48. Conversations with anthropologists Elisabeth Tooker and Bruce G. Trigger at 1986 and 1987 meetings of the American Society for Ethnohistory. See also

Trigger, *Natives and Newcomers,* pp. 10−14; and his *Children of the Aataentsic* (Montreal: McGill-Queens University Press, 1976), vol. 2, *A History of the Huron People to 1660,* 662; and Elisabeth Tooker, "The League of the Iroquois . . . ," in *Handbook of the North American Indians,* ed. Trigger, vol. 15, *The Northeast,* 434−451. Still another view of Indians and whites in *Pontiac* is expressed by Robert Shulman in a readable, provocative essay, "Parkman's Indians and American Violence," *Massachusetts Review* 12 (1971): 221−239. Shulman argues that *Pontiac* provides insight into white violence.

49. *Letters of Francis Parkman,* I, 35. My interview with Ottawa Indians, one of whom claimed direct descent from Pontiac, Indian Center, Wichita, Kansas, confirmed that Pontiac was indeed a hero among his people because of his leadership in the "Pontiac War."

50. *Pontiac,* II, 43−46; Parkman also encountered evidence of smallpox among the Hurons in writing his volumes on the *Jesuits* (see I, 176−187). He narrates incidents concerning missionaries trying desperately to baptize stricken Indian children before they died. Because the Indians feared the ceremony, suspecting that it was the cause of death, the priests were forced to adopt secret baptismal rites, almost, as Parkman says, with the stealthiness of pickpockets. Though he was concerned with the dramatic aspects of disease impact, he presents his reconstruction of events in such a manner that it is apparent that some of the Europeans (the inference being the missionaries) were themselves probably immune carriers of disease. This is a theme set forth in modern ethnohistorical research in native American population dynamics in eastern North America. See Dobyns, *Their Number Become Thinned,* pp. 7−28; Wilbur R. Jacobs, "The Tip of the Iceberg: Pre-Columbian Indian Demography and Some Implications for Revisionism," *William and Mary Quarterly* 31 (1974): 123−132; William H. McNeill, *The Great Frontier Freedom and Hierarchy in Modern Times* (Princeton, N.J.: Princeton University Press, 1983), pp. 16−22.

51. *Pontiac,* II, 43−46 and notes.

52. Ibid.

53. Bernard Knollenberg, "General Amherst and Germ Warfare," *Mississippi Valley Historical Review* 41 (December 1954): 489−494, discussed the problem of circumstantial evidence in the smallpox episode and a statement in William Trent's journal stating that Captain Simeon Ecuyler, commander at Fort Pitt, did give the Indians blankets from the smallpox hospital. This account was revealed by A. T. Volwiler, in the editing of "William Trent's Journal at Fort Pitt, 1763," *Mississippi Valley Historical Review* 11 (1924): 400.

Knollenberg, in response to criticism of his article by Donald H. Kent, acknowledged, however, that there was now "conclusive evidence" that Ecuyler ordered that blankets from the smallpox hospital be given to the Indians.

Citing the *Papers of Col. Henry Bouquet,* ser. 21654, folio 168, pp. 218−219, Knollenberg quoted the account of Levy, Trent, and Company against the Crown for June 1763. "To sundries got to replace in kind those which were taken from the people in the Hospital to Convey the Small-pox to the Indians viz[t]

2 Blankets at 20/1 OO
1 Silk Handkerchief LO/O
& Linens do 3/6."

Knollenberg also mentions that the above was certified by Captain Ecuyler, 13 August 1763, corrected by Captain Ourry on 22 May 1764, and finally endorsed by General Thomas Gage. As Donald Kent stated, the available data shows that the attempt to infect the Indians was an official action. See Kent's letter to Knollenberg, 19 January 1955, and Knollenberg to the Managing Editor, *Mississippi Valley Historical Review* (21 January 1955), and (March 1955) 41, no. 4 : 762. I am indebted to Francis Jennings for calling my attention to Kent's letter.

54. On Parkman's correspondence with the Stevens brothers, see *Letters of Francis Parkman*, I, 92–93 and n. Parkman mentions his first major revision of *Pontiac* in his letters to Lyman C. Draper, 29 January 1852, ibid., 100, and to John G. Shea, 28 March 1866, ibid., II, 7–8. Compare Parkman's completely revised treatment of "The War on the Borders," chapter 19, pp. 343–351 in *Pontiac* (Boston, 1851) with "The War on the Borders," chapter 19, *Pontiac*, Frontenac ed. (Boston: Little, Brown & Co., 1899), II, 32–60. As indicated above, the 1851 edition has no mention of the smallpox episode.

For an account of Parkman's periodic modifications of *Pontiac*, see "The Sources and Revisions of Parkman's *Pontiac*," by Howard H. Peckham, in *The Papers of the Bibliographical Society of America* 37 (Fourth Quarter, 1943) : 292–307. See also *Bibliographical Note* for criticisms of *Pontiac* and Parkman's other writings.

7. THE HERO IN THE WILDERNESS

1. In his preface to *Pioneers of France in the New World*, Frontenac ed. (Boston: Little, Brown & Co., 1899), Parkman makes the point that he wrote about "a memorable but half-forgotten chapter in the book of human life" (p. xci). For an excellent discussion of the "fact-truth" factor in literature, see Jackson K. Putnam, "Historical Fact and Literary Truth: The Problem of Authenticity in Western American Literature," *Western American Literature* 15 (Spring 1980) : 17.

2. Parkman to Pierre Margry, 6 May 1878, *Letters of Francis Parkman*, II, 113.

3. Parkman to Martin Brimmer, 1886, printed in the appendix of Sedgwick, *Francis Parkman*. Excerpts are in *Letters of Francis Parkman*, I, 184–185.

4. Ibid., I, 7–8.

5. Journals, 24 July 1841, pp. 10–14, MHS.

6. *Vassal Morton*, pp. 11, 115.

7. Ibid.

8. Journals, 24 July 1841, pp. 13–14.

9. "The Scalp-Hunter," *Knickerbocker Magazine* 25 (April 1845) : 297–303.

10. Ibid.

11. *Montcalm and Wolfe*, II, 229.

12. In my conversations with Andrew Rolle, psychoanalyst and historian, I discovered parallels in the youthful behavior of Parkman and the young John

Charles Frémont. See Rolle's analysis of Frémont in his essay, "Exploring the Explorer . . . ," cited in full in note 12, chapter 2, discussing Parkman's mental illness.

13. Ibid.

14. *The Oregon Trail*, 316.

15. *Letters of Francis Parkman*, I, 34.

16. *Pontiac*, I, 77.

17. Ibid., II, 227.

18. See chapter 7 for additional comments on Parkman's techniques in building reader suspense.

19. Handwritten MSS of Parkman's books are preserved in the Houghton Library of Harvard University and in PP, MHS.

20. *Pontiac*, II, 226–230.

21. Ibid., 230.

22. Ibid., 253–254.

23. Journals, 12–19 March 1885, pp. 25–39.

24. *Pioneers*, I, 37.

25. Ibid., 39–40.

26. Ibid., 86–95.

27. Doughty, *Francis Parkman*, pp. 395–396, comments on Parkman's reliance on Bartram.

28. See Robert C. Vitzhum, *The American Compromise: Theme and Method in the Histories of Bancroft, Parkman, and Adams* (Norman, Okla.: University of Oklahoma Press, 1974), p. 97; Doughty, *Francis Parkman*, pp. 235, 242 ff.

29. This is a basic literary theme in *The Old Régime*. The imagery of forest "suffocation" and trees "devouring" their own dead, from *The Old Régime*, was borrowed by novelist Willa Cather for her *Shadows on the Rock* (see pp. 6–8). See W. R. Jacobs, "Willa Cather and Francis Parkman: Novelistic Portrayals of New France," in J. J. Murphy, ed., *Willa Cather, Family, Community, and History* (Provo: Brigham Young University Press, 1990), pp. 253–264.

30. *A Half-Century of Conflict*, I, 34–35.

31. This theme is persistent in Cooper's *Last of the Mohicans* and other novels.

32. In a number of instances it appears that Parkman, the naturalist, the horticulturalist, was competent to give his readers a basic idea of what we now call a forest ecosystem. It can be argued that in his historical works Parkman, however, merely described vegetational assemblies in a romantic, literary manner, not scientifically or systematically, and that he did not understand ecosystems. At the same time a counterargument can be made that Parkman was an extremely able horticulturalist. And, as Clair Martin has pointed out in his essay "Francis Parkman: American Historian-Horticulturalist-Rosarian," *Sub Rosa, Southern California Heritage Roses Quarterly* (April 1982), no. 2:4–6, Parkman did systematically describe rose families so that his *The Book of Roses* (Boston: J. E. Tilton & Co., 1866, reprint 1871; reprint, Boston: William F. Gill, 1874), is still a valuable reference work for botanists concerned with identification and description of rose families. Parkman's knowledge of plants went beyond flowers. There are passages in Parkman's historical works that make it appear that he did indeed comprehend the whole process by

which herbivores and insects feed on foliage and new wood, that he comprehended what we now call the hetertrophic system in which there is a rearrangement and decomposition of complex materials. He also seems to have been aware of what is now described as the autotrophic component, the self-nourishing process in which there is use of light energy, inorganic substances, and the buildup of complex substances. See Eugene P. Odum, *Fundamentals of Ecology,* 3d ed. (Philadelphia: Sanders College Publishing, 1971), on "Principles and Concepts Pertaining to the Ecosystem," pp. 8–35. See also E. P. Odum, *Basic Ecology* (Philadelphia: Sanders College Publishing, 1980), pp. 1–60. Additionally, more detailed analysis and descriptions of forest ecosystems, food chains, food webs (complexes of interlocking food chains) is in W. D. Billings, *Plants, Man and the Ecosystem,* 2d ed. (Belmont, Ca.: Wadsworth, 1970), pp. 29–44, 81–102, 136–139; and B. R. Strain and W. D. Billings, *Vegetation and Environment: Handbook of Vegetation Science,* ed. Reinhold Tuxen (The Hague: W. Junk, 1974), pp. 9–16, 18–24. For further analyses of ecosystems, see Penelope Revelle and Charles Revelle, *The Environment: Issues and Choices for Society* (Boston: Jones and Bartlett, 1981), "Structure of Ecosystems," pp. 13–24. Herein is a discussion of "food webs" and simple "food chains." P. Revelle and C. Revelle have also written an excellent book, *Environment,* 3d ed. (Boston: Jones and Bartlett, 1988). See especially pp. 1–200.

Parkman in many of his volumes, beginning with *The Oregon Trail,* wrote about ecosystems and food webs involving decomposition, dead organisms, and life cycles of feeding fish and small carnivores. Such ecosystem structures are described for the layman in G. Tyler Miller, Jr., *Living in the Environment,* 6th ed. (Belmont, Ca.: Wadsworth, 1990), pp. 48–100. This work stresses the impact of climate on the ecosystem, especially the significance of large bodies of water as a modifier of nearby land areas. See pp. 50–57. Although Parkman was no student of climatic change, he used the images of sunsets, storms, heat and cold, and seasonal change dramatically in all his works so as to give his readers a sense of climatic reality. As Miller and others have depicted climate and its relation to the ecosystem, Parkman's *History* records changes in the weather centuries ago. For Parkman's perspectives on values of retaining what he called "primeval" forests and their drainage systems, see his "The Forests of the White Mountains," *Garden and Forest* 1 (29 February 1888): 2; "The Forests and the Census," *Atlantic Monthly* 50 (January 1885): 835–839.

Parkman even went so far as to check LaSalle's mention of a comet and wrote to a lifelong friend and astronomer, Benjamin Apthorp Gould, in 1868, "How can I ascertain if a comet—a somewhat remarkable one—was visible from the site of Peoria, Illinois, in January 1681?" Gould replied: "Dear Frank, in answer to your question:—One of the most brilliant comets of the century appeared in Dec. 1680 and was visible till the later part of Febr. 1681—being especially brilliant in January. It was . . . known as the 'Great Comet of 1680'!" See *LaSalle and the Discovery of the Great West,* Frontenac ed. (Boston: Little, Brown & Co., 1899) pp. 213, 213n, and *Letters of Francis Parkman,* II, 21.

33. *The Old Régime in Canada,* Frontenac ed. (Boston: Little, Brown & Co., 1899), II, 113–115 and n.

34. At the end of this passage Parkman made a special notation: "An Adverse French critic gives as his opinion that the sketch of the primeval wilderness on the preceding page is drawn from fancy, not from observation. It is, however, copied in every particular, without exception, from a virgin forest in a deep moist valley by the upper waters of the little river Pemigewasset in northern New Hampshire, where I spent a summer afternoon a few days before the passage was written." *The Old Régime*, II, 114–155 and n. E. Lucy Braun in her superb book, *Deciduous Forests of Eastern North America* (New York: Hafer Publishing Co., 1964), pp. 424–425, writes about the virgin Connecticut forests lamenting their falling before the saw. She quotes the ecologist, G. E. Nichols, who writes in much the same vein as Parkman: "The ecologist . . sees in such a group of trees the glorious consummation of long centuries of slow upbuilding on the part of Mother Nature. . . . They represent the survivors of that keen competition and relentless struggle for existence to which their less fit comrades of earlier years have long since succumbed. To precipitate their downfall with the axe seems little short of desecration."

35. As has been noted, Parkman made a special effort to obtain specific data on early American plant and animal life. An excellent modern volume, based upon much of the original material Parkman consulted, is William Cronon's *Changes in the Land, Indians, Colonists, and Ecology of New England* (New York: Hill and Wang, 1983). See especially Cronon's bibliographical essay, pp. 207–235. A recent book on the *coureur de bois*, which corrects much of Parkman's romanticism on these pioneers, is Philippe Jacquin's well-documented work, *Les Indiens blancs: Français et Indiens en Amérique du Nord, XVIe–XVIIIe siècle* (Paris: Payot, 1987) pp. 185–210, and his essay "Les 'Sauvages Blancs' du Canada (XVII–XIXᵉ siècles)," *L'histoire*, no. 15 (September, 1979): 18–26. In this article Jacquin stresses the feverish attraction of the woodland Indian lifestyle "la griserie de la vie sauvage. . . . la fièvre de bois," as well as the impact of intermarriage between the French fur traders and Indian women and the emergence of the Métis population. Much of his analysis of relations between the *coureur de bois* and the French colonial government is similar to Parkman's in *The Old Régime*.

8. SOME LITERARY DEVICES OF THE HERO-HISTORIAN

1. Frederick Jackson Turner, "Francis Parkman and His Work," in *The Dial* (Chicago), 16 December 1898, pp. 451–453. One of Turner's treasured possessions was a note from Parkman dated 2 May 1889, acknowledging receipt of "the Fur Trade of Wisconsin, which I have examined with much interest." Parkman to Turner, TU Box 1, Turner Papers, Huntington Library.

2. Turner, "Francis Parkman," p. 453. See also the last chapter of this book, "Epilogue: The Legend of the Hero-Historian," for Parkman's use of the episode to set forth the image of a frontier type.

3. Turner, "Francis Parkman." Turner also found Parkman lacking in understanding of frontier "institutions" (i.e., the fur trading post).

4. Turner to Herbert Eugene Bolton, 20 January 1916, Bolton Papers, Bancroft Library, University of California, Berkeley.

5. "Romance in America," Class of 1844, Harvard Archives.

6. Ibid.

7. Parkman to Francis H. Underwood, 17 September 1887; *Letters of Francis Parkman*, II, 207–208.

8. "The Wentworth Mansion" was formerly home of Benning Wentworth, colonial governor of New Hampshire. I recall its handsome seventeenth-, eighteenth-, and nineteenth-century rooms and additions when I was a visitor at the mansion some years ago.

9. Barrett Wendell, "Francis Parkman," *Proceedings of the American Academy of Arts and Sciences* 29 (1894): 445–446.

10. "Reminiscences written for Mr. Farnham at his request," [1895], PP, MHS.

11. *Montcalm and Wolfe*, II, 254.

12. Ibid., II, 286–287.

13. Ibid., III, 31.

14. Ibid., II, 42.

15. Richard Sonderegger, *Francis Parkman*, p. 27n.

16. *Pioneers*, I, 33.

17. Ibid., 195.

18. Ibid., 157.

19. *Jesuits*, II, 33–39.

20. Parkman to John G. Shea, 25 September 1857, *Letters of Francis Parkman*, I, 129–130.

21. *Pontiac*, II, 248–250. See also the Epilogue.

22. *The Oregon Trail*, p. 26.

23. Lewis Garrard, *Wah-to-yah and the Taos Trail* (Palo Alto: American West Publishing Co., 1968), p. 288. Other visitors on the plains in the 1840s tended to give a favorable view of the Delaware. A good example is the report made by the British traveler, William Fairholme, who encountered Delaware, Shawnee, and Kansas tribesmen trading at Westport in 1840. They were, Fairholme wrote, "Christians . . . and appear to be a much finer race than the Canadian and other Northern tribes, with good features, & tall slim figures . . . dressed in bright colored blankets and handkerchiefs."

Elsewhere in his illustrated manuscript diary, Fairholme describes the ideal Indian he had met, "a tall handsome fellow, with strongly marked features, & high cheekbones, a fine roman nose . . . the chivalrous scalp-lock . . . over his shoulders a blanket was carelessly thrown . . . he certainly came up to my ideal of the North American Indian." William Fairholme, "Journal of An Expedition to the Grand Prairies of the Missouri, 1840," MS diary, HM 40696, Huntington Library.

24. *Montcalm and Wolfe*, III, 93 ff.

25. Vernon Parrington, *Main Currents in American Thought* (New York: Harcourt, Brace & Co., 1927), II, 136.

26. "Mr. Parkman's Tour," a review of *The California and Oregon Trail*, in *Literary World* 4, no. 113 (31 March 1849): 291–293. This is an unsigned review. Some years ago, I discussed the internal evidence that Melville was the author with Ber-

nard Devoto, and he concluded that there is little question that Melville wrote it. I agree.

27. Ibid.

28. Ibid.

29. *Montcalm and Wolfe,* II, 181.

30. Parkman's journals and letters detail this trip as well as another, in later life, to the Illinois country of LaSalle. My criticisms of Parkman's reconstruction of the Fort William Henry scene are based upon correspondence with anthropologist Henry Dobyns in November 1986.

31. Some nature scenes were deleted in later editions of *Pontiac* because they intruded on the narrative. Parkman was severely criticized by one English reviewer for overloading his book with descriptions of forests, sunsets, waterfalls, and other scenes.

32. Copy of a letter from Parkman to Casgrain, 13 April 1889, *Letters of Francis Parkman,* II, 232.

33. Changes of this kind are observed by comparing the original manuscript of *Montcalm and Wolfe* (PP, MHS) with the printed version.

34. Parkman to Howells, 3 June 1873, *Letters of Francis Parkman,* II, 70.

35. Parkman to Howells, 15 April 1879, Ibid., 127.

36. Parkman to Howells, 6 November 1885, Ibid., 182−183.

37. Howells, *Literary Friends and Acquaintances,* pp. 141−142.

38. Ibid.

39. "Mr. Parkman's Histories," *Atlantic Monthly* 34 (November 1874) : 602−610.

40. Parkman to James, 15 September 1885, *Letters of Francis Parkman,* II, 178−179.

41. James to Parkman, 24 August 1885, Ibid., 179.

42. Turner to Herbert Eugene Bolton, 20 January 1916, Bolton Papers, Bancroft Library, University of California, Berkeley. In this letter, Turner went on to say, "Sometimes you are going to complete your Parkman-like work by putting your material in the form of interpretation and generalization suited to the general reader."

43. Parkman to Frank Parsons, 21 May 1890, *Letters of Francis Parkman,* II, 240. Parkman goes on to say in this letter: "Among the American writers to whom I owe the most I would name Cooper, Irving, and Bryant. Longfellow is a poet of the closet, and never touched me in the least."

44. See also Richard W. Cooper, "Francis Who?: Thoughts on Parkman and New York State," *New York History* 46 (July 1983) : 280−295. Cooper maintains that "Parkman can and should be read if for no other reason than the sheer joy of good writing," p. 294.

9. THE HERO-HISTORIAN AND THE ARISTOCRATIC MALE TRADITION

1. For an extended discussion of the social implications of English aristocracy, much of which was accepted by Parkman, see Jonathan Powls, *Aristocracy* (Oxford, England: Oxford University Press, 1984), pp. 44−45, 88−89, 94−95.

2. Jules Jusserand in the *Parkman Centenary Celebration at Montreal, 13th November 1923* (Montreal: McGill University, 1923), pp. 14–15; Francis Jennings, "Francis Parkman, A Brahmin among Untouchables," *William and Mary Quarterly* 42, no. 3 (July 1985): 305–325; W. J. Eccles, *Frontenac: The Courtier Governor* (Toronto: McClelland and Stewart, 1959), pp. 24, 33, 155–156, 163, 165–170; Kim Townsend, "Francis Parkman and the Male Tradition," *American Quarterly* 38, no. 1 (Spring 1986): 97–113.

3. *Vassal Morton*, p. 215.

4. Parkman to his mother, 19 April 1846, *Letters of Francis Parkman*, I, 37.

5. *Pontiac*, II, 115.

6. See Robert Bechtold Heilman's *Tragedy and Melodrama: Versions of Experience* (Seattle: University of Washington Press, 1968), pp. 7, 91, for an analysis of heroism and melodrama and the forming of literary stereotypes.

7. Francis Parkman, "The Works of James Fenimore Cooper," *North American Review* 89 (January 1852): 161.

8. Parkman's ideas on this subject are best expressed in "The Tale of the Ripe Scholar," *Nation* 20 (23 December 1869): 558–560; "The Failure of Universal Suffrage," *North American Review* 137 (July–August 1878): 1–20.

9. *A Half-Century of Conflict*, II, 108 ff.; *Montcalm and Wolfe*, I, 290 ff. Parkman's dog-eared copy of Pomeroy's journal is still preserved in vols. 107–109, "Notes on Pontiac," PP, MHS.

10. *LaSalle*, p. 363.

11. For a criticism of Parkman's inconsistency on this point, see W. J. Eccles, "The History of New France According to Francis Parkman," *William and Mary Quarterly* 17 (April 1961): 171–172, and Jean Delanglez, *Some LaSalle Journeys* (Chicago: Institute of Jesuit History, 1938), p. 99, on LaSalle's "madcap" enterprises. The extreme complexity of a tangled and distorted body of record on LaSalle is stressed by Peter Wood, "LaSalle: Discovery of a Lost Explorer," *American Historical Review* 89 (April 1984): 294–393.

12. See William Taylor, "A Journey into the Human Mind: Motivation in Parkman's LaSalle," *William and Mary Quarterly* 19 (April 1962): 220–237. This view is echoed in Carl A. Brasseux, "The Image of LaSalle in North American Historiography," in *LaSalle and His Legacy*, ed. Patricia K. Galloway (Jackson, Miss.: University Press of Mississippi, 1982), pp. 5–6.

13. Otis A. Pease, *Parkman's History: The Historian as Literary Artist* (New Haven: Yale University Press, 1953), pp. 33–34.

14. *LaSalle*, pp. 166–167.

15. Mention of Duplessis does not appear in Parkman's first edition of *LaSalle: The Discovery of the Great West* (Boston: Little, Brown & Co., 1869). See *LaSalle*, p. 153, for the paragraph where the insertion was made.

16. *LaSalle*, pp. 340–342.

17. Ibid., p. 430.

18. Ibid., pp. 431–432.

19. For an appreciative analysis of Parkman's poetic and novelistic talents, see Daniel James Sundahl, "Cunning Corridors: Parkman's LaSalle as Quest-

207

NOTES TO PAGES 127–130

Romance," *Colby Library Quarterly* 25, no. 2 (June 1989): 109–123, especially p. 122. Traditional arguments about Parkman's heroism are in Wade, *Francis Parkman,* and in the concluding pages of Samuel E. Morison's booklet, *Francis Parkman (1823–1893): A Massachusetts Historical Society Picture Book* (Boston: Massachusetts Historical Society, 1973).

20. *LaSalle,* p. 432.

21. Ibid.

22. See Bechtold Heilman, *Tragedy and Melodrama,* pp. 7, 91. For further discussion of nineteenth-century melodramatic literary forms, see Martha Vicinus' critique: "'Helpless and Unfriended,' Nineteenth-Century Domestic Melodrama," *New Literary History, A Journal of Interpretation* 13, no. 1 (Autumn 1981): 127–43.

23. *The Old Régime,* II, 59.

24. For a commentary on the importance of Maréchal de Lévis, who was clearly neglected in *Montcalm and Wolfe,* see *The French-War Papers of Maréchal de Lévis Described by Abbé Casgrain with Comments by Francis Parkman and Justin Winsor* (Cambridge, 1888).

25. "The Failure of Universal Suffrage," *North American Review* 127 (July–August 1888): 1–20.

26. Ibid.

27. Unaddressed letter, Boston, 28 September 1874, MS in possession of W. R. Jacobs.

28. "The Tale of the Ripe Scholar," *Nation* 9 (23 December 1869): 558–560.

29. "Is Universal Suffrage a Failure?" Newspaper clipping in Parkman Scrapbook, MHS.

30. Parkman to Frank Parsons, 21 May 1890, *Letters of Francis Parkman,* II, 240–241. Farnham, *Life of Francis Parkman,* pp. 347–348, mentions Parkman's intense interest in Milton, Robert L. Stevenson, Jane Austen, Charles Dickens. Dickens' melodramatic techniques may have had a considerable impact on Parkman's style.

31. See list of books borrowed by Parkman, 1850–1880, "Entry of Books borrowed," Boston Athenaeum; "Library Charging Books," Harvard Archives, 1840–1847.

32. "The Tale of the Ripe Scholar," pp. 558–560.

33. Parkman's will and codicils are in the records of the Probate Court, Suffolk County, Boston, Massachusetts. His donations to the Harvard College were moderate. He left his books and maps to Harvard and his correspondence and historical manuscripts to the MHS.

34. Parkman did defend the common schools when it came to the question of expanding parochial schools. See his essay, *Our Common Schools* (Boston, 1890).

35. Morison's elitist perspective is evident in a number of his writings, especially in his books on New England, in his writings on Harvard University, and in his Oxford University Press history of the American people. A full Morison bibliography, excluding book reviews, compiled by Karl Jack Baur, is in a special edition of NASH (*North American Society for Oceanic History,* [1975]); this same issue contains a moving eulogy by Clark G. Reynolds.

There is little doubt that Morison also shared Parkman's view of the impact of the wilderness upon pioneers. In a letter he wrote, "In one of Robert Frost's poems he describes the terror of a young couple in a Northern New England farmhouse, at the wilderness continually stalking their fields. I, too, have the feeling that man's contest with nature on the Maine coast is an unequal one; that she will prevail in the end, and that but for a few scars of granite quarries, the coast will once more look as it did when Champlain sailed along it." Letter of 4 June 1923, to Lincoln Concord, in "Portrait of a Friendship: Selected Correspondence of Samuel E. Morison and Lincoln Concord, 1921–1947," *New England Quarterly* 56, no. 2 (June 1983) : 166–199.

36. Francis Jennings, Parkman's most vocal modern critic, argues, however, that Parkman misquoted sources, "tenaciously altering details" in a deliberate effort to distort the past. "Francis Parkman, A Brahmin among Untouchables," *William and Mary Quarterly* 42, no. 3 (July 1985) : 305–328. David Levin, after having examined Jennings' charges (some of them repeated from earlier publications), vigorously defends Parkman and makes similar counter charges against Jennings in "Modern Misjudgments of Racial Imperialism in Hawthorne and Parkman," in *Yearbook of English Studies, Colonial and Imperial Themes*, vol. 13 (1983) : 145–158.

37. *Pioneers*, I, c.

38. Ibid., I, xcii.

10. THE HERO ON CATHOLICISM AND WOMEN

1. "The Woman Question," *North American Review* 139 (October 1879) : 303–321; "The Woman Question Again," *North American Review* 130 (January 1880) : 16–30; *Some Reasons Against Woman Suffrage*, printed at the request of an Association of Women (n.p., 1887). Parkman's opponents lashed out against him in newspaper articles, and he, in turn, wrote rejoinders such as "Female Suffrage, Do You See any Young Men who Advocate It?" Clipping in the Parkman Scrapbook, MHS. The nineteenth-century woman-suffrage movement was broader than the struggle for votes. See, for example, comments by Patricia C. Cohen, Joan Hoff-Wilson, and Linda Gorden on women in prison reform, temperance movements, evangelism, and club activity in the "quest for power" as seen in books by Mary B. Norton, Linda Kerber, Ruth Bordin, and others reviewed in *Signs: Journal of Women in Culture and Society* 7, no. 4 (Summer 1982) : 878–890 ff.

2. *Some Reasons Against Woman Suffrage*, p. 9.

3. *Montcalm and Wolfe*, II, 44–45.

4. To Abbé Henri-Raymond Casgrain, 13 April 1889, *Letters of Francis Parkman*, II, 231–232.

5. Ibid.

6. "Mr. Parkman and the Woman Question," undated newspaper clipping in the Parkman Scrapbook, MHS. There is the nagging question, did Parkman say it or something like it? He may have made such a comment when he was rash enough to make a public address on the "Woman Question," although we have no record of his exact speech or comments. Because he put women in his class on a pedestal,

209

implying that they were too virtuous to vote, he left himself open to hostile questions from educated women of his time.

In writing about sexual attractiveness of Indian women in *Pioneers,* I, 10–11n, Parkman dwelled on the fountain-of-youth myth. The myth was substantiated, he wrote in a naughty footnote, "by the beauty of native women, which none could resist, and which kindled the fires of youth in the veins of age."

7. "The Woman Question," *North American Review* 139: 319–321.

8. In the heat of controversy, Parkman referred to Abbé Casgrain as one who had an "emotional" and feminine view of history. See Parkman to Casgrain, 17 September 1888, *Letters of Francis Parkman,* II, 228.

9. Parkman to George Iles, 8 October 1887, ibid., 209.

10. Farnham, *A Life of Francis Parkman,* pp. 152–153.

11. *Vassal Morton,* p. 198.

12. *Jesuits,* I, 198–199.

13. Parkman stated that he believed in the "ethical side" of Christianity, which had been "a vast boon to mankind." He questioned the "superhuman origin" of Christ and argued that "the world has outgrown the dogmatic part of Christianity which has certainly been the source of misery enough in the past—especially the doctrine of exclusive salvation which is the main source of persecution." Letter to Richard M. Mitchell, n.d. September 1887, *Letters of Franics Parkman,* II, 206. For Parkman's sympathetic support of Bourke and his research, see Joseph C. Porter's lucid, well-documented biography, *Paper Medicine Man: John Gregory Bourke and His American West* (Norman, Okla.: University of Oklahoma Press, 1986), pp. 113, 189, 204–210, 226, 239, 267–269, 308.

14. "The Revocation of the Edict of Nantes," *The Critic* 7 (October 1885): 205–206.

15. *The Old Régime,* II, 203–204.

16. Sister Mary Purissima Reilly, O.P., "Francis Parkman and the Spiritual Factors at Work in New France," (Ph.D. diss., St. Louis University, 1942), p. 24. Another viewpoint is in an unpublished recent graduate seminar study, University of California, Santa Barbara, 1987, Jeffery Ross, "Francis Parkman on the Jesuits and the Catholic Church." Ross, an able young historian, discounts Sister Reilly's work as unbalanced and argues, instead, that Parkman's persistent hostility to the church placed him in a position of inner conflict because of his admiration for the courageous Jesuit missionaries. This paper is being revised for publication.

17. Casgrain is quoted in Parkman's unsigned essay, "Mr. Parkman and His Canadian Critics," *Nation* 27 (1 August 1878): 66–67.

18. Parkman to Casgrain, 10 December 1878; Parkman to Pierre Margry, 6 December 1878; Parkman to Casgrain, 2 December 1878. Casgrain believed there were political motives behind the attack of Parkman. Jules-Paul Tardivel (1851–1905), a journalist (called "Tar-Devil" by his critics), was an advocate for Canadian independence. *Letters of Francis Parkman,* II, 122–126.

19. Ibid.

20. Parkman to George Bancroft, 18 October 1878, *Letters of Francis Parkman,* II, 118.

21. Parkman in writing to Charles E. Norton, 13 February 1870, *Letters of Francis Parkman*, II, 41–42, on the appointment of John Fiske as Harvard historian, wrote: "I shall go for Fiske on one condition—that I am satisfied that, heretic or not, he will deal with serious questions in a spirit of candor and reverence, and will practically admit the accountability of man to a higher power. I take the term 'atheist,' to be rather a term of abuse than just an expression of his intellectual status." Fiske was appointed but almost immediately was replaced by Henry Adams, though Parkman seems to have supported him.

22. Conversations with the late Father John Bannon, S.J. Father Bannon edited a publication of Parkman's *Jesuits* and is the biographer of Herbert Eugene Bolton.

23. Parkman to Casgrain, 28 November 1885, *Letters of Francis Parkman*, II, 184–185.

24. Parkman to Lucy Stone, 11 January [1880], *Letters of Francis Parkman*, II, 136.

25. "An Open Letter to a Temperance Friend," [1880], *Letters of Francis Parkman*, II, 135.

26. *Pioneers*, I, 22.

27. Ibid., 49.

28. Ibid., I, 101.

29. Ibid.

30. *Frontenac*, Frontenac ed. (Boston: Little, Brown & Co., 1899), pp. 3–9.

31. *Jesuits*, I, 279–280.

32. Ibid., 287.

33. Ibid., 267, 279.

34. *The Old Régime*, II, 14–18.

35. Ibid., 18. Although he acknowledged that the "amusing" La Hontan sketch was "maliciously untrue," there were, Parkman also said, many instances of scandal. These included women who married in Canada who also had husbands in France.

36. Gerda Lerner, *The Majority Finds Its Past: Placing Women in History* (New York: Oxford University Press, 1979), 160–180, especially, pp. 169–171. Parkman's ideas about gender and women's roles have a clear resemblance to concepts on the subordination of women in sixteenth- and seventeenth-century England. See, for instance, Susan Dwyer Amussen, *An Ordered Society: Gender and Class in Early Modern England* (London: B. Blackwell, 1988), pp. 95–133, including commentary by S. D. Hammilson.

37. Parkman to Mary Dwight Parkman, [1852], *Letters of Francis Parkman*, I, 98–99.

38. See *Letters of Francis Parkman*, I, 99 and n., 152, 168–169.

39. Parkman to Mrs. Edward Twisleton, 5 February 1859, ibid., I, 136–137.

40. Parkman to Mary Dwight Parkman, 22 June 1862, ibid., I, 148–149.

41. Parkman to Eliza Parkman, 10 July [1891], ibid., II, 249.

42. Doughty, comments on this point in his *Francis Parkman*, p. 287.

43. See Parkman's letters to women in his family, *Letters of Francis Parkman*, I, 133—138.

44. See Parkman family correspondence, PP, MHS.

45. See, for example, Parkman's letter to his father of 1841 in *Letters of Francis Parkman*, I, 5.

46. Ibid., 38—51.

47. Parkman's younger brother, John Eliot, a naval officer, died in 1871.

48. Entry of 12 March 1871.

49. The photograph is reproduced in *Letters of Francis Parkman*, II, opposite p. 168, as well as in this work.

50. Ibid., II, 137n.

51. Ibid., 132—136.

52. Parkman had excellent relations with the editors of the *North American Review*, who appear to have been eager to publish anything that came from his pen. Charles Allen Thorndike Rice, owner and editor, went so far as to suggest titles for articles Parkman might write for the *Review*, such as "Political Comedies and Comedians." Some of Parkman's "Open" letters, such as "An Open Letter to a Temperance Friend," of 1880, a polemic against woman's suffrage, which would not "diminish drunkenness," was printed, according to a leaflet, by the Massachusetts Association Opposed to the Further Extension of Suffrage to Women. A secretary, Mrs. Robert W. Lord, P. O. Box 2262, Boston, would send additional pamphlets and leaflets on request.

53. Conversations with Dr. and Mrs. Frederick Merk at Harvard in the 1960s. Mrs. Frederick Merk, Lois Merk, was completing a research study on woman's suffrage in Massachusetts and had encountered the nationwide impact of Parkman's writings opposing woman's suffrage and women's participation in abolitionism, temperance, and other reform movements.

54. *The Old Régime*, II, 158.

55. Ibid., 164—165, 181—182.

56. Ibid., 181—182.

57. Ibid., 164—165.

58. Ibid.

EPILOGUE: THE LEGEND OF THE HERO-HISTORIAN

1. Sedgwick, *Francis Parkman*, p. 235.

2. Ibid., p. 239.

3. Ibid., p. 239. See also Martin, "Francis Parkman: American Historian-Horticulturalist-Rosarian," pp. 4—6; Earnest H. Wilson, *Aristocrats of the Garden*, 2 vols. (Boston: The Stratford Company, 1932), I, 21, 62, 206. Clair Martin, Rosarian of the Botanic Gardens, Huntington Library, has found that Parkman's *The Book of Roses* (Boston, 1866), is a useful work because it has a valuable list of roses with a synopsis of various rose families, their characteristics, and description of their particular traits. For instance, the Safrano rose (which graces the Huntington

Library rose gardens) has this Parkman description: "It is of a buff and apricot hue, altogether peculiar. Its buds are beautifully formed; as are also its half-opened flowers . . . it is a very profuse bloomer, easy of growth and hardy as compared with most other Tea roses." Martin maintains that Parkman's *Book of Roses* is one of the best extant reference works for the identification of roses, a daily problem in any large rose garden.

4. *Book of Roses*, p. 100. Parkman also speaks of various types of roses as being part of a "race" and describes their struggle for survival against "enemies," pp. 32-33.

5. Evidence of this kind of study during Parkman's apprenticeship is found in his reading lists, preserved by the Harvard College Library. His later fascination with novels is documented by his reading lists preserved by the Boston Athenaeum.

6. *The Oregon Trail*, pp. ix-xi.

7. *Pontiac*, II, 331.

8. *The Old Régime*, p. ix.

9. *Pontiac*, I, p. ix.

10. *The Old Régime*, II, 204.

11. *Pontiac*, II, 266.

12. *LaSalle*, pp. 340-341.

13. *Pontiac*, I, 110-111.

14. Rogers's embezzlement of goods and money appropriated for Indian presents is well documented in the Amherst papers and most certainly was known to Parkman through copies of letters he had made. What Parkman may not have known is the story of Rogers's deplorable behavior toward his wife in repeatedly hounding her for funds. This is brought out in his letters now available through the William L. Clements Library, Ann Arbor. Rogers, in short, had some traits of a scoundrel rather than a hero figure.

15. William Taylor, leading commentator and critic of Parkman's *LaSalle*, has made the argument that Parkman's natural panoramas might well be compared with the great nineteenth-century nature paintings of the American West by Albert Bierstadt, Thomas Hill, and others. See Taylor's essays, especially his "Francis Parkman," in *Pastmasters: Some Essays on American Historians,* ed. Marcus Cunliffe and Robin W. Winks (New York: Harper and Row, 1969), a work that is based in part on his earlier Parkman critiques; and "Repossessing America," *New York Review of Books* (13 October 1983) : 35-38.

16. It was Bernard DeVoto, as much as any other modern historian, who caught Parkman's spirit. In recalling DeVoto's aspirations, a close friend, Wallace Stegner, declared: "When you combine the storytelling impulse and the kinds of simultaneity and other literary tricks he played, with the romantic choice of a big subject . . . the result is Parkmanesque. He always tried to do it as Parkman had done it, in terms of personal experience, so that it was constantly evocative in the way fiction is. So far as I am concerned, that's good. I like history like that." Wallace Stegner and Richard Etulain, *Conversations with Wallace Stegner on Western History and Literature* (Salt Lake City: University of Utah Press, 1983), p. 159.

17. Samuel E. Morison in his introduction to *The Parkman Reader*, p. 16, ar-

gues that Parkman ignored the westward movement of his time because Parkman "was a gentleman; and even in the best sense of a much-abused word, an aristocrat. . . . He went west to hunt, view the scenery, and study Indians."

18. Much of what Hayden White writes about the uses of elements of suspense, plots, and emplotment in works of novelists and historians pertains to Parkman's complex novelistic strategies. See, for instance, White's *Metahistory: Historical Imagination in Nineteenth-Century Europe* (Baltimore: Johns Hopkins University Press, 1973), pp. xl, 25, 142-143 and *Topics of Discourse: Essays in Cultural Criticism* (Baltimore: Johns Hopkins University Press, 1978), p. 67. See also White's review essay on Nicola Chiaromante, *The Paradox of History: Stendhal, Tolstoy, Pasternak, and Others* (Philadelphia: University of Pennsylvania Press, 1985) in *The New York Times Book Review*, 22 September 1985, p. 7. See also Peter Novick's trenchant commentary on narrative truth and historical truth in *That Noble Dream: The "Objectivity Question" and the American Historical Profession* (New York: Cambridge University Press, 1988), pp. 560-562, 622-625. Novick argues that Parkman organized his narrative as a "stage play with a prologue, five acts and an epilogue." He, like other "gentlemen amateurs," had an 'intrusive' authorial presence." See pp. 44-46.

19. Parkman made constant use of Pomeroy's journal in telling of colonial fighting men on the move. Nowhere in Parkman's *History* is there a more eloquent and stirring narrative than in the story of the advance of William Johnson's blue-and-red-clad army of farmers and their sons, from rustic New England homesteads, as they marched through the woods toward Lake George in 1755. See *Montcalm and Wolfe*, I, 303-320.

20. *Montcalm and Wolfe*, I, 7-38.

21. See "Bibliographical Note" for William J. Eccles's work on Frontenac and critiques of Parkman.

22. Parkman relied primarily upon French sources and tended to neglect Spanish documents. The late Philip W. Powell, my former colleague, wrote extensively on early Spanish New World history and argued in his books and articles that Parkman was an advocate of the "black legend," portraying Menendez de Avilés as a typical Spaniard, cruel, Catholic, and greedy. See Powell's *Tree of Hate: Propaganda and Prejudice Affecting the United States with the Hispanic World* (New York: Basic Books, 1971), pp. 120-121, 147. In defending Parkman against Powell's criticism, one can point to the fact that Parkman was one of the first to use the copious letters of Menendez de Avilés where Menendez himself chronicles his butchering prisoners, "Lutherans . . . put to the knife." "Understanding this," he writes, "to be necessary for the service of God Our Lord, and of Your Majesty." Pedro Menendez de Avilés to the King, 15 October 1565. Letters are translated and published from Parkman's copy of Henry Ware's translation in *Proceedings of the Massachusetts Historical Society, 1892-1894*, 2d ser., 8 (1894): 416-468. See especially p. 438. Parkman had intended to edit and publish these letters before his death. Ibid.

The controversy over the Black Legend continues, as I have found in studying the history of the Father Serra Franciscan Indian policy in California. As late as the eighteenth century there are instances of incredible cruelty by some missionaries and Spanish soldiers in the maltreatment of Indians. In my judgment there is much truth in the Black Legend as it was first set forth by Bartolomé de Las Casas in his *Tears of the Indians, Being An Historical and true Account of the Cruel Massacres and Slaughters of above Twenty Millions of Innocent People Committed by Spaniards* . . . (translation printed in London, 1656). See especially pp. 11, 15, 19, and 44.

23. As Philip Powell phrased it, Parkman's *Pioneers* tells a tale of "virtuous Huguenots and Spanish devils . . . anti-Spanish prejudice—melodramatic fiction in the Gothic-Romantic manner, making the reader shiver with the thrilling confrontation of Good and Evil." *Tree of Hate,* pp. 120–121. Although Powell defends Spaniards and attacks all historians and writers who disagree with him, including Las Casas and Parkman, some modern researchers have concluded that the Spanish sources themselves reveal the barbaric and "cutthroat" behavior of the conquistadors. Among these revisionists are Henry Dobyns and Francis Jennings. Conversations with the above scholars, at Ethnohistory meetings and at the Huntington Library, 1985–1988. See also W. R. Jacobs on the veracity of the Black Legend, "Communications," *American Historical Review* 93, no. 1 (April 1988): 283, and James Axtell's reply, ibid., p. 284. For "cutthroat" successors to Cortez, Fortun Jimenez and his crew, see Harry Kelsey, "European Impact on the California Indians," *The Americas* 41 (April 1985) no. 4: 494–496.

24. See William Taylor's comments on Parkman as a literary "painter" of wilderness panoramas in note 15.

25. We know Parkman was aware of all Indian-white-Quaker peacemaking and peace treaties because he cites *The Pennsylvania Colonial Records* and Indian treaties and journals of Conrad Weiser, Pennsylvania Indian agent. See for instance, *Pontiac,* I, 93n. Parkman barely mentions the long negotiations and treaty making for peace at Easton in 1756–1758. Ibid., p. 151. Parkman's hostility to the Quakers was such that he argued they had a "blind prejudice in favor of the Indians." Ibid., p. 111. Moreover, he cited, without reservation, the writings of the anti-Quaker clergyman, William Smith. See Francis Jennings's comments on Smith in *Empire of Fortune* (New York: W. W. Norton, 1988), pp. 226–227.

26. See W. R. Jacobs, *Wilderness Politics and Indian Gifts* (Lincoln, Neb.: University of Nebraska Press, 1967), pp. 98 ff.

27. W. R. Jacobs, *Dispossessing the American Indian* (Norman, Okla.: University of Oklahoma Press, 1985), pp. 12–13, 83–90, 92–93, 201n, 203n.

28. *Pontiac,* II, 403. Weiser and his journals and a letter he wrote are also mentioned in *Montcalm and Wolfe* (I, 70, 71, 166; and II, 206), but in connection with ongoing military affairs.

29. *Pontiac,* II, 153, and Parkman's view that Quakers were "scared . . . into their senses." Ibid., 219.

30. *Letters of Francis Parkman,* I, 97–98.

31. See chapter 1 and the discussion of Parkman's illness, and Parkman's correspondence with Francis Underwood, *Letters of Francis Parkman,* II, 79 and 79n–80n, 207. Underwood, a lawyer with literary talents, wrote about Parkman and recalled his "blue spectacles" and Parkman's "suffering from a pain like a pressure

from an iron crown." Ibid., 209n. Parkman used this "iron crown" analogy in interviews with journalists and in his autobiographical letters.

32. Parkman, in a letter to fellow-historian John G. Shea, 29 April 1872, wrote, "I don't think LaSalle a great man, though I do think him a remarkable one. In writing of him, as of others, I tried to be as candid and impartial as possible and to state both sides of his character as far as I could make it out on a careful study of the evidence." *Letters of Francis Parkman,* II, 59–60.

33. Parkman's conclusion is that LaSalle, "beset by a throng of enemies . . . stands like a King of Israel, head and shoulders above them all." *LaSalle,* pp. 431–432.

34. Parkman "walked out to Cambridge" sometime in the early 1870s. See *Letters of Francis Parkman,* II, 70. For Parkman's astonishing ride through the October snow and rainstorm in the New Hampshire mountains and his Batiscan camping trip, see ibid., pp. 159, 189–190.

35. Ibid., 97–191.

36. Parkman told his readers in January 1865 that his eighteen years of "slowness" in publishing was "unavoidable" because of his "state of health" and that any "bookish occupation would have been merely suicidal." Introduction to the *Pioneers,* I, ci.

37. Mitchell, famed Philadelphia physician, wrote Parkman 9 June 1878, (PP, MHS) mildly complaining that Parkman "had so thoroughly studied his own case." Mitchell's "rest cure" concept no doubt did help Parkman. My friends, professionals in the field of psychoanalysis, tell me that Mitchell was ahead of his time. There are many of us who, like Parkman, could avoid headaches and mental tension by taking a good nap.

38. Special Meeting, 21 November 1893, *Proceedings of the Massachusetts Historical Society, 1892–1894* 2d ser., 8 : 349–369.

39. Parkman's very personal letters to Mary Dwight Parkman were not available to early biographers and were later given to the Harvard College Library and catalogued with other manuscripts as the "Parkman Family Papers." These letters have since been published in Jacobs, ed., *Letters of Francis Parkman.* See indexes in vols. I and II.

40. See note 38, above.

41. Ibid.

42. Ibid.

43. Farnham, *Life of Francis Parkman,* p. 317.

44. Ibid.

45. Farnham did irritate Parkman's sister, Eliza, by refusing to allow her to examine his MS until it was completed. When she finally saw the biography she complained that it was too severe in portraying Parkman as cold and reserved. Yet Eliza did not hesitate to send out copies of the book to friends stating that it was her "pleasure" to do so. See E. S. Parkman to Annie Adamsfield [1900], FI5406, Huntington Library. Barrett Wendell was enthusiastic about the book's fidelity and wrote that Parkman himself was "hovering about." *Letters of Francis Parkman,* II, 190n.

46. O. B. Frothingham, "Memoir of Francis Parkman," *Proceedings of the Massachusetts Historical Society,* 2d ser., 7:545.

47. Farnham, *Life of Francis Parkman,* p. 308.

48. Sedgwick, *Francis Parkman,* pp. 327–338.

49. *Letters of Francis Parkman,* II, 175, 181.

50. Ibid., 184.

51. *Pioneers,* I, lxxiii–lxxiv.

52. *Proceedings of the Massachusetts Historical Society,* n.s., 7:551–552.

53. Ibid.

54. *Pioneers,* I, lxxxvi.

55. Wade, *Francis Parkman,* pp. 316 ff.

56. Ibid., p. 443.

57. See, for example, Kim Townsend's critique of Parkman's role in stressing the masculine viewpoint in "Francis Parkman and the Male Tradition," *American Quarterly* 38, no. 1 (Spring 1986):97–113.

58. "The Germanic race, and especially the Anglo-Saxon branch of it, is peculiarly masculine, and, therefore, peculiarly fitted for self-government." *The Old Régime,* II, 201.

59. W. R. Jacobs, "Turner, Merk, and Billington, and the Interpretation of Frontier History," unpublished paper read at the March 1990 meeting of the Organization of American Historians, Washington, D.C.; Jacobs, "Frederick Jackson Turner," in *Readers Encyclopedia of the American West,* ed. Howard Lamar (New York: Crowell, 1977), pp. 199–200.

60. I am indebted to Wallace Stegner for use of the term "Parkmanesque." See, above, note 16.

61. To Pierre Margry, 14 July 1885, *Letters of Francis Parkman,* II, 176–177.

62. Quoted in Eugenia Kaledin's sensitive and thoroughly documented biography, *The Education of Mrs. Henry Adams* (Philadelphia: Temple University Press, 1981), p. 160, from a letter written to Dr. William Hooper, 22 March 1873.

63. There are three books that have influenced my thinking about Parkman and his fashioning a hero image of himself through his writings. The late Douglas Adair in his perceptive essay, "Fame and the Founding Fathers," in a book with the same title, argued that a number of historians, including Allan Nevins, Lawrence H. Gipson, and Julian Boyd attempted to build enduring literary monuments that would give them fame and praise by posterity. Adair, in conversations with me before his death, said that Parkman could easily be included among the writers who had a "love of fame." See Adair's comments in Trevor Colbourn, ed., *Fame and the Founding Fathers* (Williamsburg, Va.: Institute of Early American History and Culture, 1974), pp. 25–26.

A second volume, Stephen Greenblatt's probing study, *Renaissance Self-Fashioning: From More to Shakespeare* (Chicago: University of Chicago Press, 1980), pp. 7–9, 115 ff., has astute observations on a number of aristocratic male writers. Greenblatt maintains that they "represented themselves in fashioning characters." See, for example, his discussion of Sir Thomas Wyatt. Ibid.

A third book, John Steadman's *Milton and the Renaissance Hero* (Oxford: Clarendon Press, 1967), has given me insight on the Parkmanesque concept of "heroic constancy," which Parkman may well have taken from John Milton. See Steadman's comments on heroic prototypes with descriptions of heroic wisdom, virtue, and constancy. Two powerful challenges to heroic constancy were erotic temptation and lawless passion. See pp. 4, 10, 43, 66, 111. LaSalle and Parkman, maintaining heroic constancy, were, as far as we know, able to avoid the kind of erotic temptation described by Milton and other poets.

Parkman, according to the Reverend O. B. Frothingham (as well as other early biographers who knew him), "had great enthusiasm for Milton" (*Proceedings of the Massachusetts Historical Society*, 2d ser., 7:560). The blind poet, often considered a "tragic hero," actually wrote *Paradise Lost* after he had lost his sight. This fact suggests that Milton may well have influenced Parkman in fashioning the heroic constancy of himself as well as LaSalle. On Milton's blindness, see James Holly Hanford, ed., *A Milton Handbook*, 3d ed. (New York: Crafts & Co., 1941), p. 378, where Milton defends himself against critics of his blindness: "the most distinguished and virtuous persons of history" had also been victims of blindness.

We also know that Parkman believed he had been a greater hero than William H. Prescott, who lost the use of one eye. "Prescott could see a little—confound him he could even look over his proofs, but I am no better off than an owl in the sunlight." Parkman to Charles Elliot Norton, 22 September 1850, *Letters of Francis Parkman*, I, 77.

APPENDIX: PARKMAN'S
COMMENCEMENT ORATION, ''ROMANCE IN AMERICA''

1. Harvard Archives (HUC) 6843.55. The essay is in Parkman's handwriting, and the date, 19 August 1844, is inscribed on the archives folder.

2. Boston and Berkshire MS Journal, July [21], MHS.

3. *Vassal Morton*, p. 112.

4. *Montcalm and Wolfe*, II, 181.

5. Parkman to Abbé Henri-Raymond Casgrain, 5 October 1892, *Letters of Francis Parkman*, II, 265.

BIBLIOGRAPHICAL
NOTE

PARKMAN CAN BE STUDIED THROUGH his collected writings, particularly in David Levin, ed., *France and England in North America*, published in the Literary Classics series, Library of America ed., 2 vols. (New York: Viking Press, 1983, 1991), or the Frontenac edition of 1899 (reprinted in 1906). Parkman's novel, *Vassal Morton* (Boston, 1856), was, at Parkman's wish, not included in his collected writings. In addition to Parkman's published correspondence and journals, there are contemporary memoirs written by authors who knew Parkman during his lifetime. The best of these is by Parkman's copyist, Charles H. Farnham, who also served as his secretary and became a friend and fishing companion in later life. Farnham's *A Life of Francis Parkman* (Boston: Little, Brown & Co., 1899, published in the Frontenac edition of Parkman's works), depicts him as a lonely isolated figure, a viewpoint that is contested in Henry Dwight Sedgwick, *Francis Parkman* (Boston: Houghton Mifflin, 1904); in the introduction of Wilbur R. Jacobs, ed., *Letters of Francis Parkman*, 2 vols. (Norman: University of Oklahoma Press, 1960); and in Samuel E. Morison's introduction to *The Parkman Reader* (Boston: Little, Brown & Co., 1955). Besides Farnham, other useful contemporary memoirs are Edward Wheelwright, "Memoir of Francis Parkman," *Publications of the Colonial Society of Massachusetts* 2 (1895):104–150, and Barrett Wendell, "Francis Parkman," *Proceedings of the American Academy of Arts and Sciences* 39 (1894):435–477. John Fiske's published lecture on Parkman in volume I of the Frontenac edition of Parkman's works (*Pioneers of France in the New World* [Boston: Little, Brown & Co., 1899], pp. xi–lxxxvi) is based upon personal acquaintance with Parkman and familiarity with his writings.

More critical, expressing mild reservations about Parkman's strictures on the Canadian church and colonial society, is Abbé Henri-Raymond Casgrain's *Francis Parkman* (Quebec, 1872).

Three twentieth-century biographies of Parkman are Mason Wade's *Francis Parkman: Heroic Historian* (New York: Viking, 1942), Howard Doughty's *Francis Parkman* (New York: Macmillan, 1962), and Robert L. Gale, *Francis Parkman* (New York: Twayne Publications, 1973). Wade, who became interested in Parkman as one of Bernard DeVoto's students, accents Parkman's formative years as a writer and includes a wealth of data from Parkman's journals, which he edited: *The Journals of Francis Parkman*, 2 vols. (New York: Houghton Mifflin, 1947). Doughty has provided a stylistic analysis of Parkman's work, and Gale, in surveying Parkman's life, concludes that he was the greatest historian in an age of romanticism.

Two shorter biographical studies comment on Parkman's interpretations and style as a writer: Wilbur L. Schram's introduction to *Francis Parkman: Representative Selections* (New York: American Book Co., 1938), and Richard Sonderegger, *Francis Parkman*, a forty-one page booklet in the *Historiadores de America* series, no. 114 (Mexico, D.F.: Instituto Panamericano de Geografia e Historia, 1951).

Parkman's originality in selecting a significant historic theme is stressed by Otis A. Pease in *Parkman's History: The Historian as Literary Artist* (New Haven: Yale University Press, 1953) and in an illuminating comparative work, David Levin's *History as a Romantic Art: Bancroft, Motley, Prescott, and Parkman* (Stanford: Stanford University Press, 1959). Further analyses on Parkman as a writer are in W. R. Jacobs's two articles, "Some of Parkman's Literary Devices," *New England Quarterly* 31 (June 1958) : 244–252, and "Francis Parkman's Oration, 'Romance in America'," *American Historical Review* 68 (April 1963) : 692–698. Van Wyck Brooks's friendly critique of Parkman and his *New England: Indian Summer 1865–1915* (New York: E. P. Dutton & Co., 1940), pp. 169–183 (the work of a "Boston Spartan"), is criticized by Bernard DeVoto in *The Literary Fallacy* (Boston: Little, Brown & Co., 1944), for neglecting Parkman's illness and Parkman's theme on the clash of empires (pp. 80–81). Kenneth Rexroth stresses Parkman's frustrations as a historian of the Puritan ethic writing on the subject of the frontier in "Francis Parkman," *Saturday Review* (24 February 1968) : 35.

There has been an accumulation of criticism from historians attacking Parkman's use of sources and his interpretations. Jules Jusserand's address in the *Parkman Centenary Celebration at Montreal, 13th November, 1923* (Montreal: McGill University, 1923), pp. 14–15, points to Parkman's negative views, especially his anticlericalism. Parkman's hostility to the Roman

Catholic church is assailed by Sister Mary Purissima Reilly, O.P., "Francis Parkman and the Spiritual Factors at Work in New France," unpublished Ph.D. diss., St. Louis University, 1942. As early as 1875 Henry Adams classified Parkman "as a reconteur" of "the adventures of individuals" in reviewing *The Old Régime* in the *North American Review* 120 (January 1875):175–179. Howard H. Peckham, *Pontiac and the Indian Uprising* (Princeton: Princeton University Press, 1947), echoed Adams' criticism by arguing that Parkman gave the Indian chief, Pontiac, undeserved credit as a central figure and an originator of the Indian war of 1763. Parkman's interpretation is largely accepted by Louis Chevrette in his detailed biographical sketch, "Pontiac," in the *Dictionary of Canadian Biography,* vol. 3, *1741–1770,* ed. George W. Brown, David M. Hayne, and Francis L. Halpenny (Toronto: University of Toronto Press and Les Presses de l'université Laval, 1974), 525–531. Parkman's theories in historical causation (linking missionaries, fur traders and Indians) are examined by Bruce G. Trigger in "The Jesuits and the Fur Trade," *Ethnohistory* 12 (1965):30–53.

Criticisms of Parkman's use of oral tradition and other sources for *Pontiac* are in another piece by Howard H. Peckham, "The Sources and Revisions of Parkman's *Pontiac,*" *Papers of the Bibliographical Society of America* 37 (1943):293–307. A critique of Parkman's overrating of Moravian missionary Christian Frederick Post as a peacemaker, and his consequent neglect of Indian initiative in making peace, is found in Francis Jennings, "A Vanishing Indian, Francis Parkman and his Sources," *Pennsylvania Magazine of History and Biography* 87 (1963):306–323; Jennings, *Empire of Fortune, Crowns, Colonies & Tribes in the Seven Years War in America* (New York: W. W. Norton, 1988), pp. 391–396. Gregory E. Dowd argues against the charge that Pontiac and the Indians fought because of "manipulative French intrigue" ("Pontiac and France: The History and Historiography of a Fantasy," paper read at the November 1988 American Society for Ethnohistory Meeting in Williamsburg, Va.). Dowd's contention is that French intrigue was an official French policy. It may not have been directed from Paris, but there is ample evidence, as Parkman and Peckham have asserted, that French officers and traders did try to convince the Indians that French help was on the way in their struggle against the English. This is Parkman's argument (in *Pontiac,* I, 181–186), which is confirmed in a number of sources.

With the exceptions of Francis Jennings and the Abbé Henri-Raymond Casgrain, Parkman's contemporary critic (who wrote a five-hundred page book, *Pèlerinage au Pays d'Évangeline* to refute two chapters on the Acadians in *Montcalm and Wolfe*), Parkman has had no more persistent faultfinder than the Canadian historian, William J. Eccles. In attacking Parkman's works as a whole, particularly his portraits of Frontenac and LaSalle, Eccles argues that Parkman's *Frontenac* is unbalanced and in error. Moreover, Eccles firmly rejects Parkman's view of Frontenac as the "man for the hour." Eccles's views are set forth in his *Frontenac: The Courtier Governor* (Toronto: McClelland and Stewart, 1959), and *Canada Under Louis XIV, 1663–1701* (New York: Oxford University Press, 1964), and in articles: "The History of New France According to Francis Parkman," *William and Mary Quarterly* 17 (April 1961): 163–175; "Denonville et les galeriens Iroquois," *Revue d'Histoire de l'Amerique Francais* 14 (December 1960): 408–429. In pleading for a rejection of Parkman's works as properly belonging on the literature shelf rather than in the history stacks, Eccles concludes that Parkman wrote in themes of the nineteenth-century concept of progress. Parkman's view of inevitable progress was on the side of lightness, Anglo-Saxon liberty as opposed to forces of darkness, French Roman Catholic absolutism. Eccles maintains further that Parkman's adherence to a great-man theory caused him to skew the roles of Frontenac, LaSalle, and other prominent individuals; Parkman unknowingly used individual Pierre Margry LaSalle documents that had been bowdlerized. Eccles relies in part on a volume by the Jesuit historian, Jean Delanglez, *Some LaSalle Journeys* (Chicago: Institute of Jesuit History, 1938), pp. 14, 99, who unraveled a maze of intrigue among LaSalle's contemporaries, certain of whom thought he was engaged in "madcap" enterprises. Parkman, Delanglez argues, was confused by Margry's LaSalle autobiographical documents, which were actually not written by LaSalle himself but by others, one of whom was his agent, Abbé Vernou.

A number of Eccles's criticisms are answered by David Griffin in "The Man for the Hour: A Defense of Francis Parkman's Frontenac," *New England Quarterly* 42, no. 4 (December 1970): 605–620, who maintains that Eccles knows little more than Parkman about Frontenac's motives and that Eccles's own writings have some of the same faults as Parkman's. Nor should there necessarily be a separation of history and literature, Griffin states, because Parkman's portrait of Frontenac and the body of his *History* shows that at their best, history and literature are one and the same.

It is ironic that one of Eccles's strictures on Parkman's *History* ("lengthy sections of his volumes were put together with scissors and paste, being little more than translations of long passages from documents," in "The History of New France According to Francis Parkman" is used to defend Parkman's skill as a master narrator. Richard C. Vitzthum in "The Historian as Editor: Francis Parkman's Reconstruction of the Sources in Montcalm and

Wolfe," *Journal of American History* 53 (December 1966): 471–486, maintains that condemning Parkman for following his sources is to ignore his art. Indeed, Parkman told us in the introduction to his *Pioneers* that the narrator should be, as it were, "a sharer or a spectator of the action he describes."

Samuel Eliot Morison has perhaps given us the most perceptive analysis of Parkman's talents as a writer who caught the spirit of the past: "That is it—the gift of vitality. Parkman's work is forever young . . . his men and women are alive . . . the forests ever murmur . . . people have parts and passions." Morison, *The Parkman Reader: From the Works of Francis Parkman* (Boston: Little, Brown & Co., 1955), pp. x–xi. Even greater praise was given Parkman by a leading British historian: "The men he describes . . . have passed into history very much as Parkman portrayed them; they are in the truest sense his recreations." Esmond Wright makes this observation in his historical forward to a reprinting of *Montcalm and Wolfe* (Frontier Library [Cambridge, England: Eyre & Spottiswoode, 1965]), p. xviii.

The Oregon Trail in particular provokes discussion about America's old and new frontiers. An Italian translation of the book caused Louis Dermigy to comment on just this point in an essay-review, "Aux Etats-Unis: 'Frontiers' et Jouvelle 'Frontier,'" *Annales, Economies, Sociétés, Civilisations* 18 (1963): 561–567.

E. N. Feltskog's edition of *The Oregon Trail* (Madison: University of Wisconsin Press, 1969), has a full collation of editions of the book appearing in Parkman's lifetime. Feltskog's extensive notes on Parkman's mention of plants, animals, Indians, and individual travelers on the plains in 1846 are particularly valuable for understanding the detail that Parkman gave us in one volume.

Samuel E. Morison in *Francis Parkman (1823–1893): A Massachusetts Historical Society Picture Book* (Boston: Massachusetts Historical Society, 1973), p. 3ff., stresses Parkman's identification with "the life and . . . the open air . . . as well as 'the library table.'" Robert C. Vitzthum in *The American Compromise: Theme and Method in the Histories of Bancroft, Parkman, and Adams* (Norman, Okla.: University of Oklahoma Press, 1974) argues that LaSalle's career was in part a war against the wilderness, although the impact of the "savage liberty of the backwoods" was significant in Canadian frontier history.

Increasing interest is expressed in Parkman as a historian of the wilderness in America as indicated in Roderick Nash's *Wilderness and the American Mind* (rev. ed., New Haven: Yale University Press, 1982). Parkman's unique contribution to environmental history is stressed in an unpublished senior thesis in environmental studies at the University of California, Santa Barbara, "Limits of Romance in America: Francis Parkman's Encounter with American Environments" by Michele Joyce (1981).

Because Parkman's writings show him to be an early ethnohistorian, it is not surprising that his interpretations are hotly debated. Francis Jennings, in his lucidly argued work *The Invasion of America: Indians, Colonialism, and the Cant of Conquest* (Chapel Hill: University of North Carolina Press, 1975), maintains that Parkman consistently overstated the savagery of Indians in order to improve the dramatic flavor of his narrative. Attacking Parkman on a variety of fronts, Jennings has, for instance, argued that Parkman's explanation of the virtual disappearance of the Susquehanna Indians was actually a bit of fiction thought up by early New York politicians. But Elisabeth Tooker, at a meeting of the American Society for Ethnohistory (Colorado Springs, 1981), in a paper, "The Susquehanna Indians, 'A Who Done It,'" states that Parkman was correct in his explanation because he relied upon Jesuit testimony as a source. A published version of this paper is "The Demise of the Susquehannochs: A 17th-Century Mystery," *Pennsylvania Archeologist* 54, nos. 3–4 (1984) : 1–10.

In another book containing criticisms of Parkman, Jennings dwells on racist themes in writings of both Parkman and Lewis H. Morgan. Parkman, Jennings maintains, deliberately built an image of Iroquois Indians as "the highest type" to support his "myth" of their conquests. These views, in heavily documented chapters, are set forth in *The Ambiguous Iroquois Empire: The Covenant Chain Confederation of Indian Tribes with English Colonies from Its Beginnings to the Lancaster Treaty of 1744* (New York: W. W. Norton, 1984).

Jennings's positions on a whole range of interpretations, including criticism of Parkman and Morgan, are contested by Calvin Martin in a review essay of *The Ambiguous Iroquois Empire*, in *Reviews in American History* (March 1985) : 14–20. Additional argumentation questioning Jennings's views is in David Levin, "Modern Misjudgments of Racial Imperialism in Hawthorne and Parkman," *The Yearbook of English Studies* 12 (1983) : 145–148. Probably one of the most succinct recent appraisals of Parkman's significance is by Robert Middlekauf, a distinguished historian of early America, who states that Parkman told a "magnificent story in grand and compelling prose," in the *Smithsonian* 14, no. 7 (October 1983) : 192–194. Francis Jennings, notwithstanding these accolades on Parkman's behalf, has renewed his attack on Parkman's shortcomings in "Francis Parkman, A Brahmin Among Untouchables," *William and Mary Quarterly*

BIBLIOGRAPHICAL NOTE

42, no. 3 (July 1985):305–328 and in *Empire of Fortune: Crowns, Colonies and Tribes* (New York: W. W. Norton, 1988), pp. xvii, 68, 126n., 171, 480. Criticism of Parkman's racism and attitudes toward women is in Kim Townsend, "Francis Parkman and the Male Tradition," *American Quarterly* 38, no. 1 (Spring 1936):97–113.

A more favorable view of Parkman's status as an ethnohistorian is in W. R. Jacobs, *Dispossessing the American Indians*, 2d ed. (Norman, Okla.: University of Oklahoma Press, 1985). Anthropologists writing ethnohistory have relied upon Parkman's work as a source in Iroquois studies as seen in the writings of William F. Fenton and Elisabeth Tooker. A formidable volume on the Northeastern Indians, *The Northeast*, vol. 15 in *Handbook of the North American Indians*, edited by the Canadian anthropologist Bruce Trigger (Washington, D.C.: Smithsonian Institute, 1978), mentions Parkman's individual volumes in *France and England in North America*. It is noteworthy that other Canadians are often writing the kind of history that has been at least partly told before by Parkman. For example, see Cornelius J. Jaenen, author of *Friend and Foe: Aspects of French-American Cultural Contact in the Sixteenth and Seventeenth Centuries* (New York: Columbia University Press, 1976), an excellent, well-documented study. This echo of Parkman's work is certainly a compliment, but not when Parkman is ignored in notes or in bibliography. Although Parkman has had rough handling by Francis Jennings and by others mentioned above, his version of certain events, as David Hawke argues in a learned survey of early American history, *The Colonial Experience* (Indianapolis: Bobbs-Merril, 1966), will remain the best for many readers. This is the opinion of Victor G. Hopwood, writing in the *Literary History of Canada: Canadian Literature in English*, ed. Carl Frederick Klinck, 2d ed., 3 vols. (Toronto, Canada: University of Toronto Press, 1977), I, 22, who states that "Parkman's ability to grasp the conflicts in the life of New France made this American historian the outstanding interpreter of early French-Canadian society to readers of English." Kenneth Windsor, also writing in this edition of the *Literary History* (I, 247), makes the point that Parkman did not please later generations of French Canadians when he stressed that the British victory was not a war of conquest but of liberation.

American literary historians have been among the enthusiastic critics of Parkman's *History* as witnessed by appreciative essays by David Levin and William Taylor. Levin, editor of Parkman's *France and England in North America*, considers Parkman the best of the romantic historians, judging his completed work as a masterpiece, in "Reconsideration: Francis Parkman, Romantic Historian," *The New Republic* (15 and 22 August 1983):

37–40. Taylor, in a review essay, "Repossessing America," *New York Review of Books* (13 October 1983) : 35–38, asserts that Parkman's talent in maintaining a readable narrative was his greatest achievement. Literary historians have also given us assessments of Parkman the man, the narrator, and the Bostonian on the Oregon Trail. Among those who are attracted to these themes are Howard Mumford Jones, "The Allure of the West," *Harvard Library Bulletin* 28, no. 1 (January 1980) : 19–32; Harold Beaver, "Parkman's Crackup: A Bostonian on the Oregon Trail," *New England Quarterly* 48, no. 1 (March 1975) : 80–103; and an earlier study, Russel B. Nye, "Parkman, Red Fate, and White Civilization," in *Essays in American Literature* in honor of Jay B. Hubbell, ed. Clarence Gohdes (Durham, N.C.: Durham Press, 1967), pp. 152–163.

Recent commentaries on Parkman deserve mention. Martin Ridge in an essay review acknowledges Parkman's shortcomings as well as those of his critics in Frank M. Magill, ed., *Magill's Literary Annual, 1989*, 2 vols. (Englewood Cliffs, N.J.: Salem Press, 1989), I, 273–277. In addition, two appreciative evaluations of Parkman as a writer are John P. McWilliams's analysis of Parkman's role in recasting the demise of the Indian as heroic history rather than as epic romance in McWilliams's *The American Epic: Transforming a Genre, 1770–1860* (New York: Cambridge University Press, 1989), pp. 152–156; Daniel James Sundahl's tribute to Parkman's talents as a poet and novelist-historian in "Cunning Corridors: Parkman's LaSalle as Quest-Romance," in *Colby Library Quarterly* 25, no. 2 (June 1989) : 109–159; and Simon Schama's eloquent assessment of Parkman's identification with General James Wolfe in *Dead Certainties: (Unwarranted Speculations)* (New York: Alfred Knopf, 1991).

As the above bibliographical commentary demonstrates, Parkman in the last decades of the twentieth century is alive and well. His works are read and persist in sparking controversies and discussions about what kind of American history should be written. I have no doubt that my book will provoke further debate, arguing among other things that Parkman, enveloped by a mental illness, wrote narratives that had elements of historical fiction.

INDEX

INDEX

INDEX